The Greatness of WOODROW WILSON

The Greatness of
WOODROW
WILSON
1856-1956

Introduction by

DWIGHT D. EISENHOWER
PRESIDENT OF THE UNITED STATES

Arranged and edited by

EM BOWLES ALSOP *Member,*
WOODROW WILSON CENTENNIAL CELEBRATION COMMISSION

Rinehart & Company, Inc.
NEW YORK TORONTO

Grateful acknowledgment is made to the following publishers for permission to reprint material from their copyrighted works:

HOUGHTON MIFFLIN COMPANY, Boston, Massachusetts, for permission to reprint excerpts from WOODROW WILSON, by William Allen White, copyright, 1924, by Houghton Mifflin Company.

MERIDIAN BOOKS, New York, N.Y., for permission to reprint Walter Lippmann's Introduction to CONGRESSIONAL GOVERNMENT, by Woodrow Wilson, published by Meridian Books Inc. Copyright, 1956.

SIMON AND SCHUSTER, INC., New York, N.Y., for permission to reprint selections from JOURNEY THROUGH MY YEARS, by James Cox, Copyright, 1946, by James M. Cox.

INTERNATIONAL NEWS PHOTOS, New York, N.Y., for permission to reprint the photograph of President Wilson on the train steps at St. Paul, Minnesota.

PUBLISHED SIMULTANEOUSLY IN CANADA BY

CLARKE, IRWIN & COMPANY, LTD., TORONTO

© 1956 BY EM BOWLES ALSOP

PRINTED IN THE UNITED STATES OF AMERICA

LIBRARY OF CONGRESS CATALOG NUMBER: 56-11640

To

A Known Soldier

the editor's brother
Willis Clyde Locker, Jr.

born 1921, the year after the United States
rejected Wilson's proposed League of Nations;

killed in action 1943, in the second World War
Wilson predicted would follow if the United States
did not lead the world in planning for peace.

"I can predict with absolute certainty that within another generation there will be another world war if the nations of the world do not concert the method by which to prevent it."

WOODROW WILSON
September 1919

All royalties and proceeds from commercial sale
of this volume are contributed by editor and authors to

THE WOODROW WILSON BIRTHPLACE
MEMORIAL FUND

commemorating his centennial
in
Staunton, Virginia

AUTHORIZED BY

The Woodrow Wilson Centennial Celebration Commission
established by the Congress of the United States, 1955,
appointed by the President of the United States, 1955

WHEN President Eisenhower appointed me to the Woodrow Wilson Centennial Celebration Commission, I felt, in accepting, a grave concern for the proper acquittal of my obligation. Because the appointment had come about as a result of certain endeavors on my part to re-illumine our Virginia history, my responsibility seemed doubled. But of all Virginia's heralded heritage, I knew least of Woodrow Wilson.

Virginia's other seven sons who had been presidents of the United States were all, through my enamourment of their biographies and the wealth of anecdotal material surrounding them, like auld acquaintance. Their past seemed present in the shrines of their homes and in the vivid memory in which they were held by succeeding generations in the Old Dominion.

To me as a child at Mount Vernon, George Washington had at first seemed formidable, forbidding. But who could help knowing how human and warm-hearted he was after seeing his vegetable garden planted in a pattern for flowers or reading his teasing, affectionate letters to his nieces. Even as giddy girls at dances at "The University" in Charlottesville, we were aware of Mr. Jefferson's being up there on his mountain at Monticello; and we were conscious of his bequest to us in the beauty of "the Lawn," the Rotunda, and the echo of his eloquence. Madison's glamour—even before the word was unrefined to its now-common usage—was evident in the grandeur of Montpelier in Orange County, and Monroe's feeling for the rights of man, his desire for balance, judiciousness and protective form, were reflected in the function and symmetry of Oak Hill in Loudoun County.

Almost next door to us in Charles City County, Berkeley, the ancestral home of Benjamin and William Henry Harrison, and

Sherwood Forest, the home of John Tyler were both so familiar as residences, rather than museums, that we felt we had even discussed the "Tippecanoe and Tyler, too" campaign with its candidates.

In spite of my having a close contact with almost every other part of Virginia, I had never known Staunton at all. Vaguely I recalled that Woodrow Wilson had been born there in a Presbyterian manse. But like Zachary Taylor, the last Virginia president before him, he had not lived long in Virginia. Had not his family moved to Georgia while he was still an infant? What effect, if any, had Virginia had upon her eighth son to achieve the nation's highest honor?

Woodrow Wilson had been President of the United States when I was born. Of course I knew the over-all facts of his administration; they were too earth-shaking not to be known and their results studied. Automatically I accepted his word as a gospel of Christian faith and enlightenment.‡ Curiously, though, Wilson had always seemed but a photograph to me. His personality had never beckoned me. In his Olympian intellectualism he had seemed a kind of tragic myth; a martyr, yes, but more of a mental than a mortal one.

Yet the fact that I had been appointed by a Republican President to honor a Democratic President was so quintessentially American, so much the substance of true democracy, that my imagination was wholly captured by the sublime paradox and spurred, despite itself, to seek out Mr. Wilson, discover just what he was like, and make myself his friend.

I first met Woodrow Wilson on a rainy afternoon in Charlottesville when my husband and I had tea before a fire with the Thomas Jefferson Research Fellow from Princeton at the University of Virginia, Thomas Jefferson Wertenbaker and his gracious wife. Dr. Wertenbaker gave us our first glimpse of Wilson as he faced a torchlight parade from the porch of Prospect, the president's home on the campus at Princeton. Standing there with Mrs. Wilson and his three daughters beside him, his face alight with the flames' reflection and his own emotion—he watched the thunderous demonstration in his honor by students, faculty and townspeople, marking his election to the Governorship of New Jersey—visibly moved by the outpouring of affection and regard. When a silence fell for his reply, he spoke of his appreciation with a hesitation born of his profound reaction. Our next glimpse of him was after a similar parade following his election to the Presidency of the United States, when he stood on the porch of his residence on Cleveland Lane and with a moving humility shook the hands of a silent file of friends who thronged to congratulate him.

Then Dr. Wertenbaker took us to meet Wilson in a classroom at an earlier date, where he was wittily regaling his students with "government," inspiring them to learning. We passed him, too, at that same time, on the football practice field, hailing the players with cheers, exhorting them to win. We saw him, once more, as a friend of Dr. Wertenbaker's father—a gay, entertaining, loquacious friend, sitting on a porch in Charlottesville, sixty years before, in a happy summer mood, relaxing from a winter's academic labors.

When we left the Wertenbakers that afternoon, Mr. Wilson was no longer a mere photograph to me. He was a warm-hearted, earnest, dedicated new acquaintance.

The next morning we rode over the mountain to Staunton as Wilson himself must have done so many times while he was a law student at the university, going back to see the birthplace he was to make a shrine by his own fame. There in a continuing drizzle of good luck we were welcomed by the moving spirit behind a great number of matters Wilsonian. Emily Pancake Smith's ardent, articulate admiration for Mr. Wilson has inspired an endless series of ceremonies and celebrations in his honor, both national and local. The wife of Herbert McKeldon Smith, former state legislator, Mrs. Smith is a member of the board of trustees of the Woodrow Wilson Birthplace Foundation in Staunton, the Virginia State Woodrow Wilson Commission, and, through me, the instigator of this volume. She took us through the now-hallowed Birthplace, the ante-bellum mansion which was the Presbyterian manse, showing us the double parlors in which Woodrow Wilson's mother, the musical Mrs. Wilson, doubtless played the pianoforte, the upstairs porch on which Dr. Wilson wrote his sermons, the room in which the future President was born. As she introduced us to his gregarious preacher father, his quiet, restrained mother, and even to the congregation of the church the Reverend Mr. Wilson served, we saw as a unit the family of two sisters and two brothers which the father passionately adored and brilliantly instructed.

When we left Staunton, Mr. Wilson and his immediate family had been taken out of their album, presented to us in their first home.

Through trips which followed to Commission meetings in Washington, trips to commemorative events honoring Woodrow Wilson throughout the country, we met Mr. Wilson many times over, sometimes in his silk hat and striped trousers at the Peace Conference in Paris, sometimes in mufti in his own living room singing with his daughters.

Then, through William Allen White's biography—which in my opinion should be recommended to all beginners in the study of Wilson—Mr. Wilson and I became great friends. I say this confidently because by this time we knew each other well. His background, with its strong faith, family ties, exhortation to accomplishment and service; his scholar's search for the seclusion of thinking and deduction; his contrastingly gregarious, spontaneous, effervescent nature; his stubborn idealism and self-confident will to help the whole world; his emotional anguish in the face of unjust, unfaithful or unprincipled enemies; his galling bitterness born of physical strain and moral disillusionment; his incredulity at the conduct of the unconscienced; and finally his abiding, sustaining faith to the end—all were elements wholly comprehensible to me, many of them a part of my own nature and/or experience. I found myself filled with covetous awe of his scholastic achievements, the books, lectures, treatises on government; and with a tender admiration for the dauntless man whose warm heart, compelling sincerity and prescient wisdom had often been denied the general public by an absence of modern communication in his time. That he was my friend, as surely as I was his, I knew; not just because he was by dedication a friend to all men; but more personally because in all his relationships through life he sought friendship, searched for its bases of mutual vision and resolve, cherished its steadfastness even as he recoiled from and struck out at its intransigeances.

I felt that in a friendship with Woodrow Wilson, whatever my inadequacies, shortcomings or mistakes, if to the best of my ability, I remained loyal not to him but to his principles, I would never want for a reciprocity of affection, interest and understanding.

Having thus come to know the twenty-eighth President of the United States so well as a person, it seemed imperative that I begin the study of Woodrow Wilson's career, his part and place in history. To be done thoroughly, adequately, this task would take many years; it could not be compressed into the weeks at my disposal. Yet how else could his memory properly be served?

A diligent, albeit by its nature a cursory, commencement yielded one revelation: there was no book about Wilson viewing him from this present, compelling moment of mid-twentieth century. All of the existing biographies and appraisals of him had been written either (1) by his contemporaries who, even a few years after his death in the 'twenties, had been still too close to the scene to write with the needed objectivity; or (2) by scholars who in the 'thirties and 'forties had devoted their attention to him before the events he predicted had taken place! Two studies in the 'fifties were solely concerned with his domestic influence.

There had been no proper appraisal of Woodrow Wilson since the most important advents of the twentieth century—World War II, the atom bomb, the United Nations, Russia's cold war—had altered the face of the earth, readjusted our view of it, our life in it.

What was needed was an immediate re-evaluation of Woodrow Wilson as our first world leader.

How could this be accomplished, even by a great authority, in the time allotted? Nor could one man accomplish this feat alone. It required the minds of many men, their many viewpoints to reach a common denominator of conclusion.

Ideally, it seemed to me for the given subject, such a book should be introduced by the President of the United States, concluded by the Secretary-General of the United Nations, with— bracketed between these two—chapters of specific chronological authority by the greatest living Wilsonians.

This then seemed my obligation to the Woodrow Wilson Centennial Celebration Commission. I asked our Chairman, General Opie, only if I might "investigate the possibility of a nationally published commemorative volume." He assented.

Then began the telephoning throughout the country, and the world, which has brought me in close and inspiring touch with the contributors to this volume. Two impressions are strongest from the past months of communication and correlation on my part.

First is the response from each authority to whom I applied. The name Woodrow Wilson was like a magic elixir. Immediately hearing it the listener became attentive, responsive, acquiescent, appreciative. There seemed to be a brotherhood of peoples regardless of their geographic or political location to all of whom the password was Wilson. Anyone who used this name was automatically trusted, respected, accepted. I was never catechized as to my credentials. The fact that I, too, knew and highly regarded Wilson was sufficient to enlist co-operation from some of the most distinguished men and women of our time.

President Eisenhower, because his spirit transcends party lines, did not hesitate to honor Wilson. Ralph McGill, renowned editor of the *Atlanta Constitution* whose chapter was the most exacting because of its scope, sacrificed other work for its completion and replied when I thanked him, "I am humbly grateful to be included with such men as your contributors." My cherished friend Madame Chiang Kai-Shek, as often misunderstood in her own time as Wilson was in his, received my cable of request while on an inspection tour with the Generalissimo, returned to Taipei to fulfill my request in spite of an "inadequacy of source material" and then rejoined her husband. The honorable Claude Bowers, historian and personal friend of Wilson's, canceled a previous commitment in order to complete his manuscript on time. No one flatly declined. In an envelope bearing the impressive seal of the Prime Minister of India, Jawaharlal Nehru although unable to commit himself to the task, sent a warm note of congratulation and encouragement in which was evident his admiration of Wilson.

Not the least was I moved by Professor Arthur Link of Northwestern University, Wilson's pre-eminent if most critical biographer in the 'forties, whose manuscript was accompanied by a revealing letter which spoke of the mellowing of his judgment of Wilson in the intervening decade.

Most eternally, will I appreciate the unequivocal co-operation of my friend Virginius Dabney, Pulitzer Prize-winning Editor of the *Richmond Times-Dispatch* who, by his carte blanche trust in me, provided the leverage for my initial request to others.

Clifford Dowdey said it was impossible for him to contribute a piece because of pressure of commitments, absence of time. Yet no one knew the place and period of Wilson's birth so well. I badgered him. He did the splendid first chapter—overnight. His courtesy later in assisting with contacts anent the publication of this volume has been indispensible.

Working with such co-operative intellectuals as Dr. Frank Bell Lewis, President Dodds of Princeton, through his emissary Colonel Arthur E. Fox, Walter Lippmann and Dr. Edgar E. Robinson but confirms the Wilson precept that in a meeting of men's minds for a purpose any problem can be resolved.

The second ineradicable impression from my absorbing work is that one theme about Wilson is recurrent in each chapter. That it was unsolicited by virtue of the latitude allowed each author in the composition of his material is the more indicative. This theme is the greatness of Woodrow Wilson, his rightful succession in the Presidential line of Washington, Jefferson and Lincoln. Among the disparate authors of this volume, whether advocates, critics or dispassionate observers of Wilson, there seems no dissent on this one chief and revealing conclusion. I have left this variously caparisoned repetition intact; for emphasis.

Just as there can hardly be found in the South today a voice which does not in the honesty of time regard Lincoln as a great man, so there seems no longer to exist in North or West, as well as South and East, a voice which does not regard Wilson as a great man; a great man whose word we will no longer fail to heed.

This is, then, a "book by many hands," a book written by scholars for laymen, a book not for that minority who already know Mr. Wilson—but for that great majority of people throughout this nation and the world who do *not* know Mr. Wilson, or who know him only slightly—from his contemporaries who misjudged him to the younger generations who are yet to comprehend his influence on their own lives. It is a book designed to bring the power of Wilson's personality and the inspiration of his thought to peoples of all ages and stages; and to help them, in this time for vision, decision and salvation of the world, to a new security of individual and international integrity.

As a testament of his contribution to our heritage, and as a revealing self-portrait of the man's mind, excerpts from Wilson's own writing interstice the chapters.

Mrs. Wilson's warmth and friendship before the work began, her interest and support, her graciousness and thoughtfulness, have made this sustained effort, in the face of many difficulties unaccounted, not only possible but pleasurable.

I must take this opportunity to thank especially the Library of Congress for its aid and counsel; the Richmond Public Library and Virginia State Library for their courtesy and accuracy in replying to my countless queries. There is never a way, I am convinced, to thank one's own family for bearing the brunt of such an effort. Yet my appreciation must be recorded to my husband, Benjamin Pollard Alsop, junior, who in spite of his forbidding me to say so, was in truth my collaborator by virtue of his interest, encouragement, judgment, and indefatigable assistance. I salute our Commission Chairman, Major General E. Walton Opie, who perceived my zeal and entrusted me with the project others termed impossible.

But primarily I thank Dwight D. Eisenhower, thirty-fourth President of the United States for his "special trust . . . in my integrity . . ." as my commission reads, and for his generous contribution of the foreword which follows.

EM BOWLES ALSOP
March 1956

Upper Shirley
Charles City County
Virginia

INTRODUCTION by DWIGHT D. EISENHOWER
President of the United States

Within the span of Woodrow Wilson's lifetime—from 1856 to 1924, from before the Civil War until after World War I—our country underwent an amazing growth as a nation and as a power among the nations of the world. In this development, as teacher, writer, administrator and President he played a role of lasting significance.

To review this role is to recall the principles in which he ardently believed, and which he fearlessly upheld. He had faith in the ability of free men to arrive at sound judgments and to govern themselves. He believed in the capacity of a free system to bring forth wise and able leaders, responsible to the whole people, with whom the power in such a system ultimately rests. As president of a great university he proclaimed that the university should serve the nation; he had a keen awareness of the individual citizen's obligations to his society and his country.

As President of the United States he saw the great part which this nation should play in the community of nations; he understood the necessity of the United States' exercising leadership in working for a world in which the rights of individuals and of individual peoples would be respected, in which international law and international justice would prevail. The establishment of such a world order was to him an essential part of the establishment of a lasting peace.

For all these reasons it is gratifying that the publication of this volume in 1956 will provide Americans a new opportunity to increase their familiarity with his life, his accomplishments and his thought. In this year and in those to come his example will continue to guide and inspire our people in their support of international friendship and progress, their search for peace, and their devotion to a free and civilized way of life.

Dwight D Eisenhower

There is one thing I have got a great deal of enthusiasm about, I might almost say a reckless enthusiasm, and that is human liberty.

Indianapolis, Jan. 8, 1915 [1]

. . . The United States were founded, not to provide free homes, but to assert human rights.

Washington, D.C., Sept. 28, 1915 [2]

America is not ahead of the other nations of the world because she is rich. Nothing makes America great except her thoughts, except her ideals . . . America has all along claimed the distinction of setting this example to the civilized world—that men were to think of one another, that governments were to be set up for the service of the people, that men were to be judged by those moral standards which pay no regard to rank or birth or conditions, but which assays every man according to his single and individual value.

Denver, May 7, 1911 [3]

America is greater than any party. . . . Parties will fare well enough without nursing if the men who make them up and the men who lead them forget themselves to serve a cause and set a great people forward on the path of liberty and peace.

Letter to Frank E. Doremus, Sept. 4, 1914 [4]

—WOODROW WILSON

CONTENTS

The Birthplace

CLIFFORD DOWDEY

A man's rootage is more important than his leafage.

Baltimore, April 29, 1912.[5]

My best training came from my father.

Philadelphia, Oct. 13, 1904 [6]

—WOODROW WILSON

THERE was probably a light snowfall on the evening of December 28, 1856 in Staunton, Virginia. The encircling mountains would have been obscured by the falling flakes, and footfalls, horses' hooves, turning wheels, would have been silenced by snow on the streets. Silhouetted before the lofty white mansion on the corner of Frederick and Coalter Streets, which seemed to blend with the whiteness of its setting, would probably have been the horse and buggy of the doctor. The only contrasting color in the scene might have been the yellow candlelight sifting through drawn shutters. On the door, beside the festive holly wreath, there would still be hanging the basket for Christmas Day calling cards, which a happy expectant family had been too busy to remove. Every parishoner of Dr. Wilson's church would be represented in those cards as well as in presents for the parson's family of cookies, cakes, pies, puddings, preserves, vegetables that had been put up the summer before, and handmade, hand-knit little garments for the new arrival. For this was a Southern community, a Victorian community, close-knit, neighborly. As the doctor entered, a faint Christmas bell in the wreath might have tinkled.

As he hung his hat and coat on the hatrack in the spacious hall and disappeared into the downstairs bedroom to the left, Mrs. Wilson's hoopskirts might have been glimpsed, through the crack in the door, hanging high on the wardrobe, and a faithful mammy might well have been seen bending over the bowl and pitcher to fetch her a soothing cloth for her forehead.

Across the hall in the twin parlors there would certainly have been a Christmas tree, for the idea was new and popular, probably a red Virginia cedar, not ablaze with lights but hung here and there with a carefully placed, now unlit, candle; brightly hung with sugar cookies, painted wood-carved birds, flowered and sugared sycamore balls, festoons made of cranberries and popcorn, candy canes, gingerbread men, paper chains, painted angels and St. Nicholases. Rummaging about in the toys below it might have been two little girls in long-sleeved, high-necked white flannel nightgowns who, when apprehended by a father pacing down from his study upstairs, would have been effectively shooed back to their beds in the nursery.

Later, as the little girls lay at last asleep, the bell in the tower of the church which lay only across a lawn and ravine from the Manse would have begun to toll its midnight hour, and the pacing father in the hall would have heard the cries of pain cease, the cries of life begin, and he would have gone in to see his wife and his son.

We know that then at once he went to his study upstairs just over the bedroom and recorded in the Wilson family Bible, the birth of Thomas Woodrow Wilson at "12¾ o'clock." Then it is likely that in relief, pride, gratitude, he went out to the upstairs porch which hung aloft in the three-storied white columns on the garden side of the Manse and said a prayer of hope and thankfulness in the silent and, to him, holy night.   —The Editor.

In 1856, the eighteenth century still lingered in the South. In other regions, the new industrialized society was struggling to be born, but the South still functioned through its agrarian economy with the economic and social patterns thus created. At the heart of its character lay the strong individualism which had marked America from its beginning.

In the Shenandoah Valley of Virginia this individualism derived more directly from the frontier influence than in the more typical plantation South. The dominant Southern pattern was based on the large-scale operation of one money crop—as tobacco in eastern and southern Virginia, as rice and cotton in South Carolina, as cotton in the lower South—and on these plantations the absolute power of the masters tended to develop personal self-assertion and imperiousness in the individual. In the Valley, the plantation of the legend did not characterize the agrarian culture. There were slave-owners, but aside from some large holdings in Clarke County at the northern end of the Valley, plantations were too scattered essentially to influence the culture. Indeed, some settlers who came across the Blue Ridge from Tidewater Virginia sought sanctuary from a society dominated by the plantation pattern. Others came to re-establish and expand those very traditions which more than any others marked Virginia's character and gave it definition.

The settlers then, were both typical frontier-stock Americans who were simply seeking homesites on which to raise families, and sons of eastern families who brought with them the habits and customs already native to their state. The homesteaders came via Pennsylvania down the broad Valley, and were mostly Pennsylvania Dutch and Scotch-Irish. Entering the Valley from the north, meeting fugitives from Tidewater crossing the mountains from the east, they blended in the great fertile Valley to form a character unique in the South. Their individualism was based on a sturdy self-reliance, a proud independence.

As with the traditional frontier Americans, they fought most bloody wars with Indians for their land. They cleared the wilderness and built their farms in the beautifully contoured rolling country. The soil was rich with limestone deposits, good for horses and beef cattle. The farm people developed orchards and grains to the extent that the Valley was called "The Breadbasket of Virginia."

From the mid-eighteenth century, small towns developed around trading centers, and by 1856 many of these towns had grown into solidly prosperous communities. Typical of these integrated towns was Staunton in the middle Valley.

As with most of the towns, Staunton was located on the old Wilderness Trail, which ran from north to south along the twenty-five-mile-wide floor of "The Valley." This road, the present Route 11, was the Valley Pike, later to be famed in the marches of Stonewall Jackson's "foot cavalry." More than a century before Jackson's men marched this way, steady streams of pioneers were flowing southward across the old Big Trail toward Cumberland Gap. As they came in restless surge, many found this prairied Valley to their liking and went no further.

First to come to Augusta County was John Lewis in 1732. He built a farm three miles from the present city of Staunton, and his epitaph epitomizes the destiny of the early settlers:

"Here lie the remains of John Lewis, who settled Augusta County, laid the town of Staunton, and furnished five sons to fight the Battle of the Revolution. . . ." So commonplace was the Indian fighting that this savage warfare was not even mentioned. Other settlers followed fast, and by 1738 Augusta County was created in the Dominion of Virginia in the British Empire, named for Princess Augusta, wife of Frederick, Prince of Wales, eldest son of George II and Queen Caroline.

At that time, Augusta County extended from the Blue Ridge Mountains to the Mississippi and included nearly all of West Virginia, the states of Kentucky, Ohio, Indiana, Illinois and a part of western Pennsylvania. The deed to the present site of Pittsburgh, bearing the date of August 2, 1749, is recorded in the Clerk's office of Augusta County in Staunton, Virginia. Bills were passed in the Virginia Assembly "for encouraging persons to settle on the waters of the Mississippi in the county of Augusta."

Despite this lure to riverside sites, frontier people continued to settle in the area of the present Augusta County in the middle Valley, and its population steadily increased during the 1740's. In 1747, William Beverley caused the present city of Staunton to be laid out in his land grant of 118,491 acres. The motives are questioned in many Virginia landowners who founded cities as a means of making urban real estate out of a wilderness, but, in any event, the half-acre lots were taken up and the new community sought a charter. Its name came from the Lady Staunton, wife of the former colonial governor, William Gooch. By one of those complications with the Crown which the colonists were forced to endure, the final charter of Staunton was delayed until 1761, when the townspeople were granted permission to hold two fairs a year and forbidden to build wooden chimneys.

A proud episode in the early life of Staunton occurred in 1774. In the fierce Indian warfare preceding the Revolution, General Andrew Lewis, the most famous son of the settler, led 1,100 Augusta men from Staunton on a nineteen-day trek into Ohio. At Point Pleasant, the "Augusta Expert Riflemen" defeated a large body of assaulting Indians, at a loss to themselves of seventy-five killed. The descendants of these "Augusta Expert Riflemen" formed with other Valley troops the nucleus of the tough-bitten soldiers of Stonewall Jackson.

The young city was also "distinguished" in 1781 when the Legislature of the Revolutionary colony, fleeing westward from Richmond, finally found haven at Staunton. An early account says simply, "The town always had a stir in it with more than the ordinary variety of population. . . ."

After the Revolution, the growth of Staunton in the new republic was steady. By 1836 the town burghers felt sufficiently prosperous to build a new brick courthouse. In 1845 the congregation
of the Presbyterian church bought a lot on the Valley Pike—what
is now the southwest corner of Coalter and Frederick Streets—
on which to build a manse for their pastor. Most Protestant denominations had at that time one church in Staunton, but in Augusta County the Scotch-Irish Presbyterianism was dominant. John
Lewis, the original settler, had brought his family of Scotch Protestants from Northern Ireland. The solidarity of the Staunton Presbyterians is indicated by the impressive house they built the following year for their pastor's family. It would serve this purpose many
years until, because of a son born to an incumbent minister in 1856,
it would become, by endowment, a National Shrine.

The Presbyterians used as a model for their parsonage—called
the Manse—the architecture of the contemporary Greek Revival
period. Characteristic of large city houses in Virginia in the 1840's,
it was a style typical of ante-bellum life, with high ceilings, wide
hallways, three full floors. A basement housed dining and store-
rooms; the first story, double parlors with the usual "chamber" (or
master bedroom); and the second story, four bedrooms, two of
which converted most often to study and nursery. The front of
the house, marked by a modestly columned portico, stood but slightly
from the street, while the opposite side was opulent with the great-
columned double balconies. Across a sloping lawn, now a terraced
garden, the Manse looked to its church through what must have
been the usual assortment of outbuildings of the era—icehouse,
smokehouse, barn and shed, chicken house, stable and carriage
house, all related in arrangement to the cow pasture, high-fenced
vegetable garden, orchard, cutting garden and flower borders. More
the city mansion of a planter than the home of a pastor, the Manse
showed the status given their minister by Stauntonians. Into this
substantial twelve-room home in the summer of 1855 moved the
family of the Reverend Joseph R. Wilson.

Joseph Wilson, thirty-three years old at the time, had been
born in Ohio of a family of Scotch Presbyterians, his father one of
the newspaper printer-editors who gave color to the America of
that day. As Justice of Peace and state legislator for one term, the

elder Mr. Wilson was referred to as "Judge." Of Judge Wilson's large family, Joseph was the scholar, and he was a teacher as much as a preacher.

After his ordination, Joseph R. Wilson came to Virginia as Professor of Chemistry and Natural Science at Hampden-Sydney College. In his four years there, he also served as minister to the small churches in the neighborhood. Before his arrival in Virginia he had married Janet Woodrow, the daughter of the Reverend Dr. Woodrow, also of Scotch Presbyterian background, who had migrated from England to Ohio as a "missionary." The church in Staunton, Wilson's first regular pastorate, was a fortunate beginning. A simple but handsome edifice of brick with columned entranceway, it looked more like a Greek temple than a Presbyterian place of worship. But its well-to-do parishioners were able to build in the style of the day.

At that time, Stauntonians boasted of a population of 5,000, though the United States census returns place it as slightly under 4,000. The small city was solidly prosperous on the economic pattern which has characterized the Valley cities from that time into the present. Essentially a trading city for agriculture, its economy was balanced by commerce and small manufacturing. The "Valley people" generally resisted the large factories of heavy industry.

You can see by the occupations the structure of the society. There were blacksmiths, bookbinders, bootmakers and bakers; carpenters and tinners, carriage and wagon manufacturers, harness makers and furniture makers, distillers and mattress makers. There was a machine shop and a foundry, two banks, more than a dozen commission merchants and, surprisingly, four newspapers—of which the most stable was the *Staunton Spectator*. The city had two hotels, the Virginia and the Eagle, bowling alleys and "billiard saloons," restaurants and saloons. The Deaf and Dumb Institute was located here and a Lunatic Asylum.

In the days before public schools in the South, there were two academies for boys, which later became Staunton Military Academy and Augusta Military Academy. There were two female seminaries, one of which became Stuart Hall—named for its postbellum principal, the widow of Jeb Stuart—and the other is the present Mary Baldwin College. The Reverend Mr. Wilson's church, now called the First Presbyterian, was situated on the pleasant hillside site of Mary Baldwin's campus.

Aside from its location on the Valley Pike, Staunton had recently been connected with eastern Virginia by the Virginia Central Railroad. The line had as its ambition to connect eastern Virginia with the Ohio River—which, as the Chesapeake & Ohio Railroad, it accomplished after the Civil War. During the Civil War, the Virginia Central figured vitally and dramatically in the strategy and tactics of the Union and Confederate armies, and the road served Stonewall Jackson in his famous Valley Campaign. In 1856 the trains roared across the Virginia countryside at the rate of twenty miles an hour and charged passengers four cents a mile. Its Staunton terminus was at the foot of one of the city's many hills, and its small depot, typical of the period, was flanked by an open platform for passengers and freight.

Looking upward from the depot, the newly arriving Wilsons would have seen solidly built brick houses, some red, some white-washed, surrounded by grass plots with great shade trees. One had been designed by Thomas Jefferson, as a wedding present for a friend. With no crowding, the city spread on its rolling hills over a large area for the size of its population. The city physically suggested the substantial and unhurried life of the people.

In the hundred years since its frontier beginnings, Staunton had acquired a certain patina of age, as American communities went. Though its citizens did not affect the lordly airs of some plantation masters, their society was indelibly influenced by Virginia customs, manners, style. They esteemed graciousness of manner and generosity of spirit, and if immovably conservative, they were also sturdily self-reliant and, while following the social pattern of an aristocracy, were ruggedly determined in making destiny their own. There was about them a four-square forthrightness, softened by the courtesy which had become traditional in Virginia character. Here was a segment of the ante bellum South which seemed uniquely stable, deep-rooted in its own evolved culture.

The strife then building towards the open conflict of the Confederate War for Independence seemed off stage to the "Valley people." In 1856, the Democrats elected to the Presidency James Buchanan, a dependable party man from Pennsylvania, and the years were in the future when the lady he squired in Washington, Rose Greenhow, was to be imprisoned as the most famous of all Confederate spies. In Kansas, the personal warfare between proslavery and proabolitionists was dying down, and at the polls the people had repudiated the new sectional Republican party led by a vainglorious Fremont. Only the extremists of the North and South strove to keep alive the slavery "issue" as a bone of contention between the regions. In Virginia, despite its few highly vocal secessionists, men of substance strove for peace within the Union. In the state capital at Richmond, resolutions were passed by religious organizations to promote good fellowship, and the Reverend Mr. Wilson might well have attended there the meetings of the Presbyterian synod which strove with other denominations towards this end. In Staunton, the Reverend Mr. Wilson and his family must have felt at once at home in the Scotch-Presbyterian background of the congregation so similar to their own. There is no question that the congregation liked its new minister.

He was spoken of as "a fine-looking man"—tall, with a strong, handsome face, which he framed in the fashionable sidelocks and under-the-chin whiskers. He spoke with a resonant bass voice, a gift of eloquence and a dedicated zeal. He was an impressive preacher. And since preaching is a basic element of worship in the Presbyterian religion, his success can be judged by the fact that the church was enlarged and renovated during his two-year stay. The pulpit was rebuilt and a vestibule was added.

In addition to his preaching abilities the Reverend Mr. Wilson was gifted with a facile fund of humor, one noticeably inherited by his son. He always took great pride in his horse, keeping him beautifully groomed. One day a member of the congregation, meeting him on the street, expressed surprise at the shabbiness of the preacher's coat in contrast to the gloss of that of the horse. With his bright eyes lighting up, Mr. Wilson said, "Well, you see, I look after the horse, but the church looks after me."

Mrs. Wilson, whose Christian name was Janet, was thought by the community to be pretty, with a wreath of brown curls about her oval face. She was a reserved woman with the dignity of the shy, and apparently lacked any semblance of her husband's sense of humor. She is said to have laughed at his jokes more out of a sense of wifely duty than true amusement. She was of a fine, intensely serious nature, devoted to music and an accomplished pianist, although she would never play for strangers.

She had borne two girls before they moved to Staunton. Midway of their second year in the handsome Manse, Mrs. Wilson bore her first son in the downstairs bedroom. The child, born at quarter to one of a Sunday morning on December 28, 1856, was named Thomas Woodrow after Janet Wilson's father, Dr. Woodrow. He was called "Tommy," the future President not adopting Woodrow as his Christian name until his second year in college. As a baby, Tommy grew up in the nursery, a large, bright room immediately behind his mother's. There the crib stood between a window and a fireplace with a white woodwork mantel. No intimate detail is known of the eight-month period in which Woodrow Wilson lived in the Manse in Staunton. He was baptized in April, 1857. It can be assumed that nothing exceptional occurred to the baby, although in the home today one sees, among other Wilson possessions, many of the effects of the Wilson family which served them during this period, and indicate something of their interests: Dr. Wilson's family Bible with its records of the births of his four children; the crib in which Wilson slept; pieces of family silver and china; some of the original Manse furniture; and, as though come home to rest, Mrs. Wilson's guitar and the violin which later belonged to the Wilson boys. The double-parlor draperies of red damask, their ornate gilt cornices and tiebacks, are facsimiles of those described in Mrs. Wilson's letters.

In August of 1857, the successful minister received a call to a large church in the larger city of Augusta, Georgia, and the Wilson family left Virginia.‡‡

The connective line of the Staunton period in the Wilson family was the Scotch Presbyterianism that dominated the community in which the father began his ministry. The Reverend Joseph R. Wilson was the greatest influence in the life of his son, who wrote his father:

You have given me a love that grows, that is stronger in me now that I am a man than it was when I was a boy, and it will be stronger in me when I am an old man than it is now—a love in brief that is rooted and grounded in reason and not filial instinct merely—a love resting upon abiding foundations, of service, recognizing in you, as in a very real sense the author of all that I have to be grateful for.

The son always felt a warmth for the place where his father had started his career in the ministry, and where he had been born. In later life Woodrow Wilson showed a deep familiarity with his father's associations in Staunton. When he was at the University of Virginia Law School, Wilson tried to visit, without written permission, his attractive Woodrow cousins who were then attending Augusta Female Seminary (later Mary Baldwin). At the time of Wilson's birth in Staunton, his father had served for a year as principal of the Seminary. Since then, Miss Mary Baldwin had assumed the directorship of the school, in its low ebb during the Civil War, and had transformed the former day seminary into a fine boarding school. When Woodrow Wilson was accosted by the aged Negro who served as doorman, he identified himself as the son of a former pastor of Miss Baldwin. But despite his memories of his father's connections with Miss Baldwin, he was refused admittance.

Later, going through regular channels, he visited his cousin Hattie at the Seminary and even spent Christmas holidays in Staunton with a kinsman in order to be near her. Indeed, the family was astonished by Wilson's courtship of his cousin, which it is said continued until he made a formal proposal—and was rejected.

Many years passed before Wilson again visited the birthplace, but Stauntonians were deeply interested in the son of their former Presbyterian minister. They began talking about him for President while he was still at Princeton, and it is claimed that the first Wilson Club in the country was organized in Staunton in 1910. The following year, he visited the city, seeking out old friends of his father, and spoke at Mary Baldwin, where so long before his charming cousin had flirted with him.

Wilson always took great pride in his Virginia heritage and spoke of it with the affection of a true native. In 1912, while campaigning for the Presidency in Baltimore, Wilson, then governor of New Jersey, was accosted by a lady who asked him if he considered himself a Virginian or a Georgian.

"I am a born Virginian," said Wilson proudly, using his native state's vernacular in the reply. But, his questioner continued, he had only lived in Virginia as an infant!

"Yes," replied Wilson with zestful humor, "but a man's root-age is more important than his leafage."

In 1912, after he had been elected President, Staunton enjoyed the biggest day in its history when President-elect Woodrow Wilson revisited his birthplace for a birthday celebration. The Valley city did itself proud. Bands, dignitaries and vast crowds in a torchlight procession met Mr. and Mrs. Wilson at the depot on a cold night, December twenty-seventh. The famous Stonewall Brigade Band played "Home Sweet Home" as the Wilsons were escorted to the red brick manse, since painted white. They were received as the guests of the current occupants, Dr. and Mrs. Fraser, and, in the company of the Frasers' daughter, the President-elect visited the room where he had been born.

The next day, Woodrow Wilson celebrated his fifty-sixth birthday by giving himself over completely to the townspeople. The year was auspicious by calculation, some said, for had he not been born in '56 and elected to the Presidency in his fifty-sixth year. There were teas and receptions given at Stuart Hall and Mary Baldwin, a parade which featured the Virginia Military Institute cadets and regular cavalry from Fort Myer, and the climax of the whole grand day was a banquet at Staunton Military Academy. Beside a huge cake bearing fifty-six candles, he received his birthday present— miniatures of his father and mother done on ivory by Miss Ellie Stuart, daughter of Jeb Stuart.

Stauntonians who were present at this greatest event in the city's history remember the warmth and friendliness of the great American. The austerity, which others remember, came later, after his illness. The associations of the people of his birthplace with Woodrow Wilson are entirely pleasant. They regarded him as a great man long before he was nationally recognized. Their pride in his birthplace is no after-the-fact claim on a distinguished leader. Always feeling that he belonged to them, their pride is based on their early recognition of the man who was born in their midst.

Of the Manse, Stauntonians have made a shrine dedicated to the memory and ideals of the city's most famous son. In 1938 the

Woodrow Wilson Birthplace Foundation was established for the home's acquisition, support and maintenance. An annual appropriation from the state of Virginia assists in an endeavor to re-create in its entirety "The Birthplace" setting of 1856. Visitors from all over the world, often from surprisingly obscure areas, come as though on a pilgrimage, articulate in their gratitude, to this American monument which celebrates the man whose work was for all the peoples of the earth.

The Human Being

VIRGINIUS DABNEY

The great curse of public life is that you are not allowed to say all the things that you think. Some of my opinions about some men are extremely picturesque, and if you could only take a motion picture of them, you would think it was Vesuvius in eruption. Yet . . . I have to make believe that I have nothing but respectable and solemn thoughts all the time.

New York, Jan. 27, 1916 [7]

. . . every man who takes office in Washington either grows or swells, and when I give a man an office, I watch him carefully to see whether he is swelling or growing. The mischief of it is that when they swell they do not swell enough to burst.

Washington, D.C., May 15, 1916 [8]

I am not afraid of a knave. I am not afraid of a rascal. I am afraid of a strong man who is wrong, and whose wrong thinking can be impressed upon other persons by his own force of character and force of speech.

The New Freedom, Chapter 9 [9]

—WOODROW WILSON

A MAN who danced hornpipes on station platforms while campaigning for the Presidency and jigs in the White House after his election; who was fervently addicted to Gilbert and Sullivan, loved limericks, wrote some good ones himself, and recited nonsense verse on many occasions; was one of the best storytellers of his time and a mimic of rare talent; who doubled as a successful football coach at two universities while serving as professor; and who, although slanderously assailed in whispering campaigns from coast to coast as a rake and libertine, was, in fact, a notably affectionate husband and father.

That man was Woodrow Wilson. Admittedly the prevailing picture in the public mind is far different. Wilson is commonly regarded as having been an austere, humorless, stern, even arrogant individual, who could brook no disagreement from anyone, whose refusal to accept compromise reservations to the Covenant of the League of Nations led to its defeat in the Senate, and who broke with several long-time friends before he died. Then too, a great many people believed the ridiculous gossip regarding his personal life.

Woodrow Wilson undoubtedly was in some respects a bundle of contradictions. It would be ludicrous to picture him as behaving most of the time like an end man in a minstrel show, but it would be equally so to regard him as a ruthless, opinionated person with ice water in his veins, or as an unfaithful husband.

True, Wilson was intolerant of stupidity; he did not "suffer fools gladly." A man of great intellectual power himself, he found it difficult, at times, to restrain his scorn for his mental inferiors. Furthermore, his tragic illness and paralysis, brought on by his fight for the League of Nations against the urgent advice of his doctors, affected his attitudes, and was the chief cause of his "breaks" with several old friends.

My own acquaintance with Mr. Wilson began when he was Governor of New Jersey. He visited in the home of my parents at the University of Virginia, and I, a boy at the time, was entranced by his buoyant and witty personality. I hung around my father's study door listening to the screamingly funny anecdotes which the Governor of New Jersey was reeling off to his one-time college chum. My father, Richard Heath Dabney, a Heidelberg Ph.D. who served on the University of Virginia faculty for nearly half a century, had a sense of the ridiculous as keen as Wilson's, and their antics were something to behold.

A story Wilson told father serves to illustrate the lighter side of his nature. While President of Princeton University he was guest of honor at a dinner in the West. The host and hostess were enormously impressed by the great Dr. Wilson, and they concluded that the dinner would have to be extremely formal. And so it was, until Wilson became so bored that he inquired if the assembled company liked limericks. The hostess answered primly in the affirmative, whereupon Wilson recited the following—which was then not in the public domain as it is today, and was startlingly new:

> There was a young monk of Siberia
> Whose existence grew drearier and drearier,
> Till he burst from his cell
> With a hell of a yell
> And eloped with the Mother Superior.

A great roar went up around the table and the ice was broken. Wilson entertained the company with stories and verse for the rest of the evening.

This side of Wilson's personality had come forcibly to the attention of his fellow students on numerous occasions at the University of Virginia. For example, when he was chosen to award the prizes for foot races and similar athletic contests, he decided, egged on by his friend, Dabney, to recite some bits of doggerel which had nothing whatever to do with the occasion. Somewhere in the program he awarded the prizes, but he also included such items as the following:

> 'Twas in the gloaming by the fair Wyoming
> That I left my darling many years ago.

But memory tender brings her back in splendor
With her cheeks of roses and her brow of snow.

But where in thunder is she now, I wonder?
Oh my soul, be quiet, and my sad heart hush!
Under the umbrella of another fellow,
Ah! I think I see her paddling through the slush!

In 1885, in a letter to Miss Ellen Axson, who was to become the first Mrs. Wilson a few months later, Wilson wrote:

"It may shock you—it ought to—but I'm afraid it will not, to learn that I have a reputation (?) amongst most of my kin and certain of my friends for being irrepressible, in select circles, as a maker of grotesque addresses from the precarious elevation of chair seats, as a wearer of all varieties of comic grimaces, as a simulator of sundry unnatural, burlesque styles of voice and speech, as a lover of farces—even as a dancer of the *cancan!*"

There is universal testimony from both his college intimates and his official White House associates that despite his love of fun, which continued down the years until his final illness, Woodrow Wilson never told off-color stories.

"His wit never verged on the doubtful or the vulgar," said David F. Houston, Secretary of Agriculture in the Wilson Cabinet for eight years. Secretary Houston added that "nobody did or could tell so many apt stories as he; and yet he did not manufacture stories or lug them in by the ears—they appeared naturally, they came quickly."

Wilson began his professorial career at Bryn Mawr, and went thence to Wesleyan University at Middletown, Conn. At Wesleyan, his fame as a lecturer and public speaker was beginning to spread, and so was his fame as a football coach.

As a member of the coaching staff there (although he himself had never played football) he helped devise winning plays which gave Wesleyan a championship team. He was specifically credited, furthermore, by the college *Alumnus Magazine* with inspiring the eleven to tie Lehigh, after it had fallen two touchdowns behind. When the outlook was blackest, Professor Wilson rushed out in front of the bleachers, gave the students a going over for not cheering as they should, beat time to the college yell with his umbrella, and "continued this violently" until the players caught fire and tied the score. The Lehigh team credited him with saving the game for Wesleyan.

When he joined the Princeton faculty in 1890, he again took on the job of helping to coach the gridiron warriors. "It was a particularly welcome sight one afternoon in October to see Woodrow Wilson come striding out upon the field, take his place behind the eleven with Captain Poe, and proceed to whip the team up and down the sward, a function which Wilson continued daily to discharge through the long grind of ten weeks," said Professor Winthrop M. Daniels.

Wilson was a wildly enthusiastic fan at college athletic contests of all kinds. One observer reported that at a Princeton-Yale baseball game he "sprang to his feet and yelled like a madman."

He was greatly liked by the students at Princeton. During his twelve years as a teacher there, he was elected four times by the senior class as the most popular member of the faculty.

The principal reason seems to have lain in the brilliance of his witty and stimulating lectures on political science. More than two thirds of the students who had the right of choice elected to take one or more of his courses.

After he was chosen president of the University in 1902 by the unanimous vote of the trustees, he got into a terrific wrangle with some of the trustees, faculty and alumni over his plans for abolishing the clubs and otherwise reorganizing the institution. Yet through it all the students, whether members of clubs or not, kept a warm place in their hearts for him. When he appeared at his final commencement before resigning to run for Governor of New Jersey, they cheered him again and again. When he returned to Princeton briefly, following his election to the Presidency, he was given such an ovation by the students that the tears ran down his cheeks.

It must be conceded that Wilson broke with some of his closest friends both during his Princeton period and later, on grounds that do not impress one today as at all adequate. His break with Professor John G. Hibben, before Dr. Hibben succeeded him as president of the university, is an example. Hibben had been closer to Wilson than any other member of the faculty, but he finally decided that he could not go along with his colleague's plans for reorganizing the institution. Wilson held him in scorn forever after. It was one of the episodes which led to the conclusion in many minds that Woodrow Wilson could not tolerate disagreement of any kind.

Yet he appointed Professor Henry van Dyke, who also disagreed with him at Princeton, as Minister to the Netherlands; he named Congressman William C. Redfield, who had attacked his candidacy prior to the Baltimore Convention in 1912, to be Secretary of Commerce, and he chose George Fred Williams, who had assailed him bitterly in the campaign of 1912, as Minister to Greece.

When the "cloistered" Dr. Wilson was elected Governor of New Jersey, there was much shaking of heads by the practical politicians. They wondered whether anybody with only a theoretical knowledge of public affairs could possibly do well in the job. They were aware, however, that this "schoolmaster" was a person of great force.

"God, look at the man's jaw!" exclaimed one awestruck politician when Wilson delivered his address of acceptance.

He soon showed that he meant business, by breaking with New Jersey's Democratic bosses. In his final interview with Boss Jim Nugent, the latter shouted at Governor Wilson, "You're no gentleman!" Wilson's retort, as he showed Nugent the door was, "You're no judge!"

Wilson used a different tactic on the eve of the meeting of the State Legislature. Invited to eat fried chicken and waffles with the members of the Republican-dominated Senate at a country club, he sang songs and danced "in every comical combination anybody could think of." As he described the occasion in a letter to a friend, "the evening was one unbroken romp," and he led one Senator "several times around the big dining room in a cakewalk in which we pranced together to the perfect content of the whole company."

A few weeks later he wrote the same friend that all four of his major reform bills had passed the Senate *unanimously*, and that the hijinks at the club had undoubtedly played an important part in the result.

"I am on easy and delightful terms with all the Senators," he wrote. "They know me for something else than an 'ambitious dictator.'" He added that the newspapermen were "dazed" by his almost incredible success with the legislature.

He impressed the rank and file in New Jersey, as well as the lawmakers. One of his favorite stories concerned the comment of two laboring men who were leaving a big meeting in Newark, where the Governor had spoken.

"That's a smart guy," said one of them.

"He's smart as hell," said the other. "What I don't see is what a fellow as smart as that was doing hanging around a college so long."

Edward E. Davis, a prominent Philadelphia newspaperman who covered the New Jersey Legislature during this period, said he couldn't understand how the notion got abroad that Woodrow Wilson was cold, and he added:

"There never was a man in the Governor's chair at Trenton who had such a human way of expressing himself. . . . He seemed to be one of the happiest men I ever met. . . . No one could be in his presence for five minutes without being charmed. . . . In moments of leisure he was in the habit of joking with the newspapermen and laughingly reciting limericks."

All this contributed to his tremendous success as Governor of New Jersey and to his nomination to the Presidency in 1912.

Soon after his nomination, a whispering campaign began. It involved his friendship with attractive Mrs. Mary Hulbert Peck, whom Wilson had met in Bermuda in 1907, and with whom he had carried on an animated correspondence during the intervening years. The fact that Mrs. Peck divorced her husband in 1912 added fuel to the flames. The further fact that Mrs. Peck (or Mrs. Hulbert, as she called herself after her divorce) was a devoted friend of the whole Wilson family, that she visited them and they visited her, was largely ignored.

There is general agreement among those who have read the more than two hundred letters which Wilson wrote Mary Hulbert that they are almost entirely impersonal and concerned with public affairs. Wilson undoubtedly found Mrs. Hulbert a stimulating personality and enjoyed exchanging views with her. The substance of many of his letters to her has been published.

Wilson wrote similar letters to other able and charming women who, like Mary Hulbert, were friends of Mrs. Wilson—such as Edith Gittings Reid, wife of a Johns Hopkins professor, and Nancy Toy, who was married to a member of the Harvard faculty. There is every reason to believe that his relations with each of these talented women were completely correct. True, it was unwise for him, a public man, to carry on so extensive a correspondence with any woman other than his wife, even though—as in all these cases—Mrs. Wilson approved his doing so. She approved because she felt that she herself was "too grave," and that "since he married a wife who is not gay, I must provide for him friends who are."

William Allen White, like Wilson's other biographers, made an earnest effort to get the facts concerning Wilson and Mary Hulbert, the woman about whom the scandalous stories revolved. The noted Republican editor concluded that these were "slanders as foul and unfounded as were ever peddled in any campaign." Gamaliel Bradford, the historian, termed them "utterly baseless." Such has been the unanimous verdict of all serious students.

Dean Andrew F. West, of the Princeton Graduate School, with whom Wilson had one of his most bitter quarrels while President of the University, said:

"Heaven knows I hated Wilson like poison, but there's not one word of truth in this nonsense. It is simply not in character."

David Lawrence, the columnist, who was probably closer to Wilson throughout his public career than any other journalist, agrees that these stories had no foundation. Lawrence quotes a Princeton faculty member as having said that he (the professor) was approached by a newspaper in 1912 and offered "a large sum of money if I would write an article even hinting that Mr. Wilson's personal conduct in Princeton had been improper." The faculty member added: "You know how bitterly I despise Woodrow Wilson but I told the newspaper representative I not only would not write anything but that there was nothing to write."

Professor Stockton Axson, of the Princeton faculty and Wilson's brother-in-law, would have been the first to denounce Wilson as a faithless husband, had he been one. Wilson had no more staunch defender throughout it all than Dr. Axson, who often spoke and wrote of Wilson's deep devotion to his wife.

That devotion was beautiful and profound, and was expressed

in countless ways. It was strikingly set forth in a moving letter Wilson wrote from Bryn Mawr in 1888 to his friend Dabney, who had just informed Wilson of his own approaching wedding. "Marriage has been the *making* of me both intellectually and morally," Wilson declared. He felt the same adoration for his wife more than a quarter of a century later when she died in the White House. On that occasion, he wrote Mary Hulbert: "God has stricken me almost beyond what I can bear." Later he said of Ellen Axson: "She was the most radiant creature I have ever known. Something like an aura of light always surrounded her."

The first Mrs. Wilson was not only a lovely and talented person, but at crucial points in his career she had given her husband excellent advice. She was credited, for example, with tipping the scales in favor of his running for Governor of New Jersey, and with keeping him in the race for the Democratic nomination for the Presidency in 1912, when he was on the verge of dropping out.

Wilson's affection extended to his wife's family, as evidenced by the fact that he contributed for many years from his slender means toward the support of Mrs. Wilson's sister.

Yet he refused time and again to give any sort of government post to his relatives. Francis B. Sayre, his son-in-law, was conceded to be almost ideally equipped to render valuable service at the Paris Peace Conference, and even offered to pay his own way. Wilson told him he couldn't go, as it would be misunderstood, and nobody would believe Sayre had paid his expenses. He also declined to permit his brother, a trained newspaperman, to be elected secretary of the Senate. His brother-in-law was felt to be just the man to serve ably as solicitor of the State Department, for he had been admirably trained for this post. President Wilson conceded that he was the man he wanted, above all others, but added that he "is the one man I can't appoint because he is my brother-in-law."

Such inflexibility tended to create the impression that Wilson was so stern and unbending that there were no human juices in him. Yet this was far from true; the human qualities which contributed so largely to his success as Governor of New Jersey stood him in good stead in the Presidential campaign of 1912.

Wilson realized that many persons contrasted his scholarly

approach with the rip-roaring, virile personality of "Teddy" Roosevelt, against whom he was running. Consequently he sought to overcome this impression by getting as close to his audience as he could. Salting his speeches with punchy anecdotes, he set out deliberately to see if he could make the newspapermen laugh louder than Teddy had been able to make them do. When the veteran correspondent, Charles Willis Thompson, dropped his pencil and guffawed uproariously at a story Wilson told, the latter looked down at him from the platform with a satisfied smile. And when, on another occasion, someone in the audience yelled "That was a good one, Woody!" the candidate mentioned it later to newspapermen with obvious relish. "They called me Woody!" he said, his eyes dancing. He was clearly pleased that he was being thus hailed. Here was further evidence that he was developing the type of platform personality that would make the people feel close to him.

Later in the campaign, he made a whirlwind campaign through New Jersey. One evening he returned to his hotel at Cape May, after delivering a dozen or more speeches. He looked haggard and exhausted, and his friend, Judge John W. Wescott, told him he ought to go to bed at once.

"Judge, I haven't the slightest intention of going to bed," said Wilson. "I'm going to recuperate by having some fun with you boys."

Judge Wescott then gave the following account:

"The 'fun' consisted of an animated conversation that lasted until nearly two o'clock in the morning. I am not exaggerating in the least when I say that Mr. Wilson told us twenty or more funny stories. They came from every age and every clime. . . . In turn he told his stories with an Irish accent, a Negro dialect, a German, Italian or French accent. There was a clever point connected with each story. He had us laughing during all the time he was talking. If you had been in an adjoining room, when he was telling his Irish story, you would have sworn it was an Irishman talking, and so on with the different nationalities.

"Not one of the stories he told was shady or off-color. Indeed, this was characteristic of the man. . . . He was the cleanest-minded man I ever came in contact with."

This somewhat strenuous evening with "the boys," piled on top of twelve or fifteen speeches, would seem to have been enough to put Wilson in bed for a week. Yet very much to the contrary, when the party broke up, he looked "as if he had just come out of a refreshing sleep"!

Sometime afterward, Judge Westcott asked Dr. Cary Grayson, the White House physician, how Wilson managed to stand the strain of the Presidency. Dr. Grayson replied:

"The answer is the medical power of fun. The President lightens his labors by his wit and his enjoyment of storytelling."

One of the subjects about which Wilson joked was his own appearance. He considered himself "horse-faced," and was fond of reciting the limerick which has come to be associated with his name:

> For beauty I am not a star,
> There are others more handsome, by far.
> But my face—I don't mind it,
> For I am behind it,
> It's the people in front that I jar.

During the campaign of 1912, people who saw him for the first time were heard to remark "Well, he may be all right, but he ain't good-looking." Wilson overheard this. When, on one occasion, he was asked by a member of his party on the train for his opinion of a certain individual, Wilson replied, with a knowing grin, "Well, he may be all right, but he ain't good-looking."

And then he added:

"It reminds me of a thing that happened when I was running for governor. I stopped in front of a billboard that had my picture on it. As I looked at it I became conscious of two working men who had stopped and were staring at me. One of them said to the other, 'Bill, damned if them two ain't enough alike to be twins.' "

Wilson also liked to tell of an incident which happened in his native town of Staunton, Virginia, where he received a great ovation following his first election as President. A small boy in the crowd shoved and pushed his way to the front until he stood squarely in front of the speaker, and shouted, "Where is it? Where is it?" Wilson stopped his speech and said goodnaturedly, "Well, my boy,

I guess I'm it." "Shucks!" exclaimed the lad with a look of utter disgust. "I thought it was a dogfight."

His first years in the White House were, in the main, happy and successful. During those years, the fun-loving side of his personality was more obvious than it became later when Mrs. Wilson's death and the simultaneous outbreak of the first World War left him desperately depressed.

It is important to emphasize, however, that in the early years of his Presidency, Woodrow Wilson did not impress the average citizen as a jovial or even a lively person. In addition to the fact that he was never the back-slapping type, and might even have been termed shy, he had suffered with digestive and nervous troubles for many years. He actually came to the White House carrying a stomach pump and coal-tar headache tablets, and although Dr. Grayson managed to get him to cast these aside for golf, he was never robust.

The gayer side of his nature was not usually visible to the public. Much was made of his devout Scotch Presbyterianism and of his being "the scholar in politics," and he looked the part. He could write his friend, Robert Bridges, editor of *Scribner's* magazine, "I often long for the renewal of old comradeships . . . the old love never dies down for a moment"; he could jestingly close an affectionate letter to Heath Dabney, "Oh, thou very ass!" Yet his own son-in-law, Secretary of the Treasury William G. McAdoo, said that callers at the White House who were not congenial to Wilson's spirit "would go away with the conviction that they had met a modern impersonation of Jonathan Edwards."

The coming of the war in Europe was, of course, a great trial to him, and he felt that he had to devote himself unreservedly to his governmental duties. George Creel, head of the Committee on Public Information, wrote that "Mr. Wilson's regard for his time became an actual obsession; everything and everybody were excluded that did not bear upon the task." Contrary to the practice he had followed in New Jersey, he made no particular effort to become friendly with the leaders in Congress, and this lack of personal contact became more obvious as his responsibilities grew.

Nor were his relations with the Washington press as cordial as they had been with the correspondents in Trenton. Mr. Wilson felt that, after he became President, many of the papers were entirely too concerned with trivialities. "Sob sisters" enraged him by speculating as to the love affairs of his three daughters.

During the campaign of 1912, his press relations had suffered a slump when one of his speeches stressing the need for "thinking things through" turned up in several New York papers as an endorsement of chewing tobacco. Wilson had described a group of men sitting around a country store, conferring about the affairs of the neighborhood, and spitting into a sawdust box. "Whatever may be said against the chewing of tobacco," said the speaker (who neither chewed nor smoked himself), "this at least can be said for it, that it gives a man time to think between sentences." "Advocates the Chewing of Tobacco" was the headline next day, and the papers in question carried only a brief, garbled account, which was promptly seized upon and reproduced in advertisements of a tobacco firm!

Not long after his election, Wilson had received a large group of correspondents at Sea Girt, New Jersey. Asked by them about the mail he was getting, he replied that it was quite heavy, and that he felt somewhat like the frog in the well: "Every time he jumped up one foot he fell back two." Next morning one of the New York papers headed the story "Wilson Feels Like Frog."

This sort of thing infuriated him. So did the behavior of certain cameramen, notably one who disregarded his courteous request in Bermuda that there be no photographs of Miss Jessie Wilson, his daughter, who had just come from a bicycle ride and was somewhat disheveled. When a photographer promptly snapped her picture anyway, the supposedly cold and emotionless Woodrow Wilson "turned the color of a strawberry" and rushed the man with clenched fists. Wilson pulled up just short of punching the fellow's head, when he realized what sort of newspaper copy it would make if the President of the United States engaged in fisticuffs with a cameraman. His eyes still blazing, he shouted, "You're no gentleman! I want to give you the worst thrashing you ever had in your life; and what's more, I'm perfectly able to do it!" The episode served not only to illustrate Wilson's growing rift with the press, but it was one of several instances which might be cited to show that this "austere intellectual" was capable of enormous wrath.

As a matter of fact, Wilson disliked the frequent references to him as a glacial, unfeeling person. He told David Lawrence in this connection that, to the contrary, "my constant embarrassment is to restrain the emotions that are inside me," and added, "I sometimes feel like a fire from a far from extinct volcano."

To his secretary, Joseph P. Tumulty, he remarked, "It is no compliment to me to have it said that I am only a highly developed intellectual machine. Good God, there is more to me than that! I want people to love me, but I suppose they never will. Do you think I am cold and unfeeling?" Tumulty replied, "I think you are one of the warmest-hearted men I ever met."

Tumulty also wrote that tears of sincere grief often came into Wilson's eyes when he was being appealed to for clemency on behalf of some convicted criminal, or when he was otherwise greatly moved.

On one occasion when under the terrific strain of events on the eve of America's entry into the first World War, the President was discussing with him certain editorials that had been written by Waldo L. Cook, editor of the Springfield, Massachusetts, *Republican*. Tumulty quoted Wilson as saying with deep feeling, "That man understood me and sympathized." The private secretary then went on, "As he said this, the President drew a handkerchief from his pocket, wiped away great tears that stood in his eyes, and then laying his head on the Cabinet table, sobbed as if he had been a child."

The death of Mrs. Wilson and the outbreak of the war in Europe had subjected President Wilson to an almost constant emotional ordeal. His wife's passing left him horribly depressed, and the world crisis added greatly to his burdens.

Mrs. Wilson died on August 6, 1914. For some eight months, the President lived in "tomblike seclusion." Then, in the spring of 1915, the gloom which enveloped his spirit was gradually lifted through the companionship of a beautiful and attractive widow— Virginia-born Edith Bolling Galt. Mrs. Galt had met the President through the latter's cousin, Miss Helen Bones. Within a few months, if not weeks, he had fallen deeply in love with her, and had characteristically consulted his daughters as to how they would feel if he married again. They gave their approval.

But it was some months before Mrs. Galt overcame her hesitancy to assume the tremendous responsibilities of marrying the President of the United States. She told him she would marry him if he were defeated for re-election, but otherwise was uncertain as to whether she should do so.

Finally, on an automobile drive through Rock Creek Park she overcame her reluctance. The President had just said to her, "I have no right to ask you to help me by sharing this load that is almost breaking my back."

Mrs. Wilson tells what happened next:

"I am proud to say that despite the fact that Mr. Murphy of the Secret Service, and Robinson, the chauffeur, were on the front seat and Helen [Bones] beside me on the back seat, I put my arms around his neck and said, 'Well, if you won't ask me, I will volunteer, and be ready to be mustered in as soon as can be.'"

Although various members of the Cabinet and other leaders of the Democratic party felt that the President's remarriage so soon after his first wife's death probably would wreck his chances for a second term, he married Mrs. Galt in December, 1915. She brought cheer and warmth into his life, and they were inseparable thenceforth.

So inseparable, in fact, that President Wilson saw few other people during the succeeding years, except the minimum required by his official duties. He talked over many of his problems with his wife, whose practical cast of mind was no less useful to him than her great social charm, but otherwise retired within himself to a much greater degree than formerly. "I rarely consult anybody," he told Ida Tarbell in the autumn of 1916, when America was drawing closer and closer to involvement in the war.

This was on the eve of the Presidential election, when the whisperings against Wilson's private life were at their height. Fantastic tales were circulated that Mrs. Galt had bought off Mrs. Hulbert with a large sum of money before marrying Wilson the previous year; Colonel House had taken Mrs. Hulbert to Europe to get her out of the way; she was receiving a handsome salary from the Treasury Department; Wilson's "love letters" to her were filled with incriminating material; Louis D. Brandeis was appointed to the Supreme Court as a reward for having hushed up the letters, and so on.

How much of this nonsense was believed, it is impossible to say. At all events, Woodrow Wilson was elected for a second term, albeit by a narrow margin.

His appointment of Brandeis to the court shortly before had not borne the remotest relationship to Mrs. Hulbert, of course. He had admired Brandeis for years, and had tried to get him into his first Cabinet. In finally naming him to the nation's highest tribunal, Wilson became the first President to appoint a Jewish citizen to that court, just as in appointing Judge Samuel Kalisch to the Supreme Court of New Jersey he had been the first to choose a Jewish justice to sit on the top court of that state. His confidence in the country's minority groups had likewise been evidenced in his selection of a Roman Catholic, Joseph P. Tumulty, as his private secretary.

This latter fact enabled him to assail one Jeremiah O'Leary in the campaign of 1916 with notable effect, and without any imputation of anti-Catholicism. O'Leary, a fire-eating Irish-American and anti-British agitator, had written Wilson a sneering letter, saying that he would not vote for him. Wilson caught the imagination of the nation with his blistering retort:

"I would feel deeply mortified to have you or anybody like you vote for me. Since you have access to so many disloyal Americans, and I have not, I will ask you to convey this message to them."

During these strenuous days, when America was on the verge of entering the war, or had actually gone in, President Wilson found time for relaxation with few persons, except Mrs. Wilson. She writes:

"When he left his desk or office, he apparently closed that door in his mind, and was ready to play; then he would play with the abandon of a boy. Frequently, at night, we would go to the Oval Room upstairs after dinner and he would put a record on the Victrola and say, 'Now I'll show you how to do a jig step.' He was light on his feet, and often said he envied Primrose, the minstrel dancer, and he wished he could exchange jobs."

President and Mrs. Wilson made it a practice for years to attend Keith's Vaudeville every Saturday night. Wilson preferred vaudeville to any other type of theatrical performance. Another means of diverting his mind from his superhuman task was, he said, to "get a rattling good detective story, get after some imaginary offender, and chase him all over."

There is general agreement that the strain of the prewar and war years aged Mr. Wilson greatly. His hair was much grayer, the lines in his face much deeper. Yet when the Armistice terms were finally accepted, he was still capable of having his little joke. As the war ended, he remarked to Secretary Tumulty:

"I feel like the Confederate soldier General John B. Gordon used to tell of, soliloquizing on a long, hard march during the Civil War: 'I love my country and I am fightin' for my country, but if this war ever ends, I'll be dad-burned if I ever love another country.' "

So deep was his dedication to the cause of world peace that he refused to spare himself. He contracted a violent case of the then-deadly influenza in Paris, and Dr. Grayson was much alarmed. Before the President could get his strength back, he had to plunge into wearisome haggling with the Big Three—Clemenceau of France, Lloyd George of Great Britain, and Orlando of Italy.

While Wilson was under this almost unparalleled strain, Tumulty wrote to warn him that he might wreck his constitution. Wilson's reply was, "Constitution? Why man, I'm already living on my by-laws!"

Partly as a result of such rare humorous interludes, he managed to keep going. On his return to the United States he plunged into the fight for ratification of the League of Nations.

Unfortunately he made it clear that he would accept no amendments or reservations to the Covenant of the League. This was generally regarded by his friends as a bad mistake, since they felt that reasonable reservations ought to be accepted. They accordingly advised him that unless he swung across the country arousing the people on behalf of the League, ratification would fail in the Senate.

President Wilson was in a state of virtual exhaustion, and was told by his physicians that the trip would be dangerous, if not fatal. He had been under such pressure that he had had no time to prepare a single speech for his tour, and he expected to make something like a hundred. It was before the day of Presidential ghost writers. Weary and worn, plagued by raging headaches, he threw himself into the campaign with what little strength he had left, and refused to listen to Dr. Grayson's urgent plea that his itinerary allow for a week's rest at the Grand Canyon. He said he could not justify taking any time whatever for relaxation on so vital a mission.

His breakdown near Pueblo, Colorado, in September, 1919, was the almost inevitable result. A crippling stroke, which paralyzed his left side, followed soon after his return to Washington. He was an invalid until his death in 1924.

It was during this period of invalidism that he broke with his long-time friend and confidant, Colonel Edward M. House, and with Private Secretary Tumulty and Secretary of State Robert Lansing. Had he been in normal health, it is probable that these breaks would not have occurred. Yet it is understandable that under the circumstances, the public should have considered the rupturing of these long-standing friendships as climactic evidences of "Wilsonian arrogance."

The invalid in the White House, who was not seen at all by the public for many months, and then was glimpsed only on rare occasions when out for an automobile drive with his devoted wife, was far from being the vigorous, alert figure who had taken over the Presidency only a few years before. The closing years of his life strengthened the popular feeling that his was a cold and remote personality.

Yet even during his serious illness, when the Senate sent a delegation to confer with him, a spark of the old wit crackled to the surface. One of the group was Republican Senator Albert B. Fall, who said, "Mr. President, we have all been praying for you."

"Which way, Senator?" Wilson inquired with a chuckle.

Later, when the patient was more fully recovered, Secretary of State Bainbridge Colby arranged for an acquaintance to see him about a matter which the party in question deemed important. Colby asked Wilson after the interview what impression the man made on him. "That of a bungalow," said Wilson. "How is that?" asked Colby. "No upper story," was the reply.

Despite the strain of Inauguration Day in 1921, when the broken man turned over the Presidential office to his successor,

Warren G. Harding, Wilson came through "smilingly and with a whimsical, humorous twist to his comments," said the correspondent of the Detroit *Free Press*.

Until only a couple of months before his death, when Mr. Wilson arrived at the vaudeville on Saturday night, the street outside was usually filled with people who wanted to see the former President and cheer him. The audience always gave him and Mrs. Wilson a standing ovation as they entered and departed. Mr. Wilson's love of light comedy and slapstick humor never left him.

It was, he liked to say, the "Irish" in him that accounted for this. His "Irish" was Scotch-Irish, and he was fond of attributing his frivolous qualities to his forebears, the Wilsons, who came to this country from Northern Ireland. The Woodrows, on the other hand, were blown-in-the-bottle Scots for many generations—serious, dour, crusading preachers; intent intellectuals. Woodrow Wilson often referred to these two elements as battling for supremacy inside him.

The "Irish" in him deserves far more emphasis than it has received. Few, if any, Presidents in our history have been so adept as storytellers, so prankish in their lighter moods, quicker in repartee, more affectionate in their intimate friendships or tenderer in the family circle than Woodrow Wilson. The myths of coldness, hardness, humorlessness and ruthlessness that have grown up around his name should be dispelled in this centennial year.

The Man of Faith

FRANK BELL LEWIS

Christianity gave us in the fullness of time, the perfect image of right living, the secret of social and individual well-being; for the two are inseparable, and the man who receives and verifies that secret in his own living has discovered not only the best and only way to serve the world; but also the one happy way to satisfy himself. Then, indeed, has he come to himself.

When A Man Comes to Himself, Harper & Bros. 1915.[10]

There is a sense, I sometimes think, in which everyone of us in whose life principle forms a part is merely holding up a light which he himself did not kindle, not his own principle, not something peculiar and individual to himself, but that light which must light all mankind, the love of the truth, the love of duty, the love of those things which are not stated in the terms of personal interest.

Address on Robert E. Lee, Jan. 19, 1909 [11]

Our civilization cannot survive materially unless it be redeemed spiritually.

The Road Away from Revolution, Atlantic Monthly Press, 1923.[12]

—WOODROW WILSON

"THE stern Covenanter tradition which is behind me," President Wilson once said, "sends many an echo down the years." The Covenanter tradition was his heritage from the hard-forged faith of Scotch and Scotch-Irish forebears. It formed the foundation of his character and convictions, and accounts, largely, for his strength and achievements. It accounts, too, for some of his political weaknesses and "hateful virtues." It helps explain the strangeness that marked Wilson in the eyes of so many men in the twentieth century. To those who did not know the tradition he often seemed simply incredible. Therefore they misunderstood him in fabulous ways, and took him to be anything from "a god upon a mountain" to "a bloodless pedagogue playing a lone hand in the attic of his own soul."

The echoes of this Covenanter tradition are everywhere in Wilson's biography. He was proud of his ancestry, and liked to refer to "that unbending race" from which he had come. In the crises of his life he frequently and consciously turned back to the heritage of his people. Once he told a Bryn Mawr class, "No one who amounts to anything is without some trace of Scotch-Irish blood." He said such things in jest, yet they were also half in earnest, for he understood himself to be the child and product of this tradition.

The idea which underlies this Covenanter tradition appeared in Hebrew history when Abraham went forth from Ur of the Chaldees under the terms of a covenant with his God. Perhaps the idea is as ancient as the time when "the Lord God planted a garden eastward in Eden" and there put "the man whom he had formed." Wilson's phrase, however, referred more specifically to the tradition named after events in Edinburgh, Scotland, when Protestantism was struggling to establish itself against the religious authority of Rome and against the will of the English crown. The Scots wanted two things: political independence of England and religious independence of the Roman Catholic church. From the days of William Wallace and Robert the Bruce these two Scottish hopes had been related, and sometimes confused. Persecution of the Protestants was sporadic for a time, but began in earnest about 1557. Then a group of nobles in Edinburgh, having committed themselves to the Reformation principles, met and formed a solemn agreement. In it they pledged their lives and their fortunes to advance the cause of the Reformation by "maintaining God's true congregation and renouncing the congregation of Satan." This agreement was the first Scottish covenant, and it gave the name "Covenanter" to the Protestant Scots of that time and of succeeding generations.

These Covenanters of 1557 were guided in their undertaking, and their resolution was strengthened, by the coming of John Knox. After an enforced absence from Scotland he returned to them, iron-willed, and fortified with the teaching of John Calvin in Geneva. This Calvinistic theology, though it mightily influenced the doctrines of many Protestant denominations, came to be associated most particularly with a type of church government called Presbyterianism, a representative democracy under the authority of elders, or presbyters. Such a system of church government was established in Scotland, and the teaching of Calvin and Knox became the popular theology. The Covenanters had need of such strong doctrine as Knox offered them, for they faced a long and bitter and bloody struggle. Theirs was a good faith for hard times. It was not inviting, but it was strong. Some forms of religious faith appeal to men by their suggestions of grace and beauty. The reeds and the willows that bow, pliant with the breeze, possess a winsome charm. But oaks that stand on the headlands, unbending, are gnarled and scarred and forbidding. So was the faith of the Covenanters to become, knotty but strong. And in that faith the men of Scotland grew tough of mind and unyielding of character.

In this long struggle for independence, political and religious, there was forged a passionate, stubborn devotion to freedom's ideals. Such devotion marked the Scot, whether he remained on his own hills or emigrated to America. These men who fought for religious liberty were schooled already for the struggle to be politically free. One English sovereign learned where the will-to-freedom of his Scottish subjects lay, and how close-linked were freedom of worship and freedom in matters of government. In 1604, King James received a request that ministers of the Protestant persuasion be allowed to hold regular meetings. In refusing the request, he bestowed a tribute which has been proudly remembered: "If you aim at a Scottish Presbytery," he said, "it accordeth as well with monarchy as God and the devil."

The heritage from these Covenanters came to Woodrow Wilson direct and unrelieved. The Woodrow family was Scotch and the Wilsons were Scotch-Irish. The difference is not in kind but in degree, the Scotch-Irish being a toughened and more hard-bitten branch of the Scotch race. The combination of these two strains in Woodrow Wilson's heritage seems to justify his official biographer in referring to "one of the toughest, grittiest, hardest-knit races of men that ever walked the face of the earth." During the reign of James I there were certain native chieftains in North Ireland who showed an unco-operative attitude toward their English overlords. To subdue or displace them, thousands of Englishmen and Lowland Scots were moved into Ulster. It was hoped that they would form a permanent population there and succeed in holding at bay the native "wild Irish." It may have been true, as one historian points out, that some of these emigrants "left their country for their country's good," but in any case the Presbyterian Church and the Calvinist doctrines overtook them in Ireland and put the stamp of Covenanter character upon them. And at the same time, Ireland and the Irish taught them the art of survival in lean and rugged times. From such a background came the thousands of Scotch-Irish immigrants to America. At one period in our history they populated the frontier from New York to South Carolina and formed what Theodore Roosevelt called "a shield of sinewy men thrust in between the people of the seaboard and the red warriors of the wilderness." Holding back the "red warriors" may have seemed a mild form of exercise to men who had faced the dispossessed Irish in Ulster. In any case, John Fiske was not far from right in giving the Scotch-Irish first place among "all the pugnacious and masterful, single-minded, conscientious, and obstinate Puritans that ever lived in any country."

Both parents of Woodrow Wilson's father came from North Ireland, probably from County Down or from Antrim. In 1807, they arrived at Philadelphia, port of entry for the tide of Scotch-Irish immigrants. They established and edited newspapers, first in

Ohio and later in Pennsylvania. Their son Joseph graduated from Princeton Theological Seminary and entered the ministry of the Presbyterian church. In 1849, he married a daughter of Thomas Woodrow, the Scotch minister of the Presbyterian Church in Chillicothe, Ohio. This Woodrow family had been long distinguished in Scotland for its learning, its independence of mind, and its strength of will. Thomas, who was educated at Glasgow University and crossed the Atlantic to accept a New York pastorate, carried the family characteristics. They were conspicuous also in one of his sons, Dr. James Woodrow, who studied under Agassiz at Harvard and completed his education at Heidelberg. He distinguished himself by leading an unsuccessful fight among his brethren of the church for acceptance of ideas proposed by Charles Darwin in *The Origin of Species*.

Woodrow Wilson was born in a Presbyterian manse, at Staunton, in the Valley of Virginia. His childhood was spent in the manse at Augusta, Georgia; his youth on the campus of a theological seminary and in various of the schools established by the Presbyterians: the private grammar schools of the postwar South, Davidson College, Princeton University. However, he was not educated primarily by the schools. He was educated also at home. The fundamentals of his thought and character were shaped principally by his father's life and teaching. He described his father's mind as "God-like," and while the father lived never took a major decision without seeking his counsel. Thus the Covenanter tradition, the heritage of the faith, was brought to bear upon the life of Woodrow Wilson.

How shall we characterize, how describe, the essential content of this religious heritage? There are some names for it, technical terms of theology used to label this type of thinking. Unhappily, they tell most of us very little about its real character. To say that it is Calvinist, or that it is Reformed, may distort the truth instead of describing it. This tradition, by its very nature, invites caricature, and the caricatures have been so many that we are no longer quite sure what we saw in the original and what in the malicious copy. There are, of course, classic theological formulations produced in this tradition—the *Institutes* of Calvin, the standards of the Westminster Assembly, the works of John Knox—but they seem archaic now, sometimes quaint, sometimes repelling, sometimes incomprehensible. They serve a purpose, but no one will come to understand the real nature of Wilson's religion by a casual reading of such documents. Or we might try to identify the tradition by mentioning the churches and groups with which it has been associated: Presbyterian, Congregational, Puritan, Pilgrim. Yet this does not describe it. The real meaning lies behind the terms, the creedal affirmations, the churches and the sermons. These are the results. Behind them is a whole and comprehensive philosophy of life based upon a single fundamental sense: the sense of the Divine Presence.

That sense provided a basic attitude, an outlook, a world view, comprehending the total meaning of life. It was a way of thinking about things in general. And it was exactly this attitude, this world view, which constituted the essential of Wilson's religious heritage. No one could argue that he agreed with, or even knew about, the intricate theological propositions that have been used to express such a world view. Theological speculation had no appeal for him. He was a devout man, faithful in public and private worship and in daily reading of the Scriptures. But he felt no need to speculate upon the truths of religion. Once he said that "so far as religion is concerned discussion is adjourned." His religious convictions lay so deep within him as to be safely established below the level of argumentation and questioning. He seems to have accepted faith in such a fundamental way that questions and arguments became, in a way, simply superfluous. It is not important that he learned a system of doctrine; it is crucially important for us to understand that he absorbed from the atmosphere in which he was reared the life philosophy by which it was permeated. He absorbed it by that subtle process which, in the home, transmits from one generation to the next life's deepest and most profound meanings. Therefore the religious heritage lay at the very roots of his being, and affected every facet of his life and thought.

Now we must try to make explicit some part of what was implicit in his thought. There are periods in history when men experience a renewal of vital contact between the human and the Divine. There was such a period some five hundred years before the beginning of the Christian era when Hebrew prophets, Greek philosophers and Oriental sages almost simultaneously discerned profound truths. Another such period came in Western culture about the time of the Reformation. At such times, men are moved by a sense of living communion with the Eternal. They know that they have encountered the Goodness and Majesty at the heart of things. From such experience of the Divine there comes a fresh vitality to the human spirit. The strength of Antaeus is renewed as often as he returns to touch the ground. And from each such experience there comes a newness into history. The tradition of faith in which Wilson was nurtured had its beginning in such a period of renewal, at the dawn of our modern age. Later, as the results of this religious event, there were developed various doctrines and ecclesiastical organizations, ethical standards, patterns for personal and social life. But whatever the forms of its expression, it was in essence a reinterpretation of life in the light of an encounter with God.

This sense of the reality and priority of the Divine Presence is the first distinguishing mark of the men in Wilson's religious tradition. To his Scotch-Irish forebears God was very real. He was, in sober truth, the most real fact of existence. They knew Him as the focus and center, the ground and goal, of all that is. For "of Him, and through Him, and unto Him," they liked to quote, "are all things." God was to them no abstract principle of order, no impersonal force operating below the level of consciousness. He was a person, everywhere present and everywhere active. Their God lived with them and in them, He spoke to them in His Word, showed Himself to them in His Son, guided them by His Spirit, knew all of their ways, and set their daily tasks. They felt that they lived their whole lives, moment by moment, act by act, "as before the face of God."

Theologians use the term "the sovereignty of God." It describes in theological shorthand this sense of God's primacy in human life. It suggests that life has purpose, properly, only as it is related to the purposes of God, that life has meaning only because of the meaning which God gives to history. A man's religion was understood, in this tradition, as existing, not for man's sake primarily, but for the glory of God. These people never thought of religion as chiefly designed to bring them comfort or solace, to make them happy, to afford them peace of mind, or even to improve their characters and conduct. They knew that they existed "to glorify God and enjoy Him forever." Their religion was, if we may express the idea in modern terms, God-centered. "We are not our own," wrote John Calvin, "therefore let us as far as possible forget ourselves and all things that are ours. On the contrary, we are God's; to Him therefore let us live and die."

People in this tradition were strenuous in their devotion to the Divine will as they understood it. They sought to make themselves the agents of that will in every enterprise of human life and affairs. For it they proposed to dedicate every power of body and mind, to risk every venture and stretch every nerve. Of course it seems to us that they were sometimes overconfident that they knew God's will, both for themselves and their fellows. But vigor and courage came from their self-confidence and their single-minded devotion. Professor Gilbert Murray of Oxford once described the power of a man who is devoted wholly to what he believes to be right: "He is a dangerous and uncomfortable enemy because his body, which you can always conquer, gives you so little purchase over his soul."

These qualities of faith were preserved and passed along from Reformation days in Geneva and Edinburgh to the twentieth century in America. Edwin A. Alderman called attention to one of them when he said that Wilson was a man who "took God Almighty seriously as the Supreme Reality." Wilson himself expressed that sense of the Divine Presence so characteristic of his tradition when he said that a man must come to see himself as "not the creature of the drawing room or the stock exchange, but a lonely, awful soul confronted by the Source of all souls. . . ." And in his conviction that all things are ordered by the will of God, and in his devotion to that will, Wilson again proved himself a son of these ancient Covenanters. Alderman paid tribute to that devotion in the Memorial Address before Congress: "There was such a thing as God's will to this man: and when he thought he had divined that will, he knew the right, the absolute right, and he was prepared to stand on that, if friends deserted him or he parted company with friends, if applause came or if the blow fell."

A second, and equally characteristic mark of the Covenanter

tradition was its understanding of the nature of authority, and of human responsibility to the authority of God and of men. Because they were so intensely aware of God's presence and so single-mindedly attentive to His will, the Covenanters grew somber and stern with a sense of responsibility. But their responsibility was to God. And they had this compensation, that responsibility to God released them from subservience to their fellows or to human institutions. Their opinions took shape in some such way as this: Now that God has come to us, personally, and spoken to us individually by His Word and His Spirit, we know that men are not dependent upon human agencies for the establishment of a religious relationship. And further, since God has spoken directly to us, our answer, in the last analysis, must be given directly to Him. Each man of us is responsible for himself, and ultimately responsible only to God. Each man must decide the crucial issue of his response to the Divine. This terrible and inescapable freedom before God is the ground and guarantee of freedom among men.

Naturally, when men were filled with thoughts like these, they began to be insubordinate to bishops and kings. They rejected the claim of the bishops because they understood the soul's encounter with God to be a direct encounter, mediated only through Christ the Son. They could allow no creature to interfere in this relationship, intruding between the human and the Divine. Hence they knew themselves independent, finally, of bishop and priest. To their minds it seemed that all believers are priests, all alike responsible for their service, yet none solely dependent upon another for communion with God. Neither could any king hope to exact an ultimate allegiance from men of such convictions. Because they thought so much upon the sovereignty of God they would accept no earthly sovereignty as final. Of course it is true that they were intensely interested in political theory and had pronounced opinions upon matters of statecraft. It is also true that they were aggressive and influential in political life, in Scotland and wherever they traveled. But their political philosophy was related to the fundamental proposition that "all authority of governments on earth originates from God alone." They felt that it was dependence upon God which created the possibility of independence among men. To them it was bondage to God's will that allowed freedom from man's tyranny.

And equality they understood as based upon the equality of all men before the Sovereign Ruler of the cosmos.

To hear the echo of this tradition we need but to turn to Wilson's explanation of his belief that the Bible is "the Magna Charta of the human soul." "It reveals every man to himself as a distinct moral agent, responsible not to men, not even to those men whom he has put over him in authority, but responsible through his own conscience to his Lord and Maker. Whenever a man sees this vision he stands up a free man, whatever may be the government under which he lives. . . ."

The Covenanters believed that they could move from one idea to the next by a process which they called "good and necessary inference." One good and necessary inference from the sense of individual responsibility before God was that all individuals must be prepared by education for the discharge of their responsibilities. For religious reasons men must be able to read, to reason, to understand and to decide for themselves. After the Scottish covenant was signed, the Covenanters undertook as one of their first duties to provide means for a "virtuous and godly upbringing of the youth of this realm." Their schools were multiplied, not only to provide learned ministers for their pulpits, but also to prepare their people. They practiced the intellectual disciplines in the sternest way. Mastery of Latin, Greek and Hebrew was expected of their ministers and encouraged among their laymen. Philosophy and history were studied by the same exacting standards. They found satisfaction in rigorous intellectual exercises, in wrestling with paradoxical ideas and refractory facts. They were at times pedantic, but their discipline made for high competence in the art of handling ideas.

We can mention no other respect in which Woodrow Wilson was more obviously a child of the tradition than in this. He lived his life and did his work primarily in the realm of ideas. Most of his years were invested in education, but even in the political realm his function was largely an intellectual one. Even here, he was dealing rather with ideas than with people. Despite his prominence, he never became a political personality in the sense in which that term might describe many popular leaders. He remained rather the symbol of a set of ideas. He was never self-confident nor wholly at ease with people outside the circle of his intimate friends. But when he came to deal with ideas he was at home. There he was master of the situation.

A third and final characteristic of the Covenanter tradition was its insistence that all of life, including its political phases, must operate upon those principles of justice and righteousness established by the Creator. James Stalker, in writing of John Knox, said, "Only less important to his native land than his religious views were the Scottish Reformer's political opinions. To him, in all probability, the two appeared to be one: and, ever since, in the Scottish mind the waters of religion and political conviction have been in close proximity, with a constant tendency to mingle." We can explain this fact only in the light of what these Covenanters understood by the term "vocation." To them it meant that the will of God had meaning for every phase and function of a man's life, for the "secular" as well as for the "sacred." In fact the distinction between secular and sacred was lost in the idea of vocation. A religion confined to the church or to the cloister became impossible for them. Wherever a man might be, whatever his tasks in commerce or industry or agriculture, in art or science or philosophy, he was always engaged in the service of God. Kings and magistrates, plowmen and politicians were equally His servants.

Such an understanding of their vocation made the Covenanters both industrious and aggressive. Wilson himself expressed the sense of the tradition when he said, "We are not put into this world to sit still and know, we are put into it to act." And action, to the men of that tradition, meant the effort to make all activities of men serve the purposes of God. They called upon heaven and earth, all nations and all peoples, all orders and institutions to glorify God by doing His will, that is, by acting upon the principles of righteousness and justice which He has ordained. With these ends in view, the Covenanters were never backward in proposing changes. They felt that it was their right, their duty, even, to break the "sorry scheme of things" and reshape it according to their purposes. They could not be tame or submissive, and they had not the slightest inclination to adjust themselves to their environment. Such a notion would never have occurred to them; they were intent upon adjusting the environment to themselves and to their religious ideals. Out of such attitudes there came, eventually, a bold proposal to reorganize the world.

When that proposal was made by Wilson, it was based upon the confidence that there are principles of righteousness and justice upon which human affairs, at any level, can and should operate. He conceived of public and private morality alike as expressions of these principles, and there is no theme more regularly recurrent in his writings than that of the distinction between principle and expediency. When he had fixed upon a course of action which seemed to him right, any suggestion of compromise became odious, and he felt that he could not, that he had no right to, deviate in the least from the principle involved. Political issues in his mind were resolved into differences between right and wrong, and he could be grimly resolute and inflexible. Then he would reduce friends and enemies alike to exasperation and rage. But his stubborn integrity won the world's confidence in a unique way, and there was a time when the populace, at home and abroad, trusted him almost to idolatry.

If the Covenant of the League of Nations was in some sense the end result in history of "the stern Covenanter tradition," it was also the fruit of Wilson's lifelong interest in the covenant idea. Agreements and constitutions always intrigued him. He drew up a constitution for his boyhood gang, meeting in his father's barn beneath "a portrait in red of His Satanic Majesty, torn from an advertisement of devilled ham." He wrote or rewrote constitutions for student groups and debating societies at Davidson, Princeton, the University of Virginia, Johns Hopkins, Wesleyan. His life was profoundly influenced by a "solemn covenant" made with a fellow student during undergraduate days at Princeton. It is not strange that when the opportunity came he attempted a constitution for the human race.

The most difficult and the most intriguing problem in the study of Wilson's thought has to do with the relative importance in his mind of this Covenanter tradition and of the humanitarian and liberal ideals of our Western culture. It is, of course, obvious that the latter thought strain influenced him in many ways. An example appears in his deviation from the Covenanter tradition toward a more optimistic estimate of man and man's human possibilities. The tradition would have criticized his dream of unity and world order as unrealistic because it underestimated the seriousness of sin. Sin, the Covenanters could have pointed out, has dissolved the unity in which God intended that men should live, and the hope of a united humanity is therefore only "a looking backward after a lost paradise." Yet the dream was a product of the tradition. It can be argued, cogently perhaps, that when this hope of a united humanity appears in the Western culture it is usually based upon a humanitarian ideal and is therefore the child of Plato and his disciples. I believe it was not so with Wilson's dream, for his faith was not basically in man but in a sovereign God whose purposes of righteousness and justice were to prevail in history. The dream with which Wilson captured the imagination of modern men was, as he himself understood it, less the product of Athens than of Geneva.

This dream itself, and those qualities by which he illumined it to fire the world's imagination, were largely the fruits of his use of the religious heritage. By the depth of his conviction, by the intensity of his faith, by his integrity of character and purpose he transcended his limitations and succeeded in transplanting his dream to the hearts of men. As Alderman said, "His voice was the voice of free peoples, and all over the earth in the great capitols, among the tribes of the desert, in the islands of the sea, men felt the modeling of his thought and sensed the grandeur of his aims."

Of course, Woodrow Wilson did not create, *de novo*, this ideal of world peace and brotherhood under the rule of justice and equity. What he did was to bring it into clear focus and make it live for modern men. It is his enduring achievement, his legacy to our times. His defeat at home, and the subsequent shortcomings of the League of Nations, do not prove that Wilson failed. His ideal survived those disasters, and has grown steadily stronger. World thinking took great strides between 1919 and 1945. The ideas that seemed revolutionary at Versailles were taken for granted at San Francisco. Now we are being reminded that Wilson lives on in this ideal which we can neither realize nor relinquish. We no longer see tragedy in his defeat and death; there are possibilities of unspeakable tragedy in our own present dilemma. It is clearly imperative that we realize his dream; it is just as clearly impossible for us to do so. We see no escape from this dilemma, since the resources at hand are obviously inadequate to the dream's realization. One hope remains: that the resources may yet be found in a reappropriation of that same essential faith of which the dream itself was born.

The Educator

HAROLD W. DODDS

Education comes from association of an immature mind with a mature mind. It is a process that has to do with training minds how to handle themselves: and nothing trains a mind how to handle itself so much as association with a mind that already knows how to handle itself—as the close and daily association with masters of the mind.

Address before the New Jersey State Teachers' Association, Dec. 28, 1909 [13]

There is no discipline in information. Some of the best informed men I have met could not reason at all. You know what you mean by an extraordinarily well informed man. You mean a man who always has some fact at his command to whip you up; and you will generally find that all this man can do is to throw little chunks of fact in the way so you will stumble on them. And if you say, "Very well, please be kind enough to generalize on the matter," you will find he cannot do it. Information is not education. Information is the raw material of education, but it is not education.

Address of Jan. 9, 1909 [14]

Your enlightenment depends on the company you keep. You do not know the world until you know the men who have possessed it and tried its ways before ever you were given your brief run upon it.

Forum, Dec. 1896 [15]

The object of a liberal training is not learning, but discipline and enlightenment of the mind.

Cambridge, Mass., July 1, 1909 [16]

A college must become a community of scholars and pupils—a free community but a very real one, in which democracy may work its reasonable triumphs of accommodation, its vital processes of union.

Cambridge, Mass., July 1, 1909 [17]

Every man sent out from a university should be a man of his nation, as well as a man of his time.

Forum, Sept. 1894 [18]

—WOODROW WILSON

IT was inevitable that Woodrow Wilson's contribution to higher education in America should have been obscured by the impact of his years in public office. It is therefore most appropriate to recall in this centennial year something of the educational philosophy in which he believed so deeply and the manner in which he fulfilled it at Princeton. His analysis of what the times demanded of the colleges, and his dynamic reforms at Princeton, where most of his life as an educator was spent, were truly in the stream of history. The success of his preceptorial system and the eloquent manner in which he elaborated his faith in liberal education before all sorts of audiences promptly elevated him to the position of the leading educational statesman of his epoch.

Before addressing my attention directly to my subject I cannot deny myself one bit of personal testimony. When I became president of Princeton I had not read a single professional book on education. Indeed I have read but a handful since; and it is probably a mark of my incorrigible innocence that I have never felt the loss keenly, for I believe that what is most worth saying about education in the liberal arts can be found in no more than half a dozen volumes. So it was not until my wife and I had been enjoying the comforts of Prospect, the president's home at Princeton, well-nigh a decade, that I began seriously to examine Mr. Wilson's essays and addresses on education, as distinct from his writings on government and public affairs. It was truly a humbling experience, for it revealed to me that much of what I had been saying about the proper aims and ambitions of a university had been said by him and said much better. It also showed how effectively he had prepared both the intellectual and institutional foundations not only for the modern Princeton but for American higher education in general. He was a prophet indeed. Although he departed from his university amid bitterness and controversy, he was not a prophet crying in the wilderness, and his works live after him. His body is buried in peace, but his name liveth forevermore in education and throughout the whole world of men and nations.

To qualify as a statesman either in education or politics one must be a man of action as well as a man of ideas. Wilson was such a man. He not only advocated reform; he clothed his ideals in a vigorous living structure according to a pattern so simple and clear that all could understand. The structure he fashioned became known as the "preceptorial system." With minor variations it continues today at Princeton much as he conceived it. The "preceptor" meets regularly with small groups of six to eight students for informal discussion of the readings and lectures of the week. He strives for the utmost participation and free expression of views by all members of the "precept." The goal extends far beyond the mere transmission of subject matter. The preceptor has the larger aim of stimulating students to think and speak for themselves, through testing their ideas against those of fellow students under the moderating influence of an older and more mature mind, in informal and relaxed circumstances.

It was this happy marriage of theory and practice that raised Wilson's administration to such high visibility throughout the educational world. "Never," writes Professor Link, his chief modern biographer, "had so much new life and vigor been injected at one stroke into an established faculty." He assembled within a few months a remarkable group of young, competent and enthusiastic teachers to be the first preceptors under his new plan: the "fifty guys to make us wise" celebrated year after year in the faculty song of successive senior classes. It was an extraordinary feat that has never been surpassed in any one college. His success in choosing his fifty preceptors and his capacity to capture their enthusiasm for his new system produced prompt results which proved that the reforms he advocated were practicable as well as desirable. One need search no further for proof of his astounding success in selecting his first preceptors than to observe their subsequent careers. From them emerged the strong core of later faculty leadership which carried on the work begun by Mr. Wilson to heights beyond what he could have foreseen—for no one at his time could have prophesied in detail either the future development of Princeton or of higher education in general.

It would be a grave mistake to evaluate his influence beyond Princeton by the extent to which his particular educational device, the preceptorial system itself, was copied by other colleges. None has done so, at least in a comprehensive manner. For one thing, as President Eliot of Harvard remarked, it is very expensive. It calls for a high ratio of faculty to students, for each teacher works with relatively few "preceptees." Firmly as we at Princeton believe in it, we must admit that President Eliot was right; it is expensive. But Princeton remains steadfast in the conviction that it pays rich dividends.

No, the full sweep and force of Wilson's acomplishment for education must be measured in broader terms. It must be evaluated as the contribution which one man made toward lifting the sights of all American colleges, the majority of which could not contemplate for themselves a reproduction of his justly famed preceptorial system.

To fix correctly a man's place in history, one must consider the times in which he lived. The college world of today is not the college world of 1900, which Woodrow Wilson found wanting and which his searching diagnosis and prescribed remedies did so much to improve.

The closing decades of the nineteenth century were for American colleges in general a period of pedagogical complacency approaching intellectual narcosis; and Princeton was slumbering with the rest. Not that students of the '80's and '90's derived little profit from their four years of college. Too many men are alive today who can testify to the contrary to permit a summary treatment of the values of the education they received. Professor Santayana, whose native intellectual vigor and curiosity would have flourished in almost any environment, defended the Harvard College of his undergraduate days in words applicable to others at the time. His argument was not that the college stimulated or awakened thought in a positive manner, but rather that it enabled the undergraduate to live for a time in an atmosphere of intellectual nonintervention in which he could develop his own imagination and faculties free of distorting worldly pressures. Thus, "liberated for a time from the pursuit of money and from hypocrisy" the student could "grow according to his nature." "Mankind and sagacity," he wrote, "ripen

of themselves; it suffices not to repress or distort them." In my somewhat weather-beaten experience this is too passive and optimistic
to constitute a full guide to educational policy; yet the value of
four years spent in an environment which frees the student to cultivate self-realization are very real.

However important this side of college life may be for young
men and women, it is not the whole story, and it did not satisfy
Mr. Wilson. To him higher education meant something more active
than the mere maintenance of a sort of intellectual enclave in which
a youth could grow according to his nature. For him our colleges
were in serious need of repair. His constant theme was that this
repair could be accomplished only through the realization that "the
fundamental basis of a college community is the intellectual." His
first count in his bill of particulars against existing practices concerned the traditional curriculum. Heavily weighted, as it was, with
classical subjects, it was too limited to serve adequately the needs
of young people about to move out into a world of turbulent change.
In the words of his Princeton inaugural address, college studies
"were losing their connection with working values."

Of course others besides Mr. Wilson were dissatisfied with
the traditional and regimented program of studies inherited from
earlier decades. One powerful reaction against the rigidity of a uniform program for all took the form of a full swing to the opposite
position of complete freedom of choice by which students roamed
practically at will through the curriculum. President Eliot was the
spearhead of this movement which became known as the free-elective
system; and for many years his name and Harvard's exerted a heavy
influence upon all American colleges. To Mr. Wilson, as to his
predecessors at Princeton, such heterogeneous browsing as the free-
elective system encouraged spelled intellectual chaos for young
minds still groping to find themselves. True, it represented justi-
fiable discontent with the narrowness and excessive rigidity of the
older curriculum, but it was not the cure. In its emphasis on breadth,
it omitted depth. As someone has remarked, plants that spread
rapidly over the surface have no opportunity to strike deep roots;
and he wanted deep roots. The free-elective system failed, he insisted, to "impart intellectual discipline"; and he was a friend of
discipline. Accordingly he argued that to be liberal an education

must provide some coherent acquaintance with certain fundamental areas of human thought and experience. College programs of study should contain an element of planned order, affording a "systematic sequence" of courses which would assure that young people would not be intellectual "yokels" and "provincials" destined to a sorry servitude to sprawling superficial knowledge. He constantly insisted that a college should not merely impart information, but should inspire its students with the spirit of learning. Knowledge and information, which change from decade to decade, are the raw materials of thought—not the end product. Always for him the end product of an education was "enlightenment." Indeed, when he talked of education, enlightenment was one of his favorite words.

Bearing this in mind, let us turn to his four categories of fundamental knowledge, which together provide the content of a liberal-arts mastery of life. These categories are paralleled in Princeton's current curriculum for freshmen and sophomores, and in similar form in some other colleges.

One fundamental was "thorough drill in some part of pure science" so that "the mind can never afterward shake off the prepossession of scientific inquiry." What is currently known as "general science" he considered "futile," and so does Princeton today. He was a firm friend of science, but he was a hostile critic of "scientism." "We have not given science too big a place in our education," he declared, "but we have made a perilous mistake in giving it too great a preponderance in method in every other branch of study. . . . This is not the fault of the scientist; he has done his work with intelligence and success." The fault is "the work of the noxious, intoxicating gas which has somehow got into the lungs of the rest of us from out the crevices of his workshop." And he added this warning which Marxist communism so notoriously validated in later years: "I should fear nothing better than utter destruction from a revolution led in the scientific spirit." Therefore, he added, "We must make the humanities human again."

A second component of an educated person, he insisted, is some acquaintance with pure philosophy. "By this I mean," he said, "an explanation of nature and human life which seeks to include all essential aspects." Obviously this concept of "pure" philosophy corresponds to what has been called philosophy in its "pure and pristine sense," not philosophy restricted to "philosopher's philosophy," which, with all its merits can be as narrow and specialized as any field of science or economics.

What he had in mind was the "coordination and explanation" of the several branches of the whole corpus of learning which even in his day was assuming awesome proportions. Learning was becoming fragmentized into areas or fields which, in turn, were becoming the unique possession of noncommunicating specialists. He conceded that the synthesizing task which he prescribed for pure philosophy "is a large order." In a burst of frankness not common among educators with a mission, he admitted that "so far as my reading goes, I do not know where to look for such co-ordination and explanation." He declared that there are "no natural boundaries" to knowledge. Where they exist they are "man-made and conventional." Consequently he insisted that science must be interpreted not merely in terms of physics, for example, but in the terms of the human spirit. We may add that today the fragmentation of learning without co-ordination is as alarming as it was in Mr. Wilson's time. Indeed, despite the valiant efforts of curriculum planners to develop "co-ordination and explanation," the situation is probably more critical than fifty years ago.

Mr. Wilson's third major highway to enlightenment was "pure literature." "In my own studies," he said, "I have found more true political interpretation in the poets than I ever found in the systematic writers on political science, who," he complained, "interpret almost nothing for you."

His fourth fundamental category of learning which should always be a part of a college curriculum was, as one would expect, history and politics, meaning also political economy. These subjects are necessary "parts of a lad's introduction to the modern world." To be a full man, one must be a good citizen.

While he believed that a student's program of studies should include these four basic categories of learning, his curriculum viewed as a whole was not to be uniform, the same for all. "Faculties must establish sequences and combinations," but there must be room for individual choices within a general plan, according to the student's own "prepossessions and instinctive apprehensions of his own powers, his own tastes. . . . Students in the modern college cannot all follow the same road, and it is not desirable that they should. The college should be a place of various studies, alive with a great many different interests." The choice, however, was not to be "miscellaneous, haphazard (or) dispersed . . ." "A man needs this sort of training (in basic areas) before he becomes a special student in any field of scholarship." The constant trouble with literary and philosophical study in particular was that "the men who cultivate these special fields have not been trained and made familiar with the fields of an entirely different character which, nevertheless, so intimately relate to modern thought that every field must take cognizance of them."

However, exposure to basic areas of human thought alone was not enough. If a youth is to become an intellectually mature person, breadth must be supplemented by the discipline of depth in some one branch of learning. Accordingly students "should be allowed and encouraged to make special individual choices of particular fields of study which will give them an opportunity to develop special gifts and aptitudes, and which by calling out their powers of initiative will enable them to discover for themselves." Here lies the germ of a later and most significant development at Princeton—and of course not at Princeton alone—beyond what Mr. Wilson charted in specific form. I refer to her present plan of independent study for all juniors and seniors (of which I shall have more to say in a moment), culminating in a serious and thorough piece of original research embodied in a senior thesis.

How closely Princeton, in company with other colleges, is following his principle of a balanced diet for her liberal arts undergraduates is obvious to all familiar with her present practices. During his freshman and sophomore years a student today is required to complete one year of work in each of four areas of fundamental knowledge, which correspond essentially to Mr. Wilson's categories as I described them above. Other courses are offered in each area from which the underclassman can select the ones he prefers. Thus the student is assured of some acquaintance with the major divisions of knowledge before he begins his program of concentration and independent study in his last two years. Even then he is advised and encouraged to avoid overspecialization and lopsidedness by continuing to select courses outside his particular area of concentration.

We desire him to cultivate the capacity for creative thinking that comes with depth, but not at the expense of reasonable breadth which makes depth significant.

Let us return for a moment to Mr. Wilson's most famous contribution to educational practice, the preceptorial system, his method of giving body and action to his philosophy. To him this system was a method of welding the college into a true community of liberal learning, "of which the teacher will be as much . . . a member as the undergraduate." True education, he insisted, is by "contagion." "By associating undergraduates with men who are learned," the "infection of learning" is created. Lectures are too often formal and empty things. "Recitations," he charged, "generally prove very dull and unrewarding." "It is in conversation and mutual intercourse with scholars, chiefly, that you find how lively knowledge is, how it ties into everything that is interesting and important."

Princeton's loyalty to the preceptorial system has continued unabated over the intervening years. Approximately seven hundred preceptorial conferences held each week during the term testify to the respect in which Mr. Wilson's old university still holds this method of instruction. Princetonians are inordinately proud of their "honor system" which has proved so successful since its adoption in 1893; but the preceptorial system enjoys similar esteem by students, faculty and old grads alike. "Precepting," as it is known locally, is a difficult and exhausting technique of instruction; it demands wide knowledge on the part of the teacher and skill in guiding group discussion. Usually, however, the faculty find it a most rewarding experience. As regularly as clockwork the campus daily announces that the preceptorial plan isn't what it used to be and something must be done about it. As one who was exposed to it in the days of its youth I can say, with the classic commentator on *Punch*, it never was. Indeed the fact that it is under recurring criticism and examination, not only by the faculty but by undergraduates as well, is an evidence of lively strength rather than weakness.

As I have just suggested, Mr. Wilson repeatedly stressed the intellectual awakening which a young person catches from a stimulating environment of learning. Phrases like "contagion" and stimulation by "infection" were frequently on his lips. Reading and conversation ranked high in his mind as carriers of this desirable infection.

Yet there is room in a college education for more than is gained through contagion alone. Once contagion has done its work, the next step is to arouse and develop the self-activating capacity of good minds. The problem is to provide a method by which they can participate more positively and creatively in their own education. Accordingly Princeton has superimposed on Wilson's preceptorial system an upper-class plan of study which involves the methods, the rigors, the joys and sorrows of original research and creative scholarship on the student's part. This is education not only in how to find and evaluate facts themselves, but how to weave them into new and fresh patterns and relationships. This is more than a mere academic exercise required by the faculty for academic reasons; it is education for use in a practical world. For facts do not speak for themselves, as is often asserted. On the contrary, they speak with many voices, some good and some bad, depending upon how they are blended into final judgments. So the practice of original research and scholarship, with its severe standards of truth and clear reasoning, is but education in the methods and criteria of sound thinking, such as a lawyer employs in a brief, a doctor in diagnosing disease, or a business man in formulating policies for his business. Invigorated by the tonic which Mr. Wilson administered to the intellectual life of the University, and in fulfillment of his insistence that "no man is a man who receives his knowledge (merely) by instruction from somebody else," Princeton proceeded twenty years later to a program of independent work calculated to advance further "the spirit of learning" which, in his own words, "consists in the power to digest and interpret evidence . . . in clear and logical processes of thought . . . (and) in a deep respect for the integrity of the human mind." It all adds up to a single purpose, namely cultivation of a man of thought and action, whom Wilson so deeply respected. It supports his famous terse apothegm that "We are not put into this world to sit still and know; we are put here to act."

He was a firm friend of the American college of liberal arts. His plans for Princeton were no pale reflection of British or Continental universities; they were strictly American. His ideal for the college did not exclude the education derived from the extracurricular life of the student. He cautioned that extracurricular activities do not afford all that a college should give its students. But he likewise believed that "if young men get from their years in college manliness, *esprit de corps*, a release of their social gifts, a training in give and take, a catholic taste in men and the standards of true sportsmen, they have gained much." Nevertheless, a Yale football game was no reason for cutting his lecture, and the record shows that he severely flagellated the absentees who claimed that such an occasion justified their absence. He did not, however, go to the extreme of a Scottish predecessor, Dr. McCosh, who sent away a crowd of students serenading him at his house after a famous football victory with the acid reproof, "I am more interested in the gymnastics of the mind."

He argued that professional schools of law or medicine or theology should not be separate from a university, but should be integral elements of one institution, embodying throughout the "liberal spirit of learning." On various academic occasions he insisted that the heart of a university—or as others have added, what prevents it from decomposing into a multiversity—is the liberal arts college. Graduate schools cannot long survive in excellence on levels higher than that of the college, and they will not merit university caliber unless the college succeeds in infusing the spirit of liberal learning throughout all limbs and branches of the university.

Professional training should be postponed until after the young person has had an "antecedent" liberal education. Wilson was troubled by the spread of what he termed a "new ignorance," the opposite of the New Learning of the Renaissance, in that it was composed of piecemeal bits and specialties and was directed to the purpose of making a living. He wanted America to possess professional and business men who had acquired "the habit of carrying special cases up into the region of general principles."

Therefore he favored the four-year over the two-year college which some eminent university presidents were promoting as a preprofessional training after the analogy of Germany. In one biting sentence he dismissed those who advocated shortening the college course to two years by remarking, "I take it for granted that those who have formulated the proposals (to award the baccalaureate degree at the end of the sophomore year) really never knew a sophomore in the flesh. The sap of manhood is rising in him, but it has not yet reached his head." Always present in Wilson's mind, I repeat, was the college as a preparation for full citizenship. This was one special mission of the American college, in distinction to the narrower function of the universities of continental Europe. To accomplish it required a reasonable time, and he brooked no compromise in the interest of speed.

This is no occasion for rehearsing the conflicts which marked Mr. Wilson's final years at Princeton. Several members of the faculty who were at Princeton at the time are still alive. It was my privilege to count as friends a number of surviving trustees who had been members of the board in one or the other camps during his few tempestuous years. The universal verdict in the perspective of time is that the clash of strong personalities beclouded the educational issues involved, issues on which there was broad basic agreement.

The struggle over the location of the new Graduate College did, however, involve two contrasting philosophies regarding the future of graduate study in general in America. Organized graduate work for the Ph.D. degree was still in confusion and disorder on this side of the Atlantic. The pressure to copy the German system outright was heavy and extremely influential. Mr. Wilson was not hypnotized by German scholarship and training. Indeed he could be quite scornful and impatient in respect to the scholars and scholarship of the day. Professor Link describes his "disappointed and dissatisfied" first months as a graduate student at the Johns Hopkins University. Not until he was released to go his own way, freed from the bondage of the normal schedule of courses to devote his full attention to his first and perhaps most famous book *Congressional Government*, did he become reconciled to the life at Hopkins. As mentioned earlier, Wilson's heart was with the man of action. "Uncompromising thought is the luxury of the closeted recluse." For Wilson a graduate hall of residence away from the center of the undergraduate campus was bound to be but the home of such recluses. On the other hand, Dean West advocated a site away from the undergraduate campus by about half a mile (not the distance today it seemed then). The argument over the site was not as trivial as it appears on the surface, for it really reflected two divergent points of view as to the course along which postgraduate study for the Ph.D. should develop in America.

It was natural in the circumstances that the controversy should, as it proceeded, develop collateral issues carrying a high emotional voltage. As one who was at Princeton as a graduate student while the Graduate College was being built, I can recall how widely it was assumed that the new center was to be one of luxurious social exclusiveness. I do not remember that anyone could say why it was to be so. Perhaps the architecture of the building and its gracious amenities, unusual for the time, borrowed from Oxford and Cambridge, worked to encourage the belief that it was to be the home of social snobs and intellectual dilettantes. In any event, it soon became clear that this was not to be. On the contrary, it has proved out as intended; for it provides an atmosphere of learning and culture for a community of young men planning to be scholar-teachers, in which drives to overspecialization could be curbed and outlooks broadened by social contacts with companions cultivating other fields of learning. Surely the graduate students with whom I associated were, like graduate students today, in general an impecunious lot, ambitious to get ahead in their professions. Most of us expected to be teachers; we were innocent, as teachers had better be, of either economic or social ambition. In any event, the graduate college has not worked out as its opponents honestly feared.

Mr. Wilson desired that the new building be placed on the campus among the undergraduate dormitories. In his view the postgraduate training of future professors was to be an extension of the education policy which proved so successful at the undergraduate level. "We shall build (the graduate residential college)," he announced in his Princeton inaugural, "not apart, but as nearly as may be to the very heart, the geographical heart, of the University, and its comradeship shall be for young men and old, for the novice as well as for the graduate. . . . Its windows," he added, "must open straight upon the walks and quadrangles and lecture halls of the *studium generale*."

Mr. Wilson's view of graduate study as essentially a continuance of undergraduate methods at an advanced level did not prevail at that time when graduate schools were just emerging from the confusion and contradictions which characterized their early years of development. And his views did not prevail for a very good reason.

The rapidly expanding body of knowledge which was flowing from more specialized research than was congenial to Wilson's tastes was bringing college and university scholarship and teaching to more professional standards, calling for professional methods and training which could not be supplied within the pattern and climate of undergraduate study. Serious graduate students have passed through and beyond their undergraduate experience and point of view. As one of his students of the 'nineties has expressed it, Wilson did not seem to consider that graduate students were "supposed to get down to the serious business of life, having satisfied their herd instinct in cheering and singing, frittering and dilettanting for four years as undergrads." While this is too hard on the American college student as I know him, there is enough truth in it to indicate that Mr. Wilson's basic concept of graduate education for budding college professors would not have succeeded. It was natural and inevitable that they would do best and be happiest in a society of young colleagues associated in a common enterprise: professional preparation for the practice of their profession. So the idea of enabling young men, studying professionally to be scholars and teachers, to enjoy a community life, in a separate residential college, somewhat removed from undergraduate dormitories, prevailed at Princeton as it did generally. Three decades of experience have established the case for our Graduate College both as to where it was located and what it was to be. Since its erection, other American universities have taken steps to establish similar facilities and thereby to make possible an appropriate way of life for their graduate students. Indeed, a number of years ago the reigning vice-chancellor of Cambridge University quizzed me about this development in the United States and told me of his personal desire to erect facilities similar to ours for their graduate students, who were apt to be rather homeless people.

Let us return to the main concern in Mr. Wilson's thinking. Even when he talked most directly to Princeton and Princetonians he was addressing the college and university world in general. When he exposed the weaknesses of Princeton, he was but exposing the prevailing malaise of all American colleges. If the new methodology which he established at Princeton was not adopted in the same form elsewhere, the ideals it was designed to activate were accepted. His eloquent portrayal of what all colleges could and should achieve for America heightened their dignity and self-respect. To the mounting unrest in educational circles Wilson gave inspiration and leadership and direction. That so much for which American colleges and universities are striving today was explicit in his policies for Princeton is the greatest tribute we can pay him as a prophet and artisan of educational progress. Despite all the significant improvement over the intervening years, I should be the last to suggest that the goal he set for higher education has been attained at Princeton or anywhere else. To paraphrase Browning, education's reach must always exceed its grasp, "or what's a Heaven for?" May it always be so.

In this age of techniques and skills, characterized by respect for the operator to the neglect of the thinker, of education for money-making and getting ahead in contrast to the development of the full powers of human beings, we who believe that it is liberal learning which fits free men for freedom can be grateful to Woodrow Wilson. The popular case for liberal learning suffers because it cannot be described, either as to method or purpose, in the concrete terms of money-making skills or vocational training. At bottom it is a matter of the spirit. The acceptance of liberal learning at the valuation which Mr. Wilson placed upon it is an act of faith on the part of the individual, reinforced by the observations and experience of those who are aware that they enjoy a fuller life because they were exposed to it.

He liked to describe liberal education in terms of awareness of the world of nature and of the spirit. He would remark how inaccurate it was to say that a man who had lost his way in a jungle or a desert had lost himself. That, he insisted, is the only thing he has not lost. "What, as a matter of fact, he has lost is the rest of the world" because he has lost his relation to it. One who has not found his relation to the intellectual and moral content of the world is lost; but one who has ascertained his relation to such content knows accurately where he himself is located.

As I have already intimated, Mr. Wilson constantly emphasized that liberal learning was more than acquiring information. "The perfectly informed individual, if you can find one," he once told a high-school teachers' association, "may not be an educated person," for facts are (but) the crude raw material of the mind. The goal of liberal education is to enable one to fashion from facts the "invisible things of thought" which give enlightenment. In a memorable address he drove the point home with a story about Lincoln: "Lincoln was sending a gentleman on a very delicate mission, and this gentleman had sat up until a very late hour with Secretary Seward and the President going over all the possible contingencies of the case. When midnight came and they found themselves jaded and tired, the gentleman, rising to depart, said, 'Well, Mr. President, if there is anything that we have overlooked, are there any general instructions you can give me as to what I shall do?' Lincoln answered him in this way: 'When I was in Springfield I had a little girl neighbor who was presented with some beautiful alphabet blocks. She was so fascinated with them that she did not want to part with them even at bedtime, so she took them to bed with her. After she had played with them until she was very sleepy, she recollected that she had not said her prayers. So she got on her knees and said, 'O Lord, I am too sleepy to pray, but there are the letters, spell it out for yourself.' ''

Mr. Wilson's vision for the colleges of America was that they would send forth young people eager and equipped to spell out the mystery and grandeur and meaning of life for themselves.

The Political Philosopher

WALTER LIPPMANN

Communities are not distinguished by exceptional men. They are distinguished by the average of their citizenship. I often think of the poor man when he goes to vote: a moral unit in his lonely dignity.

Address delivered in New Jersey when candidate for governor [19]

Most of us are average men; very few of us rise, except by fortunate accident, above the general level of the community about us; and therefore the man who thinks common thoughts, the man who has had common experiences, is almost always the man who interprets America aright.

Annapolis, June 5, 1914 [20]

No group of men less than the majority has a right to tell me how I have got to live in America.

Richmond, Va., Feb. 1, 1912 [21]

Sometimes people call me an idealist. Well that is the way I know I am an American.

Richmond, Ind., Sept. 4, 1919 [22]

Democracy is unquestionably the most wholesome and livable kind of government the world has yet tried.

Atlantic Monthly, March 1901 [23]

—WOODROW WILSON

WOODROW WILSON wrote his *Congressional Government, a Study in American Politics* in 1883 and 1884. When he reread it in 1900 (in order to do a preface to the fifteenth printing), he had such serious misgivings about it that he warned his readers of new developments that "may put this whole volume hopelessly out of date." Soon thereafter he thought they had, and in 1908 he wrote another book, his *Constitutional Government in the United States*, to supersede it. In this second book are the main ideas which Wilson took with him to the White House in 1912.

The basic difference between the first book and the second is in the conception of the power of the President. When Wilson was writing his *Congressional Government*, he supposed that Congress was necessarily the central and predominant power in the American system, and that the Presidency had become an ineffectual office. But at the turn of the century and after the war with Spain and America's entrance into world politics, he took a radically opposite view: the President was again, as in the early days of the Republic, "at the front of affairs." It was because the center of power had moved from one end of Pennsylvania Avenue to the other that Wilson thought this book was out of date.

And so it was if we judge the book as Wilson himself always judged it—as an attempt to describe realistically how the American constitutional system works. The fact is that at times the system works as he describes it in this book, and at other times it works as he describes it in the second book. For what he did in this first book was to give a clinical description of a disease, not permanent but recurrent, to which the system is subject. With the fresh eye of genius, and with the intuitions of a man who is born to govern, he described the breakdown of government in the aftermath of the Civil War. The book deals with the American system in the twenty dangerous and humiliating years between the death of Lincoln and the rise of Grover Cleveland. It is the first analytical description of what happens when the President is weak and helpless, of how power and responsibility disintegrate when the members of Congress, and more specifically their standing committees, are predominant. Some of the factual details are no longer correct. But the morbid symptoms which he identified are still clearly recognizable when the disease recurs, and there is a relapse into Congressional supremacy. This was a good book to read during the Harding Administration. It was a good book to have read at the end of the Truman and at the beginning of the Eisenhower Administration. It is one to be taken to heart by all who have seen the ravages of McCarthyism.

Woodrow Wilson was a graduate student at Johns Hopkins when, in the summer of 1884, he finished writing this book. He was then twenty-eight years old. After an unhappy year of trying without much success to practice law in Atlanta, he had returned, as if from exile, to the academic life. He had escaped from the "dreadful drudgery" of the law office, he had become engaged to Ellen Axson, he was no longer "buried in humdrum life down . . . in slow, ignorant, uninteresting Georgia," and he was able again to satisfy his "passion for original work . . . to become a master of philosophical discourse, to become capable and apt in instructing as great a number of persons as possible." His "plain necessity," he wrote to his friend, Heath Dabney, was "some profession which will afford me a moderate support, favorable conditions for study, and considerable leisure; what better can I be, therefore, than a professor, a lecturer upon subjects whose study most delights me?"

This book was his first work after he had come to his decision to give up the law and to go into teaching. But he did not mean to stay there. It is evident enough from his letter to Dabney that he thought of teaching as a way station, as a means of earning a living, of having the leisure to study political philosophy and history, and of preparing himself for his true vocation in the great world. His true vocation was political leadership. He had had no doubts about that since his undergraduate days at Princeton. In the terms of his Presbyterian doctrine he had since then known himself to be a predestined and foreordained agent who was being "guided by an intelligent power outside himself." So sure was he of his vocation that in his senior year at Princeton he had entered into "a solemn covenant" with his friend and classmate, Charles Talcott.

Some four years later when he went to Johns Hopkins, he remembered the covenant. In a letter written to Ellen Axson shortly after they became engaged, he wrote that Talcott and he had pledged themselves that:

. . . we would school all our powers and passions for the work of establishing the principles we held in common; that we would acquire knowledge that we might have power; and that we would drill ourselves in all the arts of persuasion, but especially in oratory . . . that we might have facility in leading others into our ways of thinking and enlisting them in our purposes.

The covenant with his friend Charles Talcott bears upon the general feeling and animus of the book. The young Wilson believed that the American constitutional system is radically defective and that it should be made over on the British model. For Congressional government, as he describes it in this book, offers nothing but misery and frustration for the kind of public man that Wilson was preparing himself to be. He aspired to acquire power because he could shape opinion by his oratory, and under Congressional government it was in the standing committees that power was traded and manipulated.

It is interesting, I think, that ambitious as he was and dedicated to a political career, the young Wilson seems never to have aspired to be President. That was not because he thought the Presidency was too high for him. It was because he saw that power, which was what he cared about, was in Congress. The ambition of the young Wilson was to be a Senator from Virginia, and he prepared himself for his destiny by making himself, through much practice, into an effective orator. He believed that as Congress was the predominant power in the American system, oratory was, or rather that oratory should be, the means of leading Congress. In the English system, as Wilson supposed it to be, governments were made and were unmade in Parliament by the great orators, like Gladstone.

By the age of twenty-two, in the year 1879, when he was still a senior at Princeton, Wilson had reached the main ideas with which he started when he came to write this book. They are to be found in an article which was published in the *International Review* for August 1879. (The editor, curiously enough, who accepted this article was his great future adversary, Henry Cabot Lodge.) The article is entitled "Cabinet Government in the United States." A responsible cabinet, he argued, was the remedy for Congressional Government—for that "despotic authority wielded under the forms of free government" by "our national Congress . . . a despotism which uses its power with all the caprice, all the scorn for settled policy, all the wild unrestraint which marked the methods of other tyrants as hateful to freedom."

When we ask ourselves why it did not occur to him to look to Presidential leadership for a remedy, we must remember the times in which he was living. Wilson was a Southerner, born in Staunton, Virginia, on December 28, 1856. He had spent his boyhood in Augusta, Georgia, where his family moved when he was an infant. After the Civil War, the family went to South Carolina, where his father, Dr. Joseph Ruggles Wilson, became professor of theology in the seminary at Columbia. Wilson had grown up amidst the ruins of the Civil War and in the tragic aftermath of the Reconstruction. He was nine years old when Lincoln died. The Presidents during his lifetime had been Andrew Johnson, General Grant and Rutherford B. Hayes, whose title was clouded, and they were followed by Garfield and Chester Arthur. It was from these Presidents that Wilson drew the conclusion, which was decisive for the constitutional theory of his nonage, that the Presidential office is insignificant. He was disgusted with the contemporary political scene: ". . . eight words contain the sum of the present degradation of our political parties," he wrote, "no leaders, no principles; no principles, no parties."

In England, particularly in the England of Gladstone, whose portrait Wilson had hung over his desk, he saw what he missed at home. He read Green's *Short History of the English People*, and he found it had for him an "overmastering charm." He became convinced that the history of the English people is also the history of the American people. In this mood he read Walter Bagehot's *The English Constitution*, presumably in the American edition, which was published in February, 1877.

The American edition contained Bagehot's introduction to the second English edition. It is dated June 29, 1872. The whole book, but particularly, I would say, this introduction had a decisive influence on Wilson's thinking, and Wilson acknowledged it when he was working on his *Congressional Government*. In a letter to Ellen Axson he wrote that

. . . it is my purpose to show as well as I can our constitutional system as it looks in operation. My desire and ambition are to treat the American Constitution as Mr. Bagehot (do you remember Mr. Bagehot, about whom I talked to you one night on the veranda at Asheville?) has treated the English Constitution. . . . He brings to the work a fresh and original method which has made the British system much more intelligible to ordinary men than it was before, and which, if it could be successfully applied to the exposition of our federal constitution, would result in something like a revelation to those who are still reading *The Federalist* as an authoritative constitutional manual.

But it was not only Bagehot's "fresh and original method" which inspired Wilson. He had become Bagehot's disciple, and he adopted, as his own, Bagehot's critique of the American Constitution. This critique was written in 1872 and in the light of the quarrel between President Andrew Johnson and the Congress. Bagehot said that after Lincoln's assassination:

. . . the characteristic evils of the Presidential system were shown most conspicuously . . . at the moment of all their history when it was most important to them to collect and concentrate all the strength and wisdom of their policy on the pacification of the South, that policy was divided by a strife in the last degree unseemly and degrading.

In one principal respect, Bagehot went on to say, "the English system" of parliamentary government is:

. . . by far the best . . . in each stage of a public transaction there is a discussion . . . the public assists at this discussion . . . it can, through Parliament, turn out an administration which is not doing as it likes, and can put in an administration which will do as it likes. But the character of a Presidential government is, in a multitude of cases, that there is no such discussion; that when there is a discussion the fate of the government does not turn upon it and, therefore, the people do not attend to it.

The young Wilson, oppressed by the spectacle of American politics, was ready to be convinced that for the reasons given by Bagehot the English system was better than the American. The American Congress was predominant. But it governed without genuine debate. Its power, which was divided among the standing committees, was not accountable to the opinion of the nation. No one spoke for the nation. Except for Lincoln, whom he admired but who, in his view, had ignored the Constitution, there had been no President in his lifetime who represented the national interest and could cope with the overriding power of the many standing committees of Congress. So the young Wilson concluded that the normal and permanent American system had come to be what it had been in his lifetime.

If that was the American system, then drastic changes would be necessary in it. For Congressional government, which Wilson described fearlessly and faithfully in his Book, was intolerably bad government. Wilson never doubted that for good government there must be a strong Executive. If the office of President had fallen irrevocably from that "first estate of dignity" which it had among the Founding Fathers, then the remedy for the radical defect of the system would lie in making a strong Executive out of a responsible cabinet.

This had been, as I have been saying, Wilson's view since his Princeton days. In fact, just as he was starting to write this book he had published in the *Overland Monthly* for January, 1884, an article called "Committee or Cabinet Government." It concludes with a paragraph saying:

. . . Committee Government [which Wilson used as another name for Congressional Government] is too clumsy and too clandestine a system to last. Other methods of government must sooner or later be sought, a different economy established. First or last, Congress must be organized in conformity with what is now the prevailing legislative practice of the world. English precedent and the world's fashion must be followed in the institution of Cabinet Government in the United States.

But during the summer of 1884, while he was, in fact, finishing the manuscript of this book, Wilson began to undergo a fundamental change in his conception of the American system. Something happened then which caused him to refrain from mentioning the drastic reform—namely Cabinet Government on the British model —which he had advocated publicly shortly before. In the book the analysis of the evils of Congressional government still points towards Cabinet government as the remedy. But Wilson was no longer willing, as he was a year before, to draw that conclusion. "I am pointing out facts," he says in his book, "diagnosing, not prescribing remedies."

Wilson's biographer, Ray Stannard Baker, does not deal with the question why, as he was finishing *Congressional Government*, Wilson decided not to put forth the remedy which, when he started to write, he had put forward as something that "must" be applied. Yet this was a critical turning point in Wilson's development— a turning away from the constitutional notions of his nonage, and towards those which he acted upon when he became President. If I might hazard a guess, it would be to suggest that what caused him to see the problem of Congressional government in a new light was the rise of Grover Cleveland.

Cleveland was running for President in that summer of 1884 when Wilson was finishing his book. Now Cleveland was the first American public man in Wilson's own lifetime who aroused his interest in the office of President. He admired Cleveland and hoped ardently for his election. This may, then, have been why in that summer of 1884 he was no longer so sure that the remedy for the evils of Congressional government was reform on the English precedent. In Cleveland for the first time in his own experience he discerned the possibility that the office of President might be restored to that "first estate of dignity" from which it had "fallen" since "the early Presidents."

I must warn the reader that there is no hard fact known to me, no letter of Wilson's for example, which supports my hypotheses that he was influenced by the candidacy of Cleveland. It may be a mere coincidence. But it is true that until that summer Wilson had always supposed that contemporary Presidents "should wear a clean and irreproachable insignificance," that Congress was necessarily "predominant over its so-called co-ordinated branches." Since Congress "has virtually taken into its own hands all the substantial powers of government," the only way to create a strong Executive was on the English precedent: to vest the executive power in a cabinet chosen as a committee of the Congress.

Soon after that he was no longer prepared to prescribe the remedy. If it was the appearance of Cleveland that caused him to doubt the need for the remedy, it is also true that the remedy belonged to the upper layers of his mind, not to the main body of his thinking. It was something he had borrowed, not something he had worked out by his own labor. He seems not to have paid much attention to the practical question of how so radical an alteration was to be brought about. So far as I know, Wilson's only published words on how to initiate the English system are in the article, "Committee or Cabinet Government," which appeared in the *Overland Monthly* for January, 1884.

It would be necessary, he wrote, to amend Section 6 of Article I of the Constitution so as to permit members of Congress to hold offices as members of the Cabinet. . . . It would be necessary to extend the term of the President beyond four years . . . and the term of the representatives beyond two years. . . . All in all Wilson devoted less than two pages to the ways and means of carrying out the reform, and he concluded rather hastily that "the admission of members of Congress to seats in the Cabinet would be the only change of principle called for by the new order of things." He appears to have assumed that the President would have a long term and would become a kind of republican monarch, the head of the state, but no longer the Chief Executive. Apparently for no better reason than that he did not think much about it, Wilson did not regard this revolutionary change in the Presidency as "a change of principle."

The truth, I believe, is that while Wilson's description of the evils of Congressional government was deeply perceived and carefully studied from the living realities, the remedy of Cabinet government on the English precedent was taken from a little reading. He adopted the remedy on faith when he was an undergraduate at Princeton. He continued to advocate it, though in very general terms, for a few years after that. But there is nothing to show that he had studied the English system as he was studying the American, or that he took into account how much the American social order differed from the British—that he asked himself, for example, what was the role of the Crown and of the peerage and of hereditary rank in the operation of the English system. His attachment to the reform was superficial, and that was why he ceased to advocate it as soon as the advent of Cleveland gave him reason to hope that the American system might, after all, be "self-adjusting."

Wilson in his own life knew the American constitutional system in three different phases. The first was the post-Civil War era of a predominant Congress and insignificant presidents. It ended with the rise of Cleveland. *Congressional Government* belongs to that period.

The second phase included Wilson's rise as President of Princeton University, as Governor of New Jersey, and as President of the United States, and goes on until his fall in the political disaster of 1918. This second phase was an era of strong Presidents, of Cleveland, Theodore Roosevelt and Wilson himself. The book which reflects his constitutional theories in that period is *Constitutional Government in the United States*. In it, writing before he ran for President, Wilson declared:

> The President is at liberty, both in law and conscience, to be as big a man as he can . . . he cannot escape being leader of his party [being] the only party nominee for whom the whole nation votes . . . he is also the political leader of the nation, or has it in his choice to be . . . his is the only national voice in affairs. Let him once win the admiration and confidence of the country, and no other single force can withstand him, no combination of forces will easily overpower him. . . . His office is anything he has the sagacity and force to make it.

The third phase, of which Wilson did not see the end, began with the mid-term elections of 1918. It lasted until the advent of Franklin D. Roosevelt in 1933. It was another period of Congressional government.

Wilson, who died in 1924, was then a sick and broken man. But had he retained his intellectual energy, he would have come back, I believe, to his first book. He would have come back to revise it, but also to recognize its deep insight. In revising it, he might, perhaps have taken a new view of the balance of powers in the original Constitution. Growing up, as he did, in a time when the balance had been radically turned towards Congress and against the Executive, he seems to have supposed that the balance could not be righted. The experience of his own life shows, however, that the balance can be righted. His own experience had shown also that it is not a stable balance, that the tendency of the system is to become unbalanced—and especially after wars when Congress is, for a time, predominant.

There exists, one might say in limbo, a third book describing the American system in its ups and in its downs. That book, alas, Woodrow Wilson was never allowed to write. But in that book he could have brought together into one field of theory the truth of his *Congressional Government* and the truth of his *Constitutional Government*. Then he would have accounted for his own rebellion as a young man, for the disaster and his defeat at the end of his life, and for the great middle years of his power and of his triumphs, and of his enduring fame.

The President

RALPH MCGILL

This is not a day of triumph; it is a day of dedication. Here muster, not the forces of party, but the forces of humanity. Men's hearts wait upon us; men's lives hang in the balance; men's hopes call upon us to say what we will do. Who shall live up to the great trust? Who dares fail to try? I summon all honest men, all patriotic, all forward-looking men, to my side. God helping me, I will not fail them, if they will but counsel and sustain me.

Inaugural Address, March 4, 1913 [24]

No man is great who thinks himself so, and no man is good who does not strive to secure the happiness and comfort of others.

Address when Governor of New Jersey, 1911 [25]

We can have no sympathy with those who seek to seize the power of government to advance their own personal interests or ambition.

Statement regarding Latin American Affairs, March 12, 1913 [26]

—WOODROW WILSON

On that fourth of March, 1913, when Thomas Woodrow Wilson took the simple oath required of one assuming the office of President of the United States, the sun shone brightly. All Washington basked in the warmth of a cloudless day.

There are always those at great inaugurations and coronations who seek for prophetic symbolisms and who bend their ears to hear any whispers by whatever oracles. It was so on that March fourth. Many who wrote of the occasion noted the brightness of the day and the sunlight which seemed to be a great spotlight focused on a new figure in American political life and government.

Certain it is that his inauguration was more than ordinarily meaningful in the history of the Presidency. He was the first Democrat to take the oath since Grover Cleveland in 1893. He was the first native Virginian to repeat the solemn obligation since Zachary Taylor; the first Southerner since Andrew Johnson. He was the first scholar, student of government and intellectual since Thomas Jefferson.

And, as it was with Jefferson, the average citizen looked to him with hope and affection. Between Jackson's second term and Wilson's start in 1913 only Lincoln appears as a President who came to office with a positive policy which he was ready vigorously and intelligently to put forward.

Since that beautiful March fourth of forty-three years ago, there have been those who looked back at that day and sought for portents and prophecies in the events of it. On that day there was no sound of the riderless horses of the Apocalypse trampling the cloudless skies. But four years later the closing sentences of his inaugural took on new significance. He spoke of men's lives hanging then in the balance. And he said, too, "Here muster the forces of humanity." When years later, the "Great Betrayal" was accomplished there were those who, poring over that inaugural, noted that Woodrow Wilson had declared that day, "Men's hopes call upon us to say what we will do."

Whether there was inspired prophecy in it or not remains for the final unlocking of all the secrets of life. Taken as a speech, it was a good one which lifted up the hearts of those who heard it. They did not know him well, but they did know he was something new in their time. He was the product of no political machine. Indeed, as Governor of New Jersey, he had exposed the corruption of his party's own organization in that state. He was not at all bound by old prejudices, forms or customs. And as he stood there that March fourth, not merely the hearts of men were stirred but their minds, too. In a very real sense, he has never stopped doing that to the hearts and minds of his countrymen.

A tree, says an old axiom, is measured best when it is down. Though this be true, the measuring of political giants is never easy and seemingly never done. Through the years that are behind us many have been busy with yardstick and tape, not merely on Jefferson, Jackson, Lincoln, Woodrow Wilson, Franklin D. Roosevelt, but on those lesser than they. Friends, enemies and coldly calculating researchers have been active across an increasing span of years, and the measuring is by no means completed.

The difficulty would seem to be that when the real giants come down, they fall always deep in the jungle of great social and economic changes above which they towered and out of which they grew. By the time the bearers of measuring rods have hacked their way to them, the processes of change have had time to accelerate or slow down. Hindsight comes to confuse and blur the image of the times in which they lived and wrought. This sometimes causes those busy with the task of measuring the fallen great to work hurriedly, even carelessly, and perhaps, now and then, to estimate rather than apply the stick. Inevitably, the sums thus attained vary, sometimes widely.

It is so with Woodrow Wilson. Some have presented him as an enigma, which assuredly he was not. In the long weary months of his illness while still in office, he became by the very nature of things a mysterious figure. He was secluded. Only a few persons saw him. And so he became a "mystery" as the unseen, unknown always is. But save that man is without question a complex being, he was no enigma. He was, on the contrary, an almost obvious man.

When he stood to take the oath he was so new to politics as

to be relatively an unknown. Not too many Americans had followed his career at Princeton. His scholarly writings on government had enjoyed no popular circulation. His fight against "the bosses" in New Jersey and his campaign speeches had stirred the imagination of those who were weary of the old pattern and tired of the static character of the Republican Party and its principles. Theodore Roosevelt had proved that many Republicans themselves suffered from a like weariness. But, save for New Jersey and his public writings and addresses, Woodrow Wilson had then, on March 4, 1913, no record by which the public and the politicians could judge him.

He was one of the old "Blue Stocking" Covenanter family strains. They bred their children to discipline of mind and character, did those families with the Scottish traditions, and rectitude was woven into the tartan of their being. Porridge and predestination produce men who live by the rules. If they can laugh and joke, it is only in the presence of the family or a small, intimate group of close friends. His Cabinet was to know the man whose severe, Calvinist, schoolmaster's face could relax into warmth and whose tongue could tell a story reminiscent of the Lincoln tradition.

Once a Cabinet member suggested to him that a task at hand be abandoned for a diversion toward which he knew Wilson had planned.

"My Boss won't allow it," he said.

"Your Boss?"

"My conscience," said Wilson. "It drives me to do what seems my duty. It frowns on temptations."

Again, he said of himself, "So far as I could make out, I am expected, as President, to be a bloodless, thinking machine— whereas I am perfectly aware I have in me all the insurgent elements of the human race. I am sometimes, by reason of my Scottish ancestry, able to keep these rebels in restraint. The stern Covenanter tradition that is behind me sends many an echo down the years."

But as he stood there on March 4, 1913, taking the oath as the twenty-eighth President of the United States, his face was stern, his lips thin, his eyes solemn. So great was his concentration and so severely were his emotions controlled, that he did not feel the arthritic pains in his back and shoulder. For that matter, none of the familiar old aches troubled him on that day. But they were there. He was never a strong man physically. The spirit which flamed continually in his frail body was to keep him going for almost eight turbulent, testing years. It was the inaugural face which was to become most familiar to his fellow countrymen.

(Even as he took the oath and began the huge task of national reform, there were men across the seas who were moving toward a bridge and a pistol shot at Sarajevo.)

In his inaugural address Woodrow Wilson listed six specific fields requiring reform:

1. "A tariff which cuts us off from our proper part in the commerce of the world, violates the principle of just taxation and makes the Government a facile instrument in the hands of private interests."

2. "A banking and currency system based upon the necessity of the Government to sell bonds fifty years ago and perfectly adapted to concentrating cash and restricting credits."

3. "An industrial system which, take it on all its sides, financial as well as administrative, holds capital in leading strings, restricts the liberties and limits the opportunities of labor, and exploits without renewing or conserving the natural resources of the country."

4. "A body of agricultural activities never yet given the efficiency of great business undertakings or served as it should be through the instrumentality of science taken directly to the farm or afforded the facilities of credit best suited to its practical needs."

5. "Water courses undeveloped, waste places unreclaimed, forests untended, fast disappearing without plan or prospect of renewal, unregarded waste heaps at every mine."

6. We have not "perfected the means by which our government may be put at the service of humanity, in safeguarding the health of the nation, the health of its women and its children, as well as their rights in the struggle for existence," and he pointed out in his pledge of "alteration" the need for sanitary laws, pure food laws, and laws determining conditions of labor which "individuals are powerless to determine for themselves," and this fun-

damental truth that guided all he proposed: "The first duty of the law is to keep sound the society it serves."

The new President could have enumerated a seventh change. He planned to lift the Presidency itself from the low estate into which it had fallen. In his book *Congressional Government*, published six years before, he had expressed the conviction that the committees of the Congress had too long been allowed to exercise increasing power. He regarded government by Congressional committees as dangerous, even vicious. "This is the defect to which, it will be observed, I am constantly recurring; to which I recur again and again because every examination of the system, at whatever point begun, leads inevitably to it as a central secret." He did not believe anything to be wrong with the basic law. His concept of the Constitution was that the President must use all the power that is his, must, in fact, stand as sponsor for the policy of the government. Too many Presidents, he felt, allowed committees "to originate, compromise and alter it." The man, he felt, makes the Presidency, and not the Presidency the man.

He sought to gird himself, in determination to be a strong executive, with a Cabinet of progressives. An opposition newspaper ran a picture of them under the heading "Wilson's Cabinet! Who are they?"

Wilson named William Jennings Bryan as Secretary of State. He was, perhaps, a bit reluctant so to do. Certainly some powerful protests were made. Wilson, whatever his reservations, did not hesitate. Having in mind revenue and fiscal reform, the President chose William G. McAdoo. Wilson long had been concerned about "the money power" and its influence in government. A. Mitchell Palmer, floor leader of the Wilson forces in the long convention struggle at Baltimore, refused appointment as Secretary of War because he was a sincere Quaker. It went to Lindley M. Garrison, vice chancellor of New Jersey. J. C. McReynolds of Tennessee, later Associate Justice of the United States Supreme Court, was made Attorney General. McReynolds had caught Wilson's eye by his effective work as a Federal attorney in the antitrust action against the tobacco companies. Franklin K. Lane became Secretary of the Interior. He had become known to Wilson by his accomplishments on the United States Commerce Commission. Albert S. Burleson of Texas was Postmaster General. David F. Houston, old friend and college president with agricultural experience, took the post of Secretary of Agriculture. William C. Redfield, of Brooklyn, an authority on the tariff and a businessman of stature, was given the portfolio of Secretary of Commerce. William B. Wilson, former Congressman and an officer of the American Federation of Labor, was a popular choice for Secretary of Labor.

Perhaps the most unusual choice was that of a then relatively obscure newspaper publisher of Raleigh, North Carolina as Secretary of the Navy. This was Josephus Daniels. He was to become the great rock in Wilson's often weary world. His faith in people, like Wilson's, had an almost mystic quality. It never wavered. He was Puritan but never the bigot. He was simple as truth is simple. He was loyal always, and without question, to friends and principles. It is well to note he made a good Secretary of the Navy; that that branch of our armed services performed well in the great war which was to come to the Wilson Administration, and that one of his reforms, that of no liquor or wine on United States Navy vessels, has come to be accepted by even the most bibulous as a necessary restriction. And, too, this would seem to be the place to say that it was Daniels who brought an ebullient, very cocksure young man in to work as an assistant—Franklin Delano Roosevelt. Young Roosevelt thought the Secretary of the Navy to be a curious, hayseed sort of man and for a while, behind the Secretary's back, he was condescending and critical. But he, too, learned something of wisdom, loyalty and the Democratic principle from him, and all his days he was to love Josephus Daniels and call him "Chief."

This was the Cabinet.

The opposition asked, "Who are they?"

But the New York World said of it: "Whether strong or weak in its various elements, this is no Cabinet of political trade and barter. It is fashioned to placate neither sordid political interests nor sordid financial interests. Each member stands on its own merits."

The first step, Wilson and his Cabinet agreed, would be tariff reform. The sugar, steel and other commodity lobbies geared for the fight.

The battle was begun with a precedent-breaking reading of his tariff message to the Congress. It was the first time a President had so appeared since 1796. He declared for free competitive enterprise, saying, ". . . A duty was laid upon the party now in power, at the recent election, which it ought to perform promptly in order that the burden carried by the people under existing laws may be lightened as soon as possible, and in order that the business interests of the country may not be kept too long in suspense as to what the fiscal changes are to be, to which they may be required to adjust themselves . . . the sooner the tariff is altered, the sooner our men of business will be free to thrive by the nature of free business, instead of by the law of legislation and artificial arrangement."

The old tariff foe of that time was high protection. It was true then, as it still is true, that the nation had moved far from the "modest notion of protecting" the industries of the country and moved boldly forward, as Wilson said, "to the idea that they (the favored industries) were entitled to the direct patronage of the government."

Wilson routed the lobby. His personal appearance before the Congress gave to the message a dynamic it otherwise might have lacked.

Then, too, his approach made sense in that it was not an uprooting of protection but a change from a special privilege to the status originally conceived for a protective tariff. The average rate of duties was reduced from 40 to 26 per cent. (Wilson was urging then a policy which, curiously enough, the Eisenhower administration of 1952–56 found it necessary to adopt.) Wilson said, of our goods and farm products, "American energies must now be directed towards the markets of the world." Indeed, some of our present farm surplus distress may be traced to the economic theories of the Republican protectionists of the years immediately following the first great World War. When farm prices declined in 1920, they hurriedly put together the Fordney Emergency Tariff. Wilson warned that a high tariff on farm products on which the price was fixed in foreign markets could bring no relief.

On March 4, 1921, the eighth anniversary of his 1913 inaugural and his last day as President, Wilson sent a veto message (rare for him) to the Congress.

"The situation in which many of the farmers of the country find themselves," he said in this message, "cannot be remedied by a measure of this sort. There is no short way out of existing conditions, and measures of this sort can only have the effect of deceiving the farmers and raising false hopes among them. The farmer needs a better system of domestic marketing and credit, but especially larger foreign markets for his surplus products. Clearly, measures of this sort will not conduce to an expansion of the foreign market. Actual relief can come only from the adoption of constructive measures of a broader scope, from the restoration of peace elsewhere in the world, the resumption of normal industrial pursuits, the recovery particularly of Europe, and the discovery there of additional credit foundations on the basis of which her people may arrange to take from farmers and other producers of this nation, a greater part of their surplus production."

A resurgent Republican bloc sought to pass the tariff measure over the veto, but failed by twenty-one votes. So great was the determination to have such a law that President Harding, following his inauguration, called a special session of the Congress and the emergency tariff was passed with a great show of partisan piety. The substantial increases were the cornerstone of the Fordney-McCumber tariff legislation of the next year. This, and subsequent protectionist legislation, such as the Smoot-Hawley Act, was a part of the tragic mosaic of blunders which led to the economic collapse of Europe; the associated fall of the democratic governments established there following the great war; the rise of nationalisms, trade barriers and dictatorships, and the coming of the somber depression to our own shores.

Wilson used a phrase in his veto message which a people seemingly conditioned to the problem of political promises might read with profit. He said, in that historic and prophetic message, that he would not be a party to giving "the promise to the ear which has been broken to the hope."

These results of a reversal of Wilson's policies were a part of the bitter future.

The tariff reform was but one part of Wilson's over-all plan of fiscal reform. He moved next to an old idea, that of an income tax. Provision for such a levy had been voted in Grover Cleveland's second administration. It had been declared unconstitutional by a somewhat suspect overnight change of mind by a judge. Since 1896 a fight had been made by Democrats to obtain an amendment to the Constitution authorizing the levying of such a tax. They argued the cost of government ought to be apportioned on ability to pay, and not entirely on the basis of consumer consumption—as did the tariff. Wilson's floor leaders pointed out that of the hundreds of millions the government received from the tariff and internal revenue taxes, a very small percentage was paid by those who profited most from the tariff.

On February 25, 1913, the Constitution was amended to give Congress the power to levy such a tax and the Underwood-Simmons act created a graduated income-tax law. When, a few years later, the nation was pulled into the great vortex of war, necessitating the raising of billions of extra dollars, the income-tax law was the basis for finding it and for causing those industries and persons whose incomes were greatly increased by the war to pay a more equitable share than otherwise would have been the case.

In 1913, the "Schoolmaster President" turned from victories in the tariff and taxation to attack the greater citadel of reaction—the banking system. Not since Andrew Jackson in 1832–33 had boldly moved against recharter of the Bank of the United States, had any President proposed so revolutionary a revision of the currency and banking system.

His specific proposals resulted in the creation of the Federal Reserve System. He did not, of course, suggest or write the Federal Reserve Act. Senator Carter Glass of Virginia, Chairman of the House Committee on Banking and currency, was the leader of the shock troops in the great battle that ensued. It properly is said of him that he was the "father" of the act itself. But he said, after victory, the "one man more responsible for the Federal Reserve System than any living man is Woodrow Wilson. It was his infinite patience, it was his clear prescience, it was his unsurpassed courage, it was the passion of Woodrow Wilson to serve mankind, that overcame every obstacle, that surmounted every difficulty, and put the Federal Reserve Banking system on the federal statute books of this country."

It was not an easy victory.

There were those who counseled delay.

"Why should we wait to crown ourselves with consummate honor?" asked Wilson.

On June 23, 1913, Woodrow Wilson again read a message to the Congress. It was a day nagged by heat and humidity. The President noted this, but added that they, and he, were in the presence of a public duty.

His message had been long in the making. As a professor teaching political economy and "government," Woodrow Wilson had taught and written of the need of change. After the panic of 1907, a study had been made and a Central Bank recommended. But Old Hickory had put the mark of the monster on the Central Bank of his time. Wilson and his associates did not want such an institution. The existing system was, he said, "perfectly adapted to concentrating cash and restricting credit."

His currency-reform message was as lucid as one of his classroom lectures. The heart of it was this:

"We must have a currency, not rigid as now, but readily, elastically responsive to sound credit, the expanding and contracting credits of every day transactions, the normal ebb and flow of personal and corporate dealings. Our banking laws must mobilize reserves; must not permit the concentration anywhere in a few hands of the monetary resources of the country or their use for speculative purposes in such volume as to hinder or impede or stand in the way of other more legitimate, more fruitful uses. And the control of the system of banking and of issue which our new laws are to set up must be public, not private, must be vested in the Government itself, so that the banks may be the instruments, not the masters, of business and of individual enterprise and initiative."

So the battle was joined.

Having seen the rout of the tariff lobbyists, the opposition bankers were more coy. They wrote, telegraphed and sent discreet emissaries to see Senators and Congressmen. But Washington seemed surprisingly clean of lobbyists.

But at last they could endure it no longer. When the Senate was long locked in debate and stalemate, a small carefully selected group of the nation's most powerful bankers arrived unannounced and at night in Washington. They avoided the usual suites in their favorite hotels but went instead to the Army and Navy Club. Soon senators and others with "influence" but no Navy or Army backgrounds, began to answer summonses to the club. A young Navy officer was interested and puzzled by the presence there of the non-military strangers who were having so many visitors. He told a friend who held a minor post with the Wilson administration. This friend recognized the news for what it was and soon the names of all the visitors and the length of their stay were in Woodrow Wilson's hands. The Congress learned them, too.

The flushed bankers requested a White House conference.

Old Andrew Jackson would have applauded the President's answer. He, too, had curtly refused a somewhat similar request. The President was cold and formal. He informed them he knew them for what they were, and, anyhow, did not need to discuss terms with them since he intended to fight on for complete victory.

On the floor the fight was bitter. Those earnestly seeking to give the nation a flexible currency system offered strengthening amendments.

The great banking influences sought a central bank not governed by law. One of those who voiced opposition was Frank A. Vanderlip of the National City Bank of New York. In a strongly applauded address before the American Bankers Association on October thirtieth, he said, "It starts the country on an issue of fiat currency. There is no case in our history when a nation has started an issue of fiat money but the result has been a complete breakdown of the financial system of that country."

This was the majority opinion of the nation's financial interests. Senator Carter Glass, in writing of those bitterly contested days, told of how he himself originally had believed, and urged, the banks of the country should have minority representation on the Central Board at Washington which would supervise the entire system of twelve district banks. President Wilson differed. Glass was equally adamant. He was, after all, the leader of those actually in the fight. It was not possible, he thought, to win the political battle without such agreement, and so convinced was he that he put it in writing to the President.

Wilson's reply was typical. He said he did not propose to apply politics to the problem.

Two days later Senator Glass obtained a conference. He took along, by agreement, seven of the leading bankers. They argued with "fervor, force, persuasiveness" and with an air of finality. Wilson listened courteously and attentively. They concluded and sat back.

Senator Glass recalled that the President said very quietly, but with unmistakable resolution:

"Gentlemen, I challenge any one of you to point to a government board, in this country or anywhere in any other civilized country, upon which private interests are permitted to have representation.

"In other words, the Federal Reserve Board is an altruistic body representing all the people of the United States, put there for the purpose of supervising this great banking system and seeing that no section and no class is discriminated against in its administration. Its members are not permitted to have any banking affiliation or connection at all. They are not permitted to own bank stock of any description. There is no single element of acquisitiveness in the whole formation of that board or in its operation. The Board is there to represent the people of the United States; and you might as well talk about giving the railroads of this country the right of minority representation on the Interstate Commerce Commission, appointed to supervise the railroads, as to talk about giving the banks minority representation on the Federal Reserve Board—and I didn't have sense enough at first to see it."

Mr. Wilson had read his message on July twenty-third. The bill reached the Senate on September eighteenth at six P.M. On December twenty-third the gaunt, weary President signed the bill into law. "It is a Christmas present for the American people," said one of those who watched.

The old policy of concentration of reserves, carefully nurtured by the speculative interests who profited most thereby, was at an end.

Wilson was not quite finished.

Farmers historically had been the ruthlessly exploited victims of unscrupulous and harsh operators in the credit system. Under the President's leadership the Congress enacted the Federal Farm Loan Act—the nation's first long-time credit loans for farmers.

Wilson moved ahead on the more minor pledges. He obtained repeal of the law giving American ships freedom from tolls in the Panama Canal because we had pledged there would be no discrimination and the nation's integrity was at issue. It was not an easy victory. Shipping interests opposed it with the enormous influence which was theirs to command.

Among those who supported him, even, there was some muttering. The President was a very human man. But there was a quality about him which was both strength and, insofar as "practical" politics was concerned, a weakness. He had the predestined faith of the Calvinist. He instinctively trusted his own great powers. He could never accept the theory that one must convince or compromise with one's adversaries. The eight-hour day came out of such a decision.

He was well into his campaign for re-election in August, 1916, when the Railroad brotherhoods and management came close to a strike and paralysis of the country. Weeks of negotiation dragged on. The issue was an eight-hour day and no reduction in pay.

Wilson, believing the eight-hour day practical and proper, asked for legislation to obtain it. The Democrats supported it, as did many House Republicans. In the Senate all Republicans save Bob LaFollette voted against it. They made it a campaign issue. In the big industrial states the industrial and rail leaders fought Wilson with all they had and managed to put all of them into the Republican column in the all-but-dead-heat election in November.

It went his way.

He plodded ahead, determined to be a liberal, progressive President, seeking always to do what he believed best for people in general.

He put all his influence behind the Clayton Antitrust law, which established by law the fact that "labor" is not a "commodity" but a human contribution to the economy and to society.

Every measure which he had urged upon the Congress up to the time of the crippling stroke suffered at Pueblo in September, 1919, became law.

All the new legislation was standing well the test of time. Even the most violent opponents of the Federal Reserve System were convinced.

Banker Vanderlip, who had prophesied a complete breakdown of the financial system, had seen how the system had enabled the nation to finance the war and had gone to Carter Glass and said so, admitting his opinion had been wrong. All the pledges had been kept.

But on that March 4, 1913, there were no war clouds anywhere save, perhaps, in the Balkans. And already the phrase "trouble in the Balkans" had become something of a jest. They were very far away, and remote, and most Americans thought of them as somehow comic-opera countries. There was talk, too, that Germany, balked in her African colonial expansion by the French and British, was building a great navy to match that of England's. And the French still bristled over the Franco-Prussian war. But no one wanted war.

In April, 1914, the Mexican problem, which President Wilson had inherited, caused some worry and embarrassment. General Victoriana Huerta had brought off a blood coup in the closing days of William Taft's administration and that good and kindly man had soundly denounced him. President Wilson had refused to recognize Huerta, saying:

"So long as the power of recognition rests with me, the Government of the United States will refuse to extend the hand of welcome to anyone who obtains power in a sister state by treachery and violence." Huerta began a series of slights and affronts. Great pressure was put on Wilson to intervene. He refused, but in April did land naval units at Vera Cruz to prevent a large shipment of German arms from reaching Huerta. There was an uproar of criticism and applause, but the net result was Huerta's flight.

Spring in 1914 was a trying one. It was hot and humid. Mrs. Wilson was not well and obviously was failing. May seventh she attended the quiet wedding of her daughter Eleanor to Secretary McAdoo. In June she was much worse.

So it was that no one in Washington seemed to pay much attention to the news of June twenty-eighth. In Bosnia an Austrian archduke had been shot.

Secretary Bryan was busy making peace treaties. In July, while Austria and Serbia exchanged notes, Mr. Wilson sent twenty of the Secretary's treaties to the Congress. (Bryan was to obtain more

Birthplace of Woodrow Wilson, Staunton, Virginia.

oodrow Wilson's parents, Joseph R. and Janet Wilson.

aunton, Virginia, 1856.

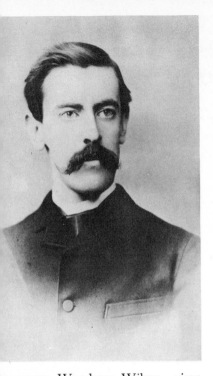

The young Woodrow Wilson, *circa* [18]86.

A cartoon from the St. Louis *Post-Dispatch*, December 29, 1910. The caption was, "Looking him over."

[Ea]rly 1919. Woodrow Wilson, Ray Stannard Baker, Georges Clemenceau, [Dr. Cary] Grayson, A. J. Balfour and others, talking together on a Paris street.

tember 9, 1919. President Wilson on the train steps at St. Paul, Minnesc
ng his last Western trip, on behalf of the League of Nations.

than thirty signatures, some of them after war had begun in Europe.)

Some of the polite foreign diplomats who signed Mr. Bryan's treaties must have had great difficulty keeping a straight face. In a sense it was a somewhat ridiculous, innocent and empty gesture. But America was an innocent country in that time, and Wilson and most of his Cabinet were, in that sense, innocent men.

The pistol shot at Sarajevo sounded the death knell of innocence. The world would never know that quality again—not as it existed in the spring of 1914. It had been a time of faith and of optimism. Christian hopes were high that perhaps, after all, the brotherhood of man was a possibility.

As Ellen Wilson lay dying in the sweltering end of July and the beginning of August, they kept from her the news that Europe had flamed into war. She, too, had believed in Mr. Bryan's pacifism; and his peace treaties, so ridiculous in later and more cynical years, did not seem at all silly to her—or to millions of wives and mothers like her. When she died in the late afternoon of August sixth, the great powers of Europe had declared war and the smaller nations were coming in fast.

By the bedside of his dying wife, Woodrow Wilson had looked at the beginning of war as incredible. The deliberate speed of her approaching death and the weariness of his frail body held him in a sort of hypnosis. All else outside that reality seemed unreal.

The war was a shock. There had been across the years of peace a flowering of idealism and belief in the goodness of human nature and of civilization. America, of course, must be neutral. Almost everyone agreed to that in the early days while the armies mobilized and began their drives across frontiers.

But as the funeral train took the long, sad road to Rome, Georgia, with the quiet, respectful crowds standing still and silent, hoping the broken man inside would somehow know how sorry they were, he did not think much about war. Ellen Axson Wilson had been wife and prop, comforter and friend. Such persons, when they go, leave a vacuum of pain and loneliness.

Back in the dreadful heat of Washington, neutrality began to be less popular. The agony of Belgium had begun two days before Ellen Wilson had died. It was at flood tide when the President returned to take up the burden of office—a burden which daily grew heavier. The shrilling of those who wanted war, and those who didn't, was beginning to grow in volume, insistent and discordant. But he clung stubbornly to neutrality.

So the steaming heat of August slowly gave way to the first cool breath of autumn, and the cold, raw wet of winter came and went, and it was spring again.

The war news had never been really good, save for the great, pulse-quickening gallantry of the allied troops at the Marne and the bloody struggle to keep the Kaiser's gray tide from flowing over all of France.

On May 7, 1915, neutrality became more difficult. The Germans sank the *Lusitania* with a torpedo from a submarine and 124 peaceful American noncombatants, men, women and children, were lost. For a day the nation seemed stunned. Then the wildly protesting wrath boiled up until the nation itself seemed to shake with the poundings from pulpit, rostrum and editorial sanctums. The grief and rage of the people were the greater because they felt betrayed. All at once those who had refused to believe all the ghastly stories of atrocities in Belgium were convinced the Germans were, indeed, Huns.

Grief and anger were a gale, buffeting the White House. Then came pictures of the dead bodies of women and children, their husbands and fathers, taken from the cold waters off Ireland where the *Lusitania* had gone down, brought ashore at Queenstown, Ireland. The gale became a storm. The hot blooded who wanted war cried "Coward." Editors who itched for battle, which others would fight, denounced the President as a human icicle, a heartless, callous man. Theodore Roosevelt, who originally had stood for neutrality, called Wilson a "Byzantine logothete," and newspaper reporters, who had hurried to their dictionaries, explained to their readers that the Rooseveltian epithet meant a person who expounded much and acted never.

Wilson, outraged and himself even less able to keep his thoughts neutral, sent a sharp-edged protest through diplomatic channels. Never again, after the *Lusitania*, did America seem so "kindly separated by nature and a wide ocean from the exterminating havoc of one-quarter of the globe."

There was a reviewing of the United States fleet off New York. It was a good show and the Secretary of the Navy began to grow in popularity.

Germany's reply was not satisfactory and in June, as the Cabinet discussed a second and sharper note, William Jennings Bryan felt the British had unfairly allowed civilians, especially it. The *Lusitania* had carried war goods and ammunition, and Bryan felt the British had unfairly allowed civilians, especially neutral Americans, to travel on her. Robert Lansing succeeded him.

Bryan's resignation made the pacifists more clamorous. Those who hated England, and they were many, accused Wilson of dragging us into war. Those who admired Germany, and they were by no means few, angrily charged Wilson was being duped by Britain. But now, Wilson was writing the notes and they were more difficult for the Germans. Their penetration and logic began to cause the American people to have a better perspective of the diplomatic struggle. Wilson, like the great mass of inarticulate people who did not want to become involved in a distant European war, was learning. A great, strong nation cannot avoid being involved, once war begins, because of its strength. Those at war will not let it be.

It was that spring, too, that Francis and Jessie Woodrow Wilson Sayre brought a grandson on a visit to the White House. A friend of the President's daughter came to call, Mrs. Edith Bolling Galt, Virginia born, widow of a successful businessman. His friends rejoiced to see the lonely, burdened man suddenly happy in her company. But, as our political history so invariably shows, the gossip against a President almost always is scurrilous and worse. Those who hate Presidents will stoop to astonishing depths of meanness if they think they can thereby do harm. They charged, among other things, the President had written indiscreet letters to another lady, an old friend, Mrs. Mary Hulbert Peck. Mrs. Galt, worried lest the gossip harm the President, suggested they see each other no more. But the President had other ideas. The formal engagement was announced. The gossips kept on. A worried Joe Tumulty, confidential secretary, went to his chief. "Don't worry, Joe," he said calmly. "There was not a single word in [those letters] that even requires an explanation." And there wasn't.

Shortly before Christmas, Saturday, December eighteenth, at eight thirty P.M., they were married at Mrs. Galt's home in Washington. The simple ceremony was performed jointly by the Reverend Herbert S. Smith, Rector of the Episcopal Church of which the bride was a Communicant, and the Reverend James H. Taylor, Pastor of Central Presbyterian Church where the President worshiped. They had two weeks at Hot Springs, Virginia, and then returned to Washington's cold, damp winter, and the shadow of the ever-darkening war clouds. Possessed of tact, wit, wisdom and graciousness, Mrs. Wilson measured up always to the high standards the American people have established for the mistress of the White House. In sickness and in health, she was by her husband's side to comfort, advise and sustain until he passed on into the great mystery and its silence.

The lonely man, the reserved man, who loved people and had for them one of the few deeply genuine compassions to be found in the history of our politics, could give personal, intimate affection only to his family and his chosen friends. He had need of such a wife and companion.

The days of neutrality were fast running out. They had begun August 4, 1914. They ended officially on April 6, 1917—a span of 197 tortured, turbulent days.

Slowly, always slowly, Wilson and the nation moved with reluctant feet toward war. Both were isolationist, he and the country. In all the history of the United States there has been no stronger, more sincere, isolationist than Woodrow Wilson.

There was a pragmatic, political argument in behalf of neutrality. More than once he said to Cabinet members that war would destroy all he was trying to do—perhaps all he had been able to accomplish—for the country. War, he said, would set the country back twenty years or more. The money changers would get back into the temple. When the people's attention was distracted by war, the corruptionists would infiltrate into war contracts, and have a field day generally. The Democratic processes would be strained. And, loving people as he did, the thought of casualties, with those of Europe terribly before him, had given him strength to announce neutrality, and to stand for it in those early months of the war.

He was by no means alone. In the September issue of the *Outlook* Theodore Roosevelt wrote, "It is certainly eminently desirable that we should remain entirely neutral and nothing but urgent need would warrant breaking our neutrality and taking sides one way or the other."

Wilson hoped, as 1916 began, that the warring nations, weary of the slaughter, would turn to a neutral United States for mediating their differences. It was in this spirit of hope he kept writing the notes and carrying on his negotiations.

But spring moved on towards summer and it was an election year. And the Democratic prognosis was not too favorable. Teddy Roosevelt, seeing no hope, refused the nomination of the Progressive Party and that organization, robust and confident in 1912, died. The Republicans went to the United States Supreme Court for their candidate and nominated Charles Evans Hughes, an Associate Justice and former Governor of New York.

The Democrats, meeting in St. Louis, had only the formality of nominating Wilson. As Vice-President they chose Thomas R. Marshall of Indiana, who described himself as "Wilson's only vice."

German elements, which had defended the sinking of the *Lusitania*, were strong in some areas of America, and the campaign began with emphasis on loyalty and an end to "hyphenated" citizenship.

The Democrats laid stress on their domestic achievements and the "Big Brother" policy toward Mexico—a policy severely strained that same year by Pancho Villa. In revolt against his old ally, Venustiano Carranza, and angry with the United States for recognition of him, Villa raided across the border at Columbus, New Mexico, killing and burning. General John J. Pershing led a punitive force into Mexico after Villa, but Carranza protested and Pershing was withdrawn. Wilson, having inherited the Mexican problem from the Taft Administration, was determined to reverse the policy of "dollar diplomacy."

In the East and along the Atlantic Seaboard generally, the sentiment was for war, was critical of Wilson. Candidate Hughes made no promise to go in, but denounced the methods employed in maintaining neutrality.

In the West there was strong sentiment against war. There the slogan "He kept us out of war," used in the nominating convention by Governor Martin H. Glynn, had meaning. Wilson made it always clear that the issue of peace or war was not in his keeping Never once did he say he had "kept us out of war."

Save for a few short trips, President Wilson remained at Shadow Lawn, New Jersey. Every Saturday afternoon he spoke from his front porch. In our time of heavy pressure campaigning, and the saturation quality of radio and television, the campaign of 1916 seems almost primitively innocent.

Candidate Hughes spoke in all parts of the country, and was carpingly critical. Wilson, reading the criticisms, said, "If you will give that gentleman rope enough, he will hang himself."

A rail strike threatened in the midst of the campaign. Wilson met it with the Adamson Law—bringing to labor the eight-hour day—which aroused all the industrial management power against him.

In the main, the candidates observed the amenities, but hardly anyone else did. It was a campaign of slander, viciousness and bitter invective. Perhaps the worst was Teddy Roosevelt. Hot for war, he called Wilson that "damned Presbyterian hypocrite," and not so openly but still not exactly privately, flayed Hughes as a "bearded iceberg."

By nine o'clock on the night of Election Day, Republicans were jubilant. Impromptu celebrations began. New York, Indiana, Connecticut and even New Jersey, traditional pivotal states, had gone to Hughes. Newspapers supporting Wilson conceded at about eleven P.M., and Charles Evans Hughes went to bed believing himself President of the United States. Wilson, Secretary Joe Tumulty recalled, seemed casual and carefree, though disappointed he had not convinced the people.

But by dawn's early light, the scene was not quite the same. In Ohio, Governor James M. Cox, progressive Democrat running on a distinguished record, was again returned to office, and Wilson, too, was partner in the triumph. Kansas went for Wilson. Minnesota swung back to Hughes and, finally, there were only the California returns incomplete. They would decide.

In Los Angeles, where the count was suspiciously slow, armed and vigilant men watched every box.

At last they were all counted and Wilson had a majority of 3,777. His electoral vote was 277 to 254 for Hughes and his popular majority was 568,822. He received a total of 9,116,296 votes, the largest vote ever given a President up to that time.

His inaugural was like a prayer:

"I pray God I may be given the wisdom and the prudence to do my duty in the true spirit of this great people——"

In the rejoicing at that second inaugural few noted the apprehension in his voice. But it was there. The patient writer of notes, the severe man who so often had tears in his eyes, knew how exorably, and with what dread feet, war was nearing. He had initiated preparedness programs, but he knew that because of the country's inertia they would not be enough. The big wide ocean had caused us to give little attention to military aircraft production plants. Our artillery was obsolete. Our training was designed for the American terrain.

Many voices were screaming at him. The congressmen and senators with German votes in their districts and states were demanding he break the British blockade. Without doubt, it was doing some violence to American traditions of freedom of the seas, but Wilson stood firm. He admired the British for their courage and they were not sinking any passenger ships with torpedoes.

The U-boats, new and frightful weapons in effectiveness, sank some ninety ships from February to early June, 1915. Among them was the *Lusitania*.

Germany pledged to give warning to all passenger ships, but the pledge was broken. In December, 1916, Wilson asked all belligerents to state their war aims—hoping to precipitate mediation.

On January twenty-second, in an eloquent address to the Senate, he made one of his most prophetic statements, "It must be peace without victory," he said. "Only a peace between equals can last——"

Nine days later the Germans answered. They announced unrestricted submarine warfare. They would sink all ships in the war zone—including those of the United States. It was an almost unbelievable, shocking decision.

Yet it was not hastily made. In Europe the war was deep in mud and blood, and bound by miles of barbed wire. The blockade was pinching German stomachs. We had no army. And if we some-how should be able to create one, the high command believed submarines could sink most of the ships transporting it. If they struck hard enough, the war might be ended before we could produce an army worth the name. So, the Germans gambled.

In Wilson's hands, known only to his Cabinet, was proof German diplomats in the Kaiser's embassy had offered Mexico the states of Texas, Arizona and New Mexico if she would join Japan in attacking us. On February 3, 1917, the German am-bassador was handed his passports.

Still, Wilson clung to the hope of peace. He would not go to war without an overt act by the Germans.

Shipping all but ceased. United States ports were crowded with ships, liners and freighters. The docks were piled high with goods. New York City had food shortages and housewives demonstrated.

Wilson asked for authority to arm merchant ships. The House passed the bill overwhelmingly. But in the Senate eleven senators, largely from states with substantial German population, filibustered until an adjournment was forced March 3, 1917. It was an angry President who denounced the "little group of wilful men" who had rendered their country "helpless and contemptible."

Then, realizing the Constitution made him Commander-in-chief of the armed forces, he armed the ships anyhow. In six days four ships were armed and steadily, then, a succession of vessels headed out toward England and France.

In March four small United States freighters daring the seas unarmed, were sunk with loss of thirty-six men. (In that same March the Russian throne fell, and a liberal provisional government was set up. Most Americans, never caring much for Kings, Kaisers or Tsars, were rather glad. At the time it seemed like a revolution leading towards democracy—as it might have, had other men done better thinking and planning, and had fortune been more benign.)

Wilson knew, after the filibuster by the "little group of wilful men," the temper of the people. They were no longer neutral. Nor was he.

Killing civilians was not regarded as "civilized" in 1914–16, and the submarine was the symbol of murder and of "the Hun."

And Wilson, and others, had begun to see that if we did not

fight in 1917 when there were allies, we would one day have to fight the Kaiser, and his dream of conquest, alone.

If we had to fight, as we did, Wilson was the man providentially provided to lead us. We were idealists. So was he. We had been isolationist. So had he. We and he were innocents together. No dreams of empire stirred in him or us as in the minds of the French, British and Germans.

True idealism, intellectual capacity and honesty lead men instinctively to say the right things, to take the right course.

On April sixth, he came before a joint session of the Congress, tense, yet convinced, though nearly all there had the feeling of Gethsemane.

Earnest, stern, his eyes grave, his gaunt face the more deeply lined, he was in appearance, voice and drama, the vehicle of the American spirit and dream awakened to the fact that they represented a great power which could not stand aside when a great moral issue was at stake.

It was to be, he told them, "a war without rancor and without selfish object, without revenge. . . ."

He held them so still one could hear the breathing in the great chamber.

"There is one choice we are incapable of making: We will not choose the path of submission and suffer the most sacred rights of our nation to be ignored or violated. . . ."

The stillness held——

"Why must we fight? Why must 'force to the utmost' be not for conquest? Why must we go to war?"

"For democracy, for the right of those who submit to authority to have a voice in their governments, for the rights and liberties of small nations, for a universal dominion of right by such concert of free peoples as shall bring peace and safety to all nations and make the world itself at last free."

There was no hymn of hate, no cry for blood or vengeance.

Then came his great peroration—and prayer:

"It is a fearful thing to lead this great, peaceful people into war, into the most terrible and disastrous of all wars, civilization itself seeming to be in the balance. But the right is more precious than peace, and we shall fight for the things which we have always carried nearest our hearts, for [this] democracy, [this right] . . . To such a task we can dedicate our lives and our fortunes, everything that we are and everything that we have, with the pride of those who know that the day has come when America is privileged to spend her blood and her might for the principles that gave her birth and happiness and peace which she has treasured. God helping her, she can do no other."

Joe Tumulty remembered that he rode back to the White House with the President, the applause of the chamber and that of the people who lined the streets still in their ears. It was the cheers of these people which seemed to bother Mr. Wilson as he sat "silent and pale" in the Cabinet room. At last he said:

"Think of what it was they were applauding. My message today was a message of death for our young men. How strange it seems they would applaud that."

Joe Tumulty wrote that this simple sentence was the key to an understanding of Wilson. "All politicians pretend to hate and dread war," he wrote in 1921, "but Woodrow Wilson really hates and dreads it in all the fibres of his human soul; hates it and dreads it because he has an imagination and a heart; an imagination which shows his sensitive perception, the anguish and the dying which war entails; a heart which yearns and aches over every dying soldier and bleeds afresh with each new made wound."

This war, to which Wilson, the pacifist and isolationist led them, had from the beginning perhaps our highest degree of unity.

And Wilson became the voice of the war and of all those opposing Germany and her allies. It was needed. The war went badly in April and May. The submarines, ordered to step up their pace, sank ships at an average of nine per day. They slowly were nullified when the Americans insisted on the convoy system, and as other antisubmarine techniques began to be developed.

The United States was prepared mentally—but otherwise there was a hopeless snarl of red tape, a confusion of effort, and a great lack of comprehension as to the size and global demands of the conflict.

"It is not an army that we must train for war," said Wilson, "but a nation."

A dismayed Congress voted the necessary authority. A war

cabinet was created. Bernard M. (Barney) Baruch was called from his office to head up the War Industries Board. It established priorities, fixed prices, cut down waste and stood off the chiselers and corruptionists with increasing success.

Slowly, surely, order emerged from chaos. Production—the vital goods to keep European allies going—began to come from the factories.

With war came high wages—silk shirts in the shipyards—and high prices. Living costs pinched the average home. There was resentment at the high war wages and the prices, and there were strikes—none serious. A National War Labor Board was established. A War Trade Board began, by license, to control exports and imports. A Fuel Administration took over the acute problem of coal. The shocked nation, never having considered the possibility of shortages, was asked to sacrifice with "heatless Mondays," "meatless Tuesdays," "wheatless Mondays and Wednesdays," "porkless Thursdays and Saturdays." "Victory gardens" sent men and women to digging in vacant lots and back yards.

They all believed in Wilson. They were inspired by his idealism, and so they did a really amazing job of following their leaders —voluntarily.

Herbert Hoover led the Food Administration, ably and well. It is somehow odd reading, in 1956, to pore over the old records and find him coming to Woodrow Wilson for help against the industrial and manufacturing groups, some of which seemed to him citadels of greed and reaction.

But over all was the keystone problem of ships. The enemy, and our allies, were across the Atlantic.

The Shipping Board, created in 1916, was joined in harness with the Emergency Fleet Corporation. Enemy ships were taken over. More than one hundred interned vessels of neutral nations were requisitioned, their owners being fully compensated.

"Ships for Victory," with haste the watchword, lost time and money with experiments in concrete ships. Yet, slowly but surely, the building program gained in momentum. Five hundred and thirty-three craft were completed in 1918.

Wilson never deviated once his mind was made up. The railroads were not doing a good job in meeting the demands on them. There were then more than thirty rail companies, and there was little co-operation between them. Indeed, so great was the competition between them, they often were at cross purposes. Management in general did not like the President because of the labor legislation he had supported over their objections. They did not like suggestions from the Government and they again came into conflict with their employees. The war machine began to slow down. Continued slowness meant a German victory.

The President took over the railroads. William G. McAdoo was made Director General. The opposition made hysterical protest and dubbed McAdoo, who had married Wilson's daughter Eleanor, "the Crown Prince." There was constant and unending carping. But the railroads ran. The rates were kept low. The moaning managements were guaranteed a high financial return. Economy was not a factor. Not too many persons knew that, if America could not work a miracle of production, the war would be lost. The ships had to be built. The railroads had to deliver steel. There had to be all possible speed. Winning the war, not running a cheap railroad, was the objective. The wartime deficit amounted to $862,000,000. But McAdoo got them out of their cross-purpose snarl. It cost money, but the job that otherwise would not have been done, was.

Victory Loans and Thrift Stamps helped finance the war. George Creel came on to head up the committee on public information, and American propaganda entered the war.

Wilson was indeed training the nation for war. There were the usual cases of disloyalty—really very few, considering the great numbers of German-Americans who believed Germany's cause just —or at least as much so as that of Britain. Many Americans had believed with them—until the submarines changed their thinking. The German-Americans proved they were, first of all, Americans.

Worst of all was the hysteria and the bigotry. Gossip, rumor and lies by hate groups, caused a revulsion against things German. Some states and cities forbade the playing of German music and the teaching of the language. Stupidity and the worst in man came to the top along with the best.

Josephus Daniels and the navy command came through with the greatest job of the war. The Secretary brought off a great building program, and fended off the armor-plate cartels with skill.

Some 2,079,880 soldiers were convoyed to France without the loss of a single man crossing on American transports. Only one troopship was lost in the crossing—an almost unbelievable record. This was an English vessel, sunk near the Orkney Islands. The United States Navy patroled the coast of France, did work in the Baltic and the Mediterranean. Late in the war it carried out a suggestion by the Assistant Secretary of Navy, Franklin D. Roosevelt, and laid a mine barrage across the North Sea. The plan accounted for 8½ per cent of the total number of enemy subs sunk or so badly damaged as to be put out of service.

Joe Tumulty, in his memoirs, wrote of the "magnificent and aggressive" leadership, so well thought-out and planned. He said that many months before war at last came, the President reached certain firm decisions. First of all, there was to be no "politics" in the conduct of the war. Secondly, no political generals were to be selected. Thirdly, all possible energy and force the nation could muster would be placed behind the Army and Navy. Fourth, every effort would be made to embargo speculators, contractors and profiteers.

All were astonishingly well kept.

Item two of those prewar plans meant that Theodore Roosevelt would not be given a command. He was still dreaming of Rough Riders, and while he and his regiment would have been picturesque, they would never have fitted into the sort of Army needed in France. Save for the most violent partisans, none questioned the wisdom of the decision.

General John J. Pershing, named commander of the American Expeditionary Force, did not ask for General Leonard Wood, a capable officer, but in poor health. Indeed, General Pershing privately said he did not want him. It was a grievous decision, and strong was the protest. But the President, refusing to reveal Pershing's request, declared he would back up his commander so long as he was doing the necessary job.

At first there had been the usual, human hope we would not need to send an army. But from England and France came the word, "We are bled white."

On July 4, 1917, for morale purposes only, General Pershing and a small force were paraded through Paris. But there was no army. Back at home, on newly scraped parade grounds, hard by the new pine barracks, an army was being manufactured. Conscription was invoked. France and Britain sent men to help with the training. The draft, which the fearful said would result in riots, worked well because it was basically fair. The drafting, recruiting and training went on at frantic speed. Russia's collapse, releasing hundreds of thousands of battle-toughened German troops to fight in France, gave the Kaiser numerical superiority.

It was October 23, 1917, before the first detachment of U. S. troops saw action. It was a small, token force. But thousands were taking two months of training in France. And America began to hear new songs—especially one about a fabulous "Mademoiselle from Armentières."

Much of our shipping, artillery, aircraft and other material was borrowed from the allies. "Send men," they said, when the United States programs in production of artillery, fighter planes and automatic weapons were delayed.

Late in May, 1918, the Germans were within forty miles of Paris. United States Marines and men of the First Division, about 30,000, were thrown into the fighting at Château-Thierry. In June, the Marines won a bloody, spectacular engagement at Belleau Wood. By July, when the second Battle of the Marne began, some 140,000 United States troops were in the lines. By September, the total was almost 200,000.

General Pershing held out for a separate United States Army, and Wilson, as usual, backed him. A large segment of the front became his responsibility—a line stretching northwestward from the Swiss border to join the French 85 miles away.

On September 26, 1918, the allies jumped off in a great assault in what was designated as the Meuse-Argonne offensive. There were 1,200,000 Americans among the millions thrown at the Germans. There were 47 days of bitter, deadly fighting and the Germans, reeling under the attack, the shortages at home, the collapse of allies, and Wilson's sledge-hammer blows of the fourteen points, agreed to an armistice. The guns ceased on November eleventh.

Some 4,000,000 Americans had been put into uniform. There were 333,734 casualties, of which 130,274 were deaths. Of these,

49,000 were killed in battle. France, in comparison, had 1,700,000 dead in battle and the British empire 900,000.

Wilson had become the allied voice when he read his eloquent war message. His fourteen points as a basis for peace proved to be as powerful as guns, perhaps more so. William Allen White, critic and admirer of the President, said that the Germans surrendered to Wilson's fourteen points, and to famine, produced by the British Navy.

The famed fourteen points were set forth in a message to Congress January 8, 1918. George Creel had them translated into all the languages of Europe and sent them by cable and wireless to every receiving office and station. Planes dropped millions of copies over Germany.

There were to be "open covenants of peace, openly arrived at," freedom of seas, removal of all possible economic barriers and equality of trade conditions. Armaments would be reduced and colonial claims impartially adjusted. Russia would receive the co-operation of the other nations for independent determination of her own political development. Belgium would be restored. All French territory would be freed and Alsace-Lorraine returned. Italy's frontiers were to be readjusted along lines of nationality. Rumania, Serbia and Montenegro were to be re-established. The Turkish portions of the Ottoman empire would be granted sovereignty. An independent Polish state would be erected.

The fourteenth point called for a "general association of nations" formed under specific covenants for the purpose of affording mutual guarantees of political independence and territorial integrity to great and small states alike.

Millions of weary, hungry, saddened, sorrowing, grieving people read them, or heard them read, and took them to their hearts.

From that time, until the bickering and visionless deeds of the peace treaty sessions began, the entire world was at a peak of idealistic hope and faith it had never known before—and has not since experienced. Neither before nor since has any other man occupied so firm a position as the moral leader of the world.

In his first inaugural in 1913 Woodrow Wilson had said, "Men's hearts wait upon us; men's lives hang in the balance; men's hopes call upon us to say what we will do. . . ."

Wilson's declarations for the self-determination of peoples, and the League of Nations, were ideas he had begun to formulate early in the war. When the pacifist, the isolationist idealist learned no great power could in fact be neutral, or hope to escape from war, he determined to find a way, if not to end war, at least to make it difficult to develop.

As usual, he acted forthrightly.

But with the silencing of the guns, the great cementing need and desire for victory crumbled. Politics, which has as its end objective the obtaining of power, reasserted itself in its most blindly partisan form. Wilson, with his mind fixed almost solely on a peace which would end war, made an appeal for a Democratic Congress to hold up his hands. Other Presidents, notably Abraham Lincoln and Theodore Roosevelt, had done so before him. But the Republicans seized on it, and called it a plea for power to establish a dictatorship—and worse.

Republican Party leaders looked ahead toward the 1920 race. Wilson, if he managed well, might enable the Democrats to win another national election. So by every known device, including the worst and most recklessly demagogic, the Republicans set out to tear him down. "Egotist" . . . "Trying to play God" . . . "hogging the whole show" . . . "mushy sentimentalist" . . . "faker" . . . "hypocrite" . . . were some of the milder phrases. They cried, when he said he would go to Paris, that he was needed at home—they, who a day before denounced him as incompetent and unfit. They said he would be "bamboozled" in Paris. At home, in the White House, they seemed to say, he could participate much more effectively.

It made no sense, but it was politically effective. Americans, quite humanly, wanted their boys hurried home. Republican speakers argued Wilson would keep them there forever. They said, too, that Europe could make her own peace. We should give attention to our own problems.

By a narrow margin the Republicans won control of the Congress. For Wilson it was a loss of face as well.

Further cries of anguish came from the resurgent GOP leaders when Wilson announced his five-man peace commission. He had been advised to place a high-ranking Republican, even two, on the list. He refused. Some argued it was one of his fatal flaws that he refused always to see he must "convince his adversaries." Whether it was flaw or not, he would never "play politics" with a principle.

He named himself to the committee; the faithful Colonel Edward House, a practical politician who could never persuade Mr. Wilson to be very practical; Secretary of State Lansing; a military adviser, General T. H. Bliss; and a Republican, Henry White completed it. This latter choice infuriated the bitter-enders all the more. They declared they did not even know that White, a retired career diplomat, was a Republican, so quiet and inactive in party affairs had he been.

In addition there were many technical advisers, economists and scholars, familiar with the history and peoples of Europe. This made the partisan critics wild. "Professors," they snorted. It has long been one of our national paradoxes that though we earnestly proclaim our devotion to education, and tax ourselves heavily for it, we have never really trusted our educators, or our well-educated people.

Nor did Wilson name a senator to the commission. And this, said the critics of the time, as well as the historians since, was sheerest folly because the Senate would have to ratify any treaty made.

It was not folly. There was but one senator he could have taken, Henry Cabot Lodge. He long before had come to hate Wilson. And hate is a destructive corrosive.

The harsh truth is the Republican chiefs, led by Lodge and Theodore Roosevelt, had met and agreed to "get" Wilson. In the first two years of his administration he had stepped on a lot of toes with his reforms of banking, currency, and his establishment of labor legislation. They had agreed that the man was politically dangerous. If he were allowed a triumph in Paris he might enable his party also to triumph—and, perish the thought—might himself run for a third term.

So, really, it did not greatly matter who made up the commission, though men still fret and theorize over "if" and "on the other hand."

Wilson sailed for Paris with just one long-run objective—the League of Nations. He landed at Brest, December 13, 1918.

Emotional demonstrations of almost incredible intensity and affection greeted him everywhere he went—in France, Great Britain and Italy. But there was no action. It was not possible immediately to begin a peace treaty. France's Georges Clemenceau, hard-bitten relic of the past, nursing a bitter dream of Old Testament revenge for the Franco-Prussian war, and Britain's canny Welshman, David Lloyd George, previously had exchanged private diplomatic views. They did not dare begin a treaty with the masses of their population so fervently, almost worshipfully, hanging on Wilson's every word.

Had there been radio in that last month of 1918, Wilson almost certainly, even with the use of interpreters, would have been able to bring the conference immediately to its task. But there was no radio. And in Britain, Lloyd George had "gone to the people" and needed time for "adjustments." France, too, had a few somewhat vague, but plausible reasons for delay.

So Wilson, at their suggestion, visited Britain and Italy—with everywhere the people looking up to him as one who might be able to bring to earth that peace and good will of which the angelic choir sang on the occasion of the birth of the Messiah at Bethlehem.

In the centennial year of Woodrow Wilson's birth, events have brought him and his vision, his intentions, his words and his views into a historical perspective rarely given one of the world's great figures. Most of what has been written of Woodrow Wilson—the biographies, the evaluations—was put down in the 'twenties and 'thirties. Those were the years of the locust. Wilson was a failure, easily discredited by the cynical and the pragmatic who so confidently "mumble the bones of the slain." He, the visionary idealist, the dreamer, who had been so helpless in contest with the strong practical men, became, in the swift rush of the 'twenties and 'thirties, a jest on the lips of those who worship the golden calf of realism. He was the "absent-minded professor." He was not realistic enough, they said. He was not a practical man. So he had failed and been left a somewhat ridiculous dreamer.

But now, it is 1956 and the centennial of his birth, and the year of vindication. One and all may see that he was the only practical man there. Of them all he was the realist, the only one dealing in cold, relentless reality.

Three days after his arrival he said, for example, replying to the French Socialist Party delegation:

"This has indeed been a people's war. It has been waged against absolutism and militarism, and these enemies of liberty must from this time forth be shut out from the possibility of working their cruel will upon mankind. In my judgment it is not sufficient to establish this principle. It is necessary that it be supported by a co-operation of the nations which shall be based upon fixed and definite covenants, and which shall be made certain of effective action through the instrumentality of a League of Nations."

This was December 16, 1918.

To the people it seemed realistic. But not to Clemenceau and George—and not to the Republican mentality then in control of Congress—all of them, in Washington, London, Paris and in Rome, were being "practical," "sound" men, looking at the future through what might be called the rear-view mirror of their experience and their political morality.

While Britain and France delayed, they sought to win Wilson to a more severe peace. They did not tell him, of course, of the imperialistic plans, of the secret treaties, already made, dividing up the rich oil land, the best of the territorial "loot." They had agreed to Wilson's fourteen points to end a war. But being "practical" men, they would not use them to make a peace. Though to be sure, they never quite said so, in so many words—the people were always demanding to see him—but then, the people, of course, were not practical either.

Speed was urgent. Wilson knew it to be so because Europe was disintegrating. Yet the Big Three worked delay so that they might obtain "title" and establish military and custom controls—to the German and Turkish colonies. The Bolsheviks had published the contents of all treaties secretly entered into by Russia. This only mildly embarrassed the European leadership of the peace conference, but did tend to make the people, suspicious of the delay, cynical, more suspicious and discontented. The Red virus was flowing westward. Already it was in the Balkans.

The peace conference was no longer truly worthy of the name. It was in the hands of "The Big Four." In truth, it usually was "The Big Three."

They shut Wilson out when they could. They did not let him know about the secret meetings, the private deals. Nonetheless, all Wilson's Scottish stubbornness came to the fore. He would not agree to their bald and bold plan for realistic imperialism—an outright division of the spoils.

This was a violation of point five—one of the more vital ones. They were three to one—but they could not break him. At last he forced a compromise. The great powers would not receive outright title to the divisions of conquered territory, but would serve as trustees of the League of Nations. They were the "mandatories" of the League.

Had the United States come into the League, these mandates would not have become, as they did, little more than subterfuges for old-fashioned imperialism.

Wilson argued, too, for a careful determination of Germany's capacity to pay reparations. He did not believe, and said so, that France could be fully compensated without imposing a burden which would destroy any possibility of Europe's economic recovery. But the "realistic" overruled the "dreamer." And, of course, Europe's economy was never sound, and the cost in human life, suffering and property loss was already large when Wilson closed his eyes in death. Four years later, when the cancer of the reparation plan adopted over Wilson's protest was making all of Europe ill, the troubled Republican administration came forward with a proposal—that Germany's capacity to pay be determined.

But Wilson had his League. Named chairman of the committee which drafted the covenant, he worked quite literally night and day. In ten long, emotional sessions, he obtained its adoption in a satisfactorily completed form, needing only a bit of editing.

The conference did not want it. There was an attempt, piously fraudulent, to make it the last item on the agenda. They wanted all the spoils divided up before any "League" cast a shadow on their plans to add to imperial possessions.

But Wilson would not agree.

One day he spoke so eloquently that the already cynical reporters, aware of the Big Three clique and its power, forgot to take notes. Even Clemenceau, "the tiger," ceased licking his chops. And Lloyd George, with his Welsh liking for music and words, appeared exalted, as if St. David had come back with a leek in his hat and a moving psalm on his lips.

In mid-February, 1919, Wilson won a really great victory. The League Covenant was not merely adopted but made an integral and major part of the final treaty impossible of surgery.

Years later, the practical men and others with guilt on their conscience, began to make their failure Wilson's. When the collapse came; when Europe's economy was being eaten away by the victories of the realists at Versailles, they began to blame it on him. They said he had not recognized the need for playing politics at home; that he had been bamboozled; that he had not gone to Paris well prepared; that his advisers were inadequate.

John Maynard Keynes, in his *Essays in Biography*, published in 1933, saw Clemenceau "plain." He wrote: "So far as possible, therefore, it was the policy of France to set the clock back and to undo what, since 1870, the progress of Germany had accomplished. . . . He sees the issues in terms of France and Germany, not of humanity and of European civilization struggling toward a new order. . . ."

Keynes, out of his memory of 1918–19, recalled Woodrow Wilson as playing "blind man's buff" in the party (conference). Keynes, remembering across a decade, said of Wilson that "he had no plan, no scheme, no constructive ideas whatever for clothing with the flesh of life the commandments which had thundered from the White House." He was, wrote Keynes, "ill-informed on European conditions."

Keynes, with his admiration remaining with the practical men, those "informed" about European conditions, noted the President could have used the financial power of the United States, and the dependence of France, Italy, England—all of Europe for that matter—to force acceptance of what he wanted.

"But the President was not capable of so clear an understanding. . . . He was too conscientious . . . he remained a man of principle . . . but insensitive to his surroundings. . . ."

And so he had. The President was indeed capable of a clear

understanding of his power. But he was not a blackmailer, nor was he "clever" as was Lloyd George, or as pragmatic as Clemenceau. He did hold to principle.

Keynes published in 1933. At that time the world was in the depths of a great economic collapse. It was the year Hitler's star began to glow on the horizon of a hungry, desperate Germany. All about Keynes was eloquently accusing evidence that neither Clemenceau's ideas, nor those of Premier George, so obvious to Mr. Keynes's eyes at the conference, had been anything but ineffective.

It was plain then to many, as it is to almost everyone in 1956, that instead of being without an idea, Wilson was the only person there with a workable one. Instead of being insensitive to his surroundings and to European conditions, he was the only man at the conference who was sensitive and aware.

But the sorry, sordid show went on. They began to tear him down. Rumor and lies were "leaked" to the French press. That press, then already largely corrupted, as so much of it was revealed to be in the opening days of the second great war, began to charge Wilson was "pro-Hun"—that he had betrayed France and was trying to rebuild Germany into a great power.

There was an interlude. The President had to go home to sign bills passed by the adjourning Congress and to attend to other business. In Washington the passions of jealousy and power were rising like the temperature of a patient suffering from some deep-seated infection. Senator Lodge was the center of it. Hatred had corroded him. The man who, as editor of the *North American Review*, had greatly admired contributor Woodrow Wilson and urged him to persevere, now led the chorus of hate. The League was denounced as "League of Nations claptrap," as a dangerous "super-state" which might destroy the sovereignty of the United States and as "the League of denationalized nations." Isolationist Senators William E. Borah and Hiram W. Johnson led their following to Lodge. They were the United States duplicates of Clemenceau.

In early March these "irreconcilables" published a Round Robin. On it were the names of thirty-nine Senators, or Senators-elect, pledged not to approve the League of Nations. They were enough to defeat it.

The Big Three were pleased. Now Wilson would have to come to them. They drove a hard bargain.

"God gave us His Ten Commandments," said Clemenceau, "and we broke them. Wilson gave us his fourteen points—we shall see."

Even here Wilson, ill and weary, held out. For an amateur diplomat he did astonishingly well. The Saar Basin would not go to the Tiger—but would be under the trusteeship of the League for fifteen years and then hold a plebiscite. France also yielded her demands for a slice of Germany to serve as a buffer state. He was the man of principle with Italy, too, and she, like France, turned against him, when he opposed her plans for territorial looting.

The Germans signed the treaty on June twenty-eighth. They, too, charged betrayal—the fourteen points on which they had agreed to surrender, had been considerably altered. It was this "stab in the back" which Hitler used as his rallying cry. Wilson had accepted compromise to save the League. He, too, was hurt and unhappy with the treaty. But the League—it would smooth out the injustices and inequities when, and if, they began to pinch.

When Wilson reached Washington, the knives were sharpened and waiting.

Teddy Roosevelt, still nursing his dream of glory, denounced all "peace-twaddle." German-Americans, Italian-Americans, the Irish-Americans, the anti-British, the liberals, the German-haters, the isolationists—they all damned the treaty.

Senator Lodge, in July, 1919, had no hope of defeating the treaty. So he set out, as chairman of the Senate Foreign Relations Committee to "love it to death" with amendments and words. Most of the press was hostile. The people had much distortion of the pact, and not much sound interpretation. The weeks dragged on.

Wilson decided to "go to the country." His wife, physician and Cabinet protested. It was a hot summer. He was ill. The long months of harassment and work despite constant pain had depleted him physically. He went.

In the Midwest the German-American influence was then strong. The Republicans sent rabble-rousing speakers in behind him. There was not much progress.

But the West was different. That region, which had supported him in 1916, turned out great and increasing crowds, all enthusiastic. He was winning—until September 25, 1919. He spoke that day at Pueblo, Colorado, a huge crowd cheering him to the echo. That night he collapsed on the train. It was routed direct to Washington. The tide turned.

Senator Lodge cynically produced his fourteen amendments. The Democrats voted to defeat this ruthless mockery. There was another ballot, and once more Lodge's amendments failed.

"The bitter-enders" had won.

The people, tired of idealism, assured they could always live in peace behind their great ocean, were apathetic, weary of the bitter arguments, not well informed. They did not see the fruits of victory were being thrown away. Nor, for that matter, did Lodge and his "Battalion of Death." To them, it was just politics—and a way to restore the Republican Party to power.

Wilson, sick and slowly dying, was out of touch with public opinion and the appeal of the slogan "Normalcy." He urged that the fight for moral principle and the League of Nations which could keep the peace, go on.

And the party found the candidates who would stand on that principle. They were James Middleton Cox of Dayton, Ohio, two-term Governor and publisher; and Franklin Delano Roosevelt, who had been Assistant Secretary of the Navy.

As a preliminary to the campaign of 1920, Governor Cox and Mr. Roosevelt called on Woodrow Wilson at the White House. In the early 1940's, while engaged in the preparation of his memoirs, *Journey Through My Years*, published in 1946, Governor Cox had a talk with the Hon. Claude Bowers, then Ambassador to Chile. The Ambassador later went on to Washington where he saw Franklin D. Roosevelt and heard from him a story. He wrote to Governor Cox so that it might be included in his book. Better than anything else, this letter provides the clue to the Democratic campaign of 1920 and the high level of principle on which it was begun, waged and lost. It was as follows:

Dear Governor:

The other day when in Washington and with President Roosevelt, I told him I had heard from you and that you had been persuaded to write some reminiscences. "Good!" he said. "I wish you would tell him for me that there is a story never yet told, that he must tell. It is this: After the convention at San Francisco I stopped off for a conference with the Governor in Columbus to discuss the character of the campaign. The Governor advised that he was going to see President Wilson the next week.

"I accompanied the Governor on the visit to Wilson. A large crowd greeted us at the station and we went directly to the White House. There we were asked to wait fifteen minutes, as they were taking the President to the portico facing the grounds. As we came in sight of the portico we saw the President in a wheel chair, his left shoulder covered with a shawl which concealed his left arm, which was paralyzed, and the Governor said to me, 'He is a very sick man.'

"The Governor went up to the President and warmly greeted him. Wilson looked up and in a very low, weak voice said, 'Thank you for coming, I am very glad you came.' His utter weakness was startling and I noticed tears in the eyes of Cox. A little later Cox said, 'Mr. President, we are going to be a million per cent with you, and your administration, and that means the League of Nations.' The President looked up again, and again in a voice scarcely audible, he said, 'I am very grateful,' and then repeated, 'I am very grateful.'

"As we passed out we came then to the Executive offices and in this very room, Cox sat down at this table"—and here Roosevelt struck the table—"and asked Tumulty for paper and a pencil, and there he wrote the statement that committed us to making the League the paramount issue of the campaign. It was one of the most impressive scenes I have ever witnessed. Tell Cox he must tell that story."

Sincerely,
Claude G. Bowers

Governor Cox and Franklin Roosevelt have been vindicated by history and events equally with Wilson. It cannot be overlooked that President Roosevelt gambled all on the United Nations, even as Wilson had on the League. He made compromises necessary to bring Russia into the United Nations, feeling, as Wilson had in 1919, that any inequities thereby created, could be ironed out by the United Nations.

Since Governor Cox, as the standard-bearer for the League in

1920, had a more direct interest in an analysis of the League and its defeat, his conclusions are necessary to round out the story. In *Journey Through My Years,* he devoted a chapter to it. It is titled "The Great Conspiracy," and with his permission, substantial portions of that chapter are herewith included:

The League of Nations in the presidential campaign of 1920 was to be the overshadowing issue. It could not have been otherwise. We had had our bitter taste of war and our people believed that its sacrifice of ten million lives was a criminal waste which should never occur again. The naked facts demanded ways to prevent further such calamities. The better instincts of mankind called for a bending of their best thought and labor in an epoch-making effort to assure world-wide peace. There could be no mistaking that this was the moving impulse of the world's peoples. America prepared to play its proper part in the fulfillment of the need.

The fact is amazing, as viewed from the present day, that almost from the beginning a conspiracy was in the making to defeat this human hope. What took place was then plain only to students of events. Twenty-five years have brought into clear view the plan and purpose of the conspiracy and the disaster which it wrought. The possible parallel between those events and gathering events of the present time gives our people a deep concern in the great betrayal of that other post-war time.

The cause of world peace was not new. . . .

At the Thirteenth Inter-Parliamentary Conference at Brussels in 1905, Representative Richard Bartholdt of Missouri presented a plan for world federation. Andrew Carnegie, in his rectorial address at St. Andrews University in Scotland soon afterward, expressed the need of such a movement. Later, he assembled a peace conference of 1,500 people in New York City in support of it. A detailed plan for a league of peace had been presented by Senor Ordoney, former President of Uruguay, to the Second Hague Conference. A vigorous sponsor came forward in Theodore Roosevelt; going beyond mere theory, he went into a detailed scheme of organization. . . . He was embarking on a project which should be a turning point in the affairs of men and nations. In ringing words he said:

"Finally it would be a master stroke if those great Powers honestly bent on peace would form a League of Peace, not only to keep the peace among themselves, but to prevent, by force, if necessary, its being broken by others . . ."

There was no quibbling here about use of police power for peace;

and the ruler or statesman who brought about this organization for peace was to earn, in his words, "his place in history for all time".

But other matters soon engrossed the mind of Theodore Roosevelt. Emerging from his journey into Africa, he declared war on the policies of the Taft administration. He tried for another term in the Presidency in 1912 and failed. Then came the First World War, with a slaughter so ghastly that civilized men were ready as never before to put into operation the plan for world order and peace which Roosevelt had so boldly presented a decade before. That the subject again took hold of Roosevelt's mind is evidenced by his assertion in 1915 that the nations in the League of Peace should "not only keep the peace among themselves, but prevent by force if necessary its being broken by others".

About this time the League to Enforce Peace, a vigorous forward movement, was formed. The conference in Philadelphia which gave it birth was presided over by former President Taft. . . .

Senator Lodge endorsed the League to Enforce Peace, both the organization and the principles which it enunciated. The League held a great meeting in Washington on May 27, 1916. Wilson and Lodge spoke. Lodge's words can be reflected upon now. He said:

"I know, and no one, I think, can know better than one who has served long in the Senate, which is charged with an important share in the ratification and confirmation of all treaties; no one can, I think, feel more deeply than I do the difficulties which confront us in the work which this league—that is, the great association extending throughout the country, known as the League to Enforce Peace—undertakes, but the difficulties cannot be overcome unless we try to overcome them. I believe such can be done. Probably it will be impossible to stop all wars, but it certainly will be possible to stop some wars, and thus diminish their number. . . . I know the difficulties which arise when we speak of anything which seems to involve an alliance, but I do not believe that when Washington warned us against entangling alliances he meant for one moment that we should not join with the other civilized nations of the world if a method could be found to diminish war and encourage peace".

When the battle against the League of Nations was on, Lodge, in numberless speeches, warned against the danger of "entangling alliances", a glaring hypocrisy, for his original views had been well matured. . . .

Even Philander C. Knox, Secretary of State under Taft, in addressing a number of conferences on international problems stressed the fact "that the common interest of nations is being recognized as superior to their special interests, and that unity of action in international matters may yet control the unrestrained, unregulated or isolated action of independent states".

With every tale of slaughter overseas came a quickening resolve in this country to accomplish two things: first, win the war; then, see that there should never be another one. President Wilson in all of his addresses made it clear that the best way to protect us against war was to write into the treaty of peace an agreement between nations to form and to maintain the peace. There were no discordant notes. The Republican leaders were here at one with President Wilson and the Democrats. The nation was united upon the greatest enterprise of all, the building of enduring peace. Who could have dreamed then that the enterprise, so supported, could fail? . . .

Wilson was now approaching the high point in his leadership. The whole world seemed to rise in approval of his Fourteen Points. Former Speaker Joseph G. Cannon said: "The President is always strong in his addresses. I wish this one could be read by every man, woman and child and thoroughly explained in Germany and Austria". Simeon D. Fees, an uncompromising partisan was "wonderfully pleased with the message. It contains no cheap diplomacy".

Even George Harvey, bitter enemy of Wilson, approved in eloquent words: "Mr. Wilson's declaration was a veritable masterpiece. He has never done, and we doubt if any other living being could have done, better. We particularly liked his definiteness. His numerical summary of the fourteen war aims was tremendously effective."

Herbert Hoover said:

"I am for President Wilson's leadership, not only in the conduct of the war, but also in the negotiations of peace and afterward in the direction of America's burden in the rehabilitation of the world. There is no greater monument to any man's genius than the conduct of negotiations with the enemy by the President".

On October 2, 1919, speaking at Stanford University, Hoover said:

"The League of Nations is an aspiration which has been rising in the hearts of all the world. It has become an insistence in the minds of all those to whom the lives of our sons are precious, to all those to whom civilization is a thing to be safeguarded, and all those who see no hope for the amelioration of the misery of those who toil if peace cannot be maintained".

Theodore Roosevelt might have been expected to welcome President Wilson as a follower—a follower of the Roosevelt faith expressed in 1910. Roosevelt could have claimed priority in presenting the principles which Wilson now proclaimed. Why did he, on the contrary, desert and help destroy the cause which he himself had proclaimed and so strongly and eloquently advanced? We deal here with one of those sad reversals of a human character and attitude with which history is tragically replete.

For Roosevelt and Lodge, those days were a stern testing time. They were both historians, familiar with the movements of the past and of the present time. They knew the lasting political consequences of special great events. They knew that from Jefferson to Lincoln, with but brief interruptions, the Democratic party had held full sway. Why? Roosevelt and Lodge, historians, knew why. It was under Democratic rule that the republic, beginning with Jefferson, had maintained its growth and expanded its democracy. . . .

Another important fact not overlooked by historians Roosevelt and Lodge was the capacity the Democrats had shown for turning great, convulsive social movements, such as those of the time of Jefferson and Jackson, into constructive, beneficent, peaceful channels. The party had recognized new needs unheeded by the reactionaries of their day. They might recognize such needs again to the detriment of existing reactionary interests. Could not historians Roosevelt and Lodge see in President Wilson another Jackson or Jefferson? He had come to the Presidency in the midst of a political turmoil growing out of the remissness of Republican regimes. He had recognized and supplied long-neglected needs. Jefferson and Jackson had accomplished hardly more than Wilson in resolving social and economic strains. To his credit stood the first income tax law, the establishment of the Federal Trade Commission, the Smith-Lever Act, the Keating-Owen Labor Act, the Underwood tariff law, the LaFollette seamen's law, the Jones Act for the government of the Philippines, the Adamson railway labor law, the Federal Land Bank System, the Overman Act, the Federal Reserve System and the National Defense Act of 1916.

Such leadership could not but impress and direct the mood of the nation for years to come. Roosevelt and Lodge well knew this. And there were added to these achievements the establishment of world peace, the supreme event in the history of nations, the name of Wilson and the prestige of this party might be as invincible as after Jackson and Jefferson. What but dread of all this could have caused the strange reversal of attitude later to appear?

Lodge had been unhappy with the whole world situation. He mourned in 1914 that the leadership of the Roosevelt era had been lost both in the Old World and the New. "Rightly or wrongly", he said, "they have come to believe we are not to be trusted; that we make our international relations the sport of politics and treat them as if they were in no wise different from domestic legislation". But now under

Wilson's leadership, skies had cleared. We, with the other nations, were building an accord which held great promise for the world. But all of this was under auspices which only aroused the partisan envy and wrath of Roosevelt and Lodge.

Roosevelt's partisan interest may have been excited by a surviving hope for the Presidency. In 1916, when the Republican leaders at their national convention had tentatively agreed to nominate Charles E. Hughes, they asked Nicholas Murray Butler to get Roosevelt by telephone, advise him what was going on and, if possible, get his agreement. Before Butler could utter half a dozen words, Roosevelt asked him "What about me?" Butler had to tell him that there was no chance. Roosevelt's speeches during the war, and his whole attitude immediately afterwards, created the impression in the minds of political observers that the presidential bug still lived. The path of politics and the path of peace had, for both these leaders, parted company. They chose the path of politics. This historic conversation was related to me by Mr. Butler.

It is strangely impressive how time throws light on situations not clear at first. Mark Sullivan, writer and historian, said almost ten years afterwards in an article in *World's Work*:

"The League as we looked upon it in the Senate fight and in the Presidential campaign of 1920, was bound up with the personality of Woodrow Wilson and his political position. It carried the liability of the partisan bias against him and of the unwillingness of the opposing political party to take a step which would have exalted him in history, which would have labeled him as a great leader and his work as a success, and would have implied such an approval of him as should logically have been followed by keeping his party in power. All that burden the League question carried in 1920".

Thus the peace effort of a war-weary world was sacrificed on the altar of partisan politics. There was, moreover, a personal bitterness of the two Republican leaders towards Wilson to add to their partisanship in explaining their desertion of the cause of world peace.

Wilson, seeking to keep politics out of the war, had supported Newton D. Baker's decision not to put Roosevelt in command of troops overseas, thus enraging Roosevelt. Wilson, grievously hurt by a statement made by Lodge in connection with the Lusitania affair, had insisted that it was so full of falsehood it could only be deliberately false. He refused later to appear on the same platform with Lodge at a public meeting. From that time Lodge hated Wilson and Wilson held only contempt for Lodge.

At whatever cost, Lodge and Baker, with their personal grievances, their partisan passion, felt Wilson must be destroyed. The way to destroy him was to discredit and defeat the great project which he had brought to the verge of success. Their own words of former days would come back to belie them, but they were too angry and desperate to care for that. It was a titanic task, but Lodge was a master at manipulating the forces which could be worked to confuse the people and defeat their desires.

A movement to take direction of the war from Wilson was launched. A coalition cabinet was proposed to take the command of our armed forces largely from the President. Then it was urged that a joint committee of both houses be created to "assist" the President. This was a companion piece to the measure his enemies in Congress launched against Lincoln in the War Between the States.

In 1918, Wilson had appealed for a politically friendly Congress. The elements behind Roosevelt and Lodge indulged in a war dance of indignation. The patriotism of the Republicans, they cried, had been impugned. They did not remind the country that long before Wilson's appeal was made in October, plans for a Republican Congress were formed in the previous May. Later in the summer, Roosevelt and Taft, who had re-established cordial relations, both addressed an unofficial Republican state convention at Saratoga, New York. The former Presidents said it was necessary to elect a Republican Congress to stimulate the President, as they put it, on to victory in the war and the reconstruction afterwards. The effort for a Republican Congress even included the joint endorsement by Taft and Roosevelt of the candidacy of Truman Newberry, who afterwards resigned under fire, for United States senator from Michigan.

Lodge wanted a Republican Senate which would make him head of the Committee on Foreign Relations, in position to cut the throat of the League. President Wilson was assailed for not appointing one or more members of the Senate to the peace commission to meet at Versailles. The failure to include senators on the commission was ascribed to Wilson's despotic way with public matters and to this same cause was ascribed the failure of the Senate to ratify the League.

The employment of senators in treaty-making had in fact been tried and discarded by Republican administrations long before. President McKinley had made a practice of including senators on commissions that negotiated treaties. This was cited as a precedent in the League argument. The precedent, in fact, had been abandoned by McKinley himself. . . .

It was about this time that President Wilson's breakdown came. Time and its revelations have shown very definitely and beyond the slightest question that such reservations as Lodge proposed were mischievous and sinister in purpose. Senator James Watson, a strong partisan but always a very truthful man, says in his autobiography that at the beginning of the discussion in the Senate he told Lodge that it was futile to attempt to kill the Covenant because public opinion, influenced by the tragedies of the war, was strongly behind it. Lodge then frankly disclosed the strategy which he had planned for his attack. He would insist that he was in favor of the peace plan in principle—which of course he was not. He said bluntly that he would kill it with reservations. . . . Ratification was finally blocked. The cabal had won. Wilson was destroyed. The Republican Party was, for the time being, saved—saved at what a cost these prophetic words of Woodrow Wilson in next to his last public speech attest:

"I can predict with absolute certainty that within another generation there will be another world war if the nations of the world do not concert the method by which to prevent it . . . and America has, if I may take the liberty of saying so, a greater interest in the prevention of that war than any other nation. . . ."

Since the end of World War II the people have given evidence of a resolve not to permit another conspiracy here against world peace. Confusing situations have arisen as was to be expected in the wake of a war in which the whole world has been in turmoil. It should be evident to anyone now that it would have been much easier to bind nations together into a charter for peace under the consideration of twenty-five years ago than it will be now. Yet it can be done. The important thing is to keep going in the right direction with patience and understanding.

Such are the conclusions of the man who carried the battle for the League into the 1920 campaign.

Among the many letters and telegrams which came to Governor Cox when the votes were counted, and the nation had turned its back on the future, was this one:

THE WHITE HOUSE
Washington

5 November, 1920

My dear Governor Cox:

I hope that you know that no Democrat attributes the defeat of Tuesday to anything that you did or omitted to do. We have all admired the fight that you made with the greatest sincerity, and believe that the whole country honors you for the frank and courageous way in which you conducted the campaign.

With the most cordial good wishes and, of course, with unabated confidence,

Cordially and sincerely yours,
(Signed) Woodrow Wilson

Hon. James M. Cox
Executive Office
Columbus, Ohio

The election of 1920 found the people in one of those compulsive moods which mark our political history, both at the local and national level, in which reason is unable to assert itself as a factor. They were determined to escape back into the good old days when America was without international problems and responsibilities. So they stampeded through the door marked "Normalcy," following a bumbling second-rate President, himself soon to be betrayed by those who created him.

Now when events have re-established Woodrow Wilson, we know that our spurning of the League was a tragedy of blindness and a hate-corroded Republican Senate leadership.

No one can prove that a League, strongly supported by the United States, would have averted the second, and greater, world war. But there is a formidable array of evidence that it would have done so. A stable Europe, with a German Republic paying reparations within its capacity so to do, and, therefore, economically strong enough to maintain itself politically, would likely have avoided the collapse of the 'thirties. Woodrow Wilson, in his last veto message, just before leaving office, had predicted that failure. The inability of the small, new democracies created by the principle of self-determination of peoples, might well have endured instead of being forced, as they were, to erect trade barriers in a futile effort to survive economically. The rise of angry nationalisms, and of the dictators, was the fruit of our shortsightedness.

The peace treaty was constructed with American participation as an integral part of its machinery. Its collapse was grist in the Hitler mill.

Those who had believed so greatly in the morality of American demands for peace could say in truth we wanted it only if we could have it without cost or responsibility for maintaining it.

Had we assumed the war-created responsibilities and followed through on Wilson's fourteen points and the League, we could have shaped the future of Europe toward peace and trade—and away from the path which was inevitably set toward the great depression of the 'thirties and the second great war.

Wilson, who had said, when the League was defeated, that "the job would have to be done over in twenty years and at ten times the cost," knew that. So did many others who shared his vision.

The sick man whom the candidates Cox and Roosevelt saw on the portico in the autumn of 1920 carried grimly on until his term was ended on March 4, 1921. Once a coarse and arrogant Senate committee, headed by Albert B. Fall, forced their way into the sickroom to investigate the President's mental condition. The political scavengers had never let up on him. The committee had to report, with obvious disappointment, that Woodrow Wilson was entirely sane and rational in every respect.

This same Fall was to be Secretary of the Interior in Harding's "Normalcy" Cabinet and was to go to prison as a convicted felon in the great oil steal. Nor was he the only one of that administration, which conspired to defeat the peace and loot the treasury, to have that experience.

On March fourth, Wilson rode to the Capitol with Warren Gamaliel Harding. Chief Justice Edward Douglass White, who twice had administered the oath to Wilson, swore in the new President.

The public career of Woodrow Wilson was done.

When he died, many in the crowd waiting devotedly outside the house on S Street, to which he and Mrs. Wilson had retired on March fourth, knelt in the snow and prayed—for the soul of the man who was dead—and for the future of their country which had rejected him and his principles.

The principles lived. And events have vindicated them, the man who proclaimed them, and those who believed in and struggled for them.

The Husband and Father

WILLIAM ALLEN WHITE

Although it was the express purpose of this volume not to use material written prior to 1956, the following excerpts from William Allen White's *Woodrow Wilson*, 1924, are included because no living biographer could give so swift and sure a personal picture of President Wilson and his family as the late Emporia editor who was both contemporary and friend.   THE EDITOR

U PON his inauguration he [Wilson] stood before the throng, in the plaza of the Capitol, composed, even placid. A generation as a schoolmaster had obliterated stage fright in him. He took the oath and delivered his inaugural with no self-conscious attitude, as a gentleman performing a conventional function. Mrs. Wilson was tremendously proud of him; that was obvious. And the Wilson girls, standing near by, were big-eyed with joy and wonder. There was the fairy story. In Princeton, where they had grown from girlhood through their teens into young womanhood, they had lived in the college circle. Plain living and high thinking had surrounded their childhood and youth. A family horse with a family surrey coming down country lanes had been their equipage during most of their lives. It was a family habit to pick up wayfarers along the road; the carpenter going to his work, the washerwoman with her bundle, the messenger on his errand, the neighbor on his way. The college boy was no high treat to these girls, but he was their fairy prince; not much of a prince. Then suddenly we have three Cinderellas in Washington in the White House, riding about in three White House cars, golden coaches, and with fairy princes— young army officers, young navy officers, young diplomats, young statesmen, all varieties of desirable young gods—lined up to do their beck and call. And they knew that they could wear their crystal slippers for at least four years. No dancing was allowed in the White House—the ruling elder of the Second Presbyterian Church in Princeton saw to that; but outside they could go to the prince's ball any night they chose. It was a fairy story come true. And no small part of the sustaining delight of the Presidential office to the Wilson elders was found watching this story of the three Cinderellas dancing through their happy days . . . Margaret, Jessie and Eleanor, who, during all of the eight years of the Wilson's occupancy of the White House, bore their part with their father's good taste, good sense, and good humor. . . .

Three of Mrs. Wilson's pictures were entered anonymously in the New York Academy of Art, the most exclusive of all yearly art exhibits in America, and admitted to a place there. Mrs. Wilson was too modest to send her pictures, but the President and the three Wilson girls forced her to send them. She was amazed and exultant when they were accepted; and the whole family was happy for weeks. It was that kind of a family. That picture of an exulting family, proud of its mother, bright, full of gibes and quips and gayety, we must hold in our minds as we see the Wilson of those first White House years going forward under the deepening shadow of his responsibility to the dark days that came afterward. . . .

It was Ellen Axson [Wilson] upon whom the impact of duties and obligations at the White House fell heavily. Her serious soul was racked by a thousand cares, a thousand dreads, a thousand duties, that came processioning through her life. The White House is no place for a New England conscience. The months wore upon her. She went out into the city of Washington (the first city, by the way, in which the Wilsons ever had lived, for they were country-town people), and there she saw the poor and neglected, the underprivileged. With all the might of her sensitive heart she set out to relieve them. She stretched eager hands to every duty that beckoned to her. As the months came, the social obligations of the place, necessary enough, crushed her, sapping her strength. She was a sweet and beautiful White House hostess; the academic woman, wise and gentle and unsophisticated amid a hard and formal whirl that had ruthlessly destroyed scores of women before her and took no heed of its toll. While her husband was fighting his battles, and they were many and hard and soul-trying, Ellen Axson tried to stand by, tried to help, tried to strengthen . . .

But the time came when he saw that, if he bore all his burdens unto her, the load would break her. So White House people say that often at night he sat at his typewriter alone, hammering out letters to friends. . . . Wherever he could find a sympathetic and understanding heart, he was liable to pour himself out. . . .

Always he shrank from strangers. Yet he cried out in his loneliness to Robert Bender, a reporter for the United Press: "It is no compliment to me to have it said that I am a 'great intellectual machine.' Good Heavens, is there no more to me than that? I want people to love me—but I suppose they never will." He liked men in the mass, but was finical about his associates among men in particular. Above everything he disliked to talk shop out of shop. In the White House he had no politicians about him. He feared two things about politicians: first, that they would bore him: second, that they would quote him and so betray him. He refused an invitation to join the Chevy Chase Golf Club, the haunt of the rich and the powerful; and men said he was a consistent democrat when he played upon a public course. Members of his family say he was merely trying to avoid people who would bother him with shop talk. He went regularly to the Keith Vaudeville house for somewhat the same reason that he went to the public golf course. He did not want to meet smart or important people. When he closed his office door, he shut in his official life. Yet he wrote letters full of shop. . . . But with strangers he had no confidence; it was his way.

The threat of the Mexican war bore terribly down upon Ellen Axson, his wife. Her soul had no Irish resilience, and the image of her husband bringing on war which should send thousands of her countrymen to death beat upon her like a great spiritual flail and winnowed all the joy out of her heart.

Under the strain of it all, Ellen Axson died, just before the world realized the horror of the Great War.

Then and there came the dread messenger unto this Man of Uz, with his evil tidings. For nearly thirty years he and Ellen Axson had lived together, grown together in mind and spirit. . . . Inevitably their aspirations were held in common; the visions of their heart were one. . . . Each had made the other. She had done her part to steady his gay spirit and temper the iron of the Woodrow soul to useful steel. Every true marriage of the spirit affects men and women thus at the end of many years. . . .

"I want you to be the first to know from me," he declared to Mrs. Hulbert a few hours after Ellen Axson's death, "of Ellen's passing."

He wrote a beautiful letter to this old friend out of a heart deeply wounded. She was a family friend who had visited in the White House during Mrs. Wilson's lifetime. . . .

Of course he did not try to replace [Ellen] in his second marriage. No man ever can restore a life's companionship which goes. . . .

In Mrs. Edith Bolling Galt, Woodrow Wilson found devotion [and] high spirits. . . . She gave him these, together with an untiring, beautiful, self-merging common sense that sustained him for nine years. The wife of a man like Woodrow Wilson is necessarily as much a part of him as any attribute of his mind or heart. Marriage with a domestic man is more than a sacrament, more than a partnership, closer than a fellowship; it is a deep, infrangible union. So that when Edith Bolling Galt came into his life, she also became a part of him; became one with him; became an essence of the Wilson story. Again Woodrow Wilson said to his old friend, Mary Hulbert, "I want you to be the first to know," but this time it was "of my great happiness!"

[The] attitude of the politicians to the President never was entirely changed during his eight years. His [Wilson's] academic habit of thought, his desire for factual reasons, rather than intuitive, for an opinion, his impatience with convictions that were based upon another man's thought, his loathing of guesses, hunches and willow-withe-witching of the waters of truth which in politics men follow, put them "at arm's length," as Fitzgerald [Tammany Democratic Congressman from New York] said. Sometimes his dealings with his Cabinet were almost as aloof as his relations with Congressmen and the smaller fry in politics. At the Cabinet meeting in which Wilson read the message in 1917, wherein he asked Congress to put other commodities as well as coal under the Lever Act, which controlled coal, after he had finished, the Cabinet sat in awed silence without comment. Victor Murdock, who had been invited in with other members of the Federal Trade Commission to the meeting, blurted out an objection to the way labor had been treated. Clearly the Cabinet was disturbed by the Murdock impertinence. But Tumulty, who stood in no great awe of his chief, agreed with Murdock, and the change was made. Wilson recognized Murdock as the expert. The Wilsonian austerity was only for those who had shown emotion in their disagreement with him, or those who wore out his patience: men who told him the same thing over and over at one interview or came back to repeat it at another interview.

"Oh, yes, I remember you," he said to Congressman Lewis, of Maryland, who was calling. "You are the man who paid me the high compliment of assuming that I could absorb an idea in five minutes."

Lewis had organized his presentation, spoken his piece, and turned around and left the White House without palaver. The President made him a Tariff Commissioner as a token of appreciation. But speaking broadly, one may say that in those days of the President's first term, when he was getting used to Congressmen and their ways, his life was hard and full of trouble. He gave the impression by his brusqueness that he was conceited, arrogant, impatient; that he knew it all, and desired no information, or advice. Yet in truth he was not insulating himself against information or advice. He was taxing every ounce of his strength to get information, to receive advice. But most of the people who came to him, came to tell him what he already knew, and to advise him to do what he had already done or would do if he could. So he had a curt, self-protective phrase, "I know that," which he stabbed into many a conversation and ended it. This would hurt. But sometimes he was too busy to be courteous. We must not forget that he was frail, and had to defend his strength savagely. This protective armor of inconsideration, that passed as arrogance, was only for those whom he cared to call strangers. At home, or among his friends, he unbuckled his breastplate, and threw it aside. . . .

In the four years that passed after March 3, 1913, the house of Wilson had been completely changed. The wife of his youth was gone, and the children of the home he had been building for nearly thirty years were married or out in the world upon their own resources. Mrs. Edith Bolling Wilson had come into his life. She made a bright home for him, and comfortable—the only home in which he could have found strength to endure the stress of the days that were bringing their crushing burden upon him. He had, in addition to his work as legislative leader, his national premiership, if one may so say, the work of administration that here he could not ignore. It required him to open new areas of his mind, to develop latent talents, to let a new man rise in him who had a giant's task. The exalted schoolmaster at Trenton was becoming an international figure—the teacher turned preacher, his rostrum set high above the world; his pupils and congregation, civilized humanity. Amid all this change, why should not the man sometimes seem unnatural, impatient, preoccupied, remote from the commonality of men? Maybe he was puzzled at himself. Perhaps in his heart's heart he saw little Tommy and the amiable professor of jurisprudence at Princeton standing apart asking each other who is this strange man in this strange house, in this strange life that has crowded in upon us?

The Progressive

ARTHUR S. LINK

We have to realize that the right is not partisan and that what is for the good of one class, if properly understood, is for the good of all classes.

Staunton, Virginia, Dec. 28, 1912 [27]

I think that in public affairs stupidity is more dangerous than knavery, because harder to fight and dislodge.

Article in the *Fortnightly Review*, Feb. 1913 [28]

The interesting and inspiring thing about America . . . is that she asks nothing for herself except what she has a right to ask for humanity itself. We want no nation's property. We mean to question no nation's honor. We do not wish to stand selfishly in the way of the development of any nation. We want nothing that we cannot get by our own legitimate enterprise and by the inspiration of our own example.

New York, May 17, 1915 [29]

What difference does party make when mankind is involved?

Richmond, Ind., Sept. 4, 1919 [30]

—WOODROW WILSON

Any evaluation of Woodrow Wilson and his place in American history demands some ingenuity in reconciling apparent contradictions. He is venerated by progressives today as the leading reformer of the prewar period, the man who seized control of the progressive movement and brought it to full flower before 1917; yet the conservatism that he imbibed from the society in which he matured and from his study of history and politics was always a powerful influence in his life. No American leader since Lincoln has been motivated in his public actions by high ideals as much as Wilson, and none has been better able to give voice to them; yet at numerous critical junctures in his career his decisions were dictated at least in part by considerations of political expediency. He was endowed with an immense capacity for leadership and an ability to inspire loyalty in his followers; yet when pressed too hard by his opponents he could be fierce and passionately bitter in conflict. Essentially a pacifist at heart, he became America's great war leader. A provincial Southerner and Easterner who knew little about Europe and the politics of the great powers, he became the symbol throughout the world of the hope for collective security and a lasting peace among nations.

These paradoxes become less enigmatic, indeed they largely disappear, if one is willing to take Woodrow Wilson for what he was—a man intensely human, a product more than a molder of his times, a leader who grew in stature and effectiveness because he changed his techniques and goals in response both to historic circumstances and his own growing understanding. Let it be said in the beginning, however, that there were certain things about the adult Wilson that never changed. He was always a man of intense religious faith, whose ideals derived from his belief in the morality of the universe and whose chief motivation was a desire to serve God by serving his fellow men. He was always a man of integrity, with high ideals of public service and a passion for justice. He was always a democrat, convinced that government existed only to serve mankind. Wilson never abandoned these beliefs and principles; they formed the basis of his political philosophy and guided his public career. But he often changed his mind about the most effective methods of leadership and the proper goals of a democracy.

There were many things about Wilson's childhood inheritance that must have decisively shaped his thought and ideals in later years. There was the contribution of a brilliant father, whose reading and conversation ranged far beyond the realm of the average clergyman of that day. There was the experience of growing up in a Presbyterian manse, of maturing, as it were, in the bosom of the church. There was the inheritance of a genteel society, conservative socially and conscious of tradition. There was, finally, the traumatic experience of growing up in a South wracked by Civil War and Reconstruction. Tradition, social status, religion, and the tumultuous events of Reconstruction all combined to produce in the young Wilson a deep suspicion of radical social and political change, an attitude confirmed by his undergraduate training at Princeton and his worshipful study of Adam Smith, Edmund Burke, Walter Bagehot, and the English Liberal leaders of the Victorian era.

The conservative theme is dominant throughout Wilson's early political writings, but it was largely an academic or theoretical conservatism that evinced itself during his adult years before 1902, because he had meanwhile found a career. Wanting to be a "statesman," he went to the University of Virginia Law School after his graduation from Princeton and then tried briefly to practice law in Atlanta. Driven from this metropolis of the New South by failure and boredom, he abandoned the hope of a political career, studied history and political science at Johns Hopkins University, and, from 1885 to 1902, taught successively at Bryn Mawr, Wesleyan in Connecticut, and Princeton.

During this long period of teaching, study and reflection Wilson emerged rapidly as a penetrating student of American political history and practice. He was still profoundly conservative in approach; but he grew increasingly concerned with the practical problems of democracy—problems of sectional adjustment, the wise exercise of governmental power, public administration, and, above all, of leadership on all levels of politics. By 1902, he had developed a mature program for a new system of leadership in the American political system. In the place of Presidential weakness and congressional irresponsibility he proposed to substitute responsible party leadership in Washington by the institution of the English cabinet system, which concentrated all initiative and responsibility in a single body.

In 1902, Wilson gained his first opportunity to put his ideal of responsible leadership to practice. In that year the trustees of Princeton University, rebelling against an inept administration, named Wilson to the presidency of his alma mater. Like a prime minister he went to work, organizing his constituents—the alumni and trustees, and his cabinet, the faculty—in a drive that transformed Princeton from a provincial college into one of the leaders among institutions of higher learning in the United States. Inspiring and driving, he pushed through a reform of the curriculum, established the preceptorial, or conference, system of instruction, and brought to the faculty a large number of distinguished young scholars and teachers. While gaining a national reputation in the educational field, Wilson also emerged as a militantly conservative Democratic spokesman on national issues, by lashing out at Bryan and condemning Theodore Roosevelt's crusade for the effective regulation of business.

Although he had already effected a revolution at Princeton by 1906, Wilson had too much driving force and too imaginative a mind to stand still and consolidate his gains. Instead, in 1906 and 1907, he launched an ambitious drive to reorganize the social life of the Princeton undergraduates. This he proposed to do by abolishing the eating clubs, which the upperclassmen had erected, and incorporating them into quadrangles in which members of all classes and some of the faculty would live, eat and mingle socially. There is a legend, which is far from true, that Wilson's objective was to democratize the social life of the undergraduates. Undoubtedly the club system as it was then constituted was undemocratic because exclusive; undoubtedly Wilson's proposals had democratic implications, and the social issues involved were hotly debated. Yet Wilson himself time and again protested that he was not making a fight on social grounds; time and again he insisted that he was seeking only the intellectual advancement of the university.

Defeat was certain when it became apparent that an overwhelming majority of the students and alumni were opposed to the quadrangle plan. It was the first defeat that Wilson had suffered as prime minister of Princeton, and the shock was so bitterly profound that he began slowly to change fundamentally in his social and political attitudes. For the first time in his personal experience he saw the intimate connection between wealth and status and resistance to social change.

Yet for all the social dynamite inherent in the quadrangle fight, it required the experience of another bitter defeat before Wilson's latent democratic idealism was to burst forth in its full fury. The struggle, in which Wilson ostensibly launched a crusade to democratize American universities in general, centered about the location of a graduate college at Princeton. At the root of the controversy was a personal struggle between Wilson and Andrew F. West, dean of the Graduate School, over control of the establishment. Wilson admitted that the personal question was the important one, yet he insisted upon confusing the debate by injecting other issues. Finally, after Dean West had won the support of a majority of the trustees, Wilson made the fight openly on personal grounds, by accusing West and his friends of holding exclusive, snobbish, antidemocratic ideals, and by asserting that he, Wilson, was fighting for the future of educational democracy in the United States. But this appeal failed in the end, especially after West obtained a large endowment for the Graduate College.

It was for Wilson the hardest blow of all, and yet it is not too much to say that the momentous struggles and bitter defeats at Princeton were decisive turning points in his growth as a practical leader and his evolution toward a liberal political philosophy. For one thing, Wilson learned his first hard lessons in practical politics at Princeton. For another, he came to believe that the selfsame forces of wealth and privilege that he thought were attempting to corrupt his alma mater were also at work corrupting and controlling the American democracy. Out of this awakening, consequently, came his first sympathy for the progressive movement, which he had hitherto either condemned or ignored.

Meanwhile, Wilson had been propelled into a political career through no direct action of his own. It began when George Harvey, conservative editor of *Harper's Weekly*, conceived the idea of pushing the Princetonian for leadership in the Democratic Party to offset Bryan and, ultimately, for the Presidency itself. As the first step in his master plan, Harvey won the support of the Democratic bosses of New Jersey for Wilson's nomination as Governor in 1910. The Democratic leaders agreed, not because they wanted to please Harvey, but because they thought Wilson would be a respectable front man and could win.

Wilson won the election in November 1910, to be sure, but not in the manner that the bosses had planned. Since he felt no obligation to the men who had nominated him and perceived that the masses of voters were on the verge of rebellion against machine rule and conservative policies, Wilson cut loose from his quondam associates early in the campaign. Through a series of brilliant speeches he then went on to take control of the progressive movement in New Jersey.

Wilson's election and subsequent administration represented the culmination of the reform movement in the state. He originated no program, for every one of the measures that he pushed through the legislature had been the object of progressive agitation for many years. In this respect Wilson's career at Princeton, Trenton, and even in Washington is remarkably similar. In none of these instances was he a pioneer in the reform movements which came to full flower during his administrations. But in this fact lies his significance as a popular leader: he was a catalytic agent of change, who succeeded where others had failed because he combined great capacity for leadership with a rare ability to feel the popular pulse and to adjust his program to the majority demand. At least this was true until conflict descended to the personal level, as during the graduate-school fight and the controversy over the Versailles Treaty.

But to return to events following Wilson's election as Governor of New Jersey. They moved in kaleidoscopic fashion. Forced against his personal wishes into a fight to prevent the election of James Smith, Jr., Democratic boss of Newark, to the United States Senate, Wilson not only defeated Smith but took personal command of the party in the state. Then in the spring of 1911 he pushed through boss-ridden legislature bills providing for sweeping election and primary reforms, a workmen's compensation system, and a public utilities commission with power to set rates. It was all done with such sureness and rapidity as to leave the people gasping and to cause Democrats throughout the country to look toward Trenton for encouragement.

There has never been anything like Wilson's subsequent rise to national leadership before or since in our history. But it was no accident that he progressed from an untried, local politician to leadership of the national Democratic Party in the space of eighteen brief months. He had made good in New Jersey; he had given the nation a demonstration of responsible leadership in action. He was a figure entirely new in American politics, and the people definitely were tired of professional politicians. Most important of all, he had come upon the political scene at a time when the decline of Bryan's leadership and the paucity of talent in the Democratic Party had created a political vacuum.

Yet it seemed certain that Wilson's bid for the Presidential nomination would be frustrated by a campaign led by reactionaries on the one hand and by professional politicians, William Randolph Hearst, and the followers of Champ Clark of Missouri, Speaker of the House of Representatives, on the other. That Wilson was nominated in the face of such powerful opposition at the Baltimore convention in July 1912 is one of the miracles of modern politics. But nominated he was, and thus began a new era in American political history. Theodore Roosevelt's disruption of the Republican Party had already made Wilson's election inevitable.

The fact that he was the leader of a minority party and was, besides, inaugurated a minority President was not lost upon Woodrow Wilson. He had a large majority in the House of Representatives and a working majority in the Senate only because the Republicans had momentarily committed political suicide, and he was determined to make the most of the opportunity at hand. Consequently Wilson applied all the powers of his leadership from the outset of his administration. In conjunction with his advisers he formulated policy and helped to draft legislation, pleaded with representatives and senators to support this measure or that, appealed to the people for assistance, and was chiefly responsible for the fulfillment of what soon came to be known as the New Freedom program.

Tariff revision had top priority, because the Democrats had made drastic reduction in rates one of their principal promises since the Civil War. It was a dangerous issue, because disagreement over certain rates threatened to disrupt the Democratic ranks and ruin Wilson's leadership in the beginning. But the new President led boldly by insisting upon sweeping reductions and a large free list, including sugar and wool, and by attacking and exposing an industrious lobby. The Underwood Tariff Act as finally approved in 1913 was all and even more than Wilson had demanded, for it included a provision for a moderate income tax. It was also a tremendous vindication of the President's leadership at a crucial time when the success or failure of the new administration hung in the balance.

In the case of three other great reforms of the prewar years—the Federal Reserve Act, the Clayton Antitrust Law, and the Federal Trade Commission Act—Wilson's leadership was the decisive factor. He pushed the Federal Reserve measure through an unwilling Congress almost in spite of many of his party leaders. There had been some popular demand for currency reform and banking control before, but it had been incoherent and entirely unorganized. The establishment of the Federal Reserve system was, therefore, clearly Wilson's own accomplishment, because the measure would certainly have failed without his leadership. In like manner he guided the men who rewrote the antitrust laws and established a federal commission to administer them; and he marshaled the majorities in Congress that put these bills across.

It was a great program, and its enactment alone would have sufficed to secure Wilson's permanent stature as a liberal statesman. But the President's contribution should not be measured merely in terms of the bill that he signed. Even more important was his contribution to the expansion of the powers of the Presidency. That institution could never afterward be the same because of his success in fusing the powers of President, party leader and popular spokesman.

Now we come to the hardest task of all in this account of Wilson's evolution as a domestic leader. It is a task with two necessities, first, of determining the degree to which the New Freedom program of 1913 and 1914 represented and satisfied the popular demand for fundamental national reform and, second, of showing how Wilson subsequently changed this program in response to historic events and became one of the prime forces in the growth of modern American progressivism.

Substantial though the New Freedom's achievements were, it can be properly understood only in its relation to the general progressive movement of the prewar years. As Herbert Croly pointed out in 1909 and reiterated afterward, the progressive movement during these years was, at least in national affairs, divided against itself by a fundamental disagreement over the objectives of reform and the proper exercise of collective power. A large element, concentrated principally in the Democratic Party, desired to reduce tariffs, destroy the so-called Money Trust, restore competition in business and industry, and, generally, free the economic energies of the people. But these progressives, suspecting public aggregations of power as much as they feared private aggrandizement, opposed positive federal intervention in economic affairs. Standing in opposition to all forms of class or special-interest legislation, they opposed all measures that would confer special benefits, whether they be conceived in the interest of manufacturers on the one hand or, on the other, of labor unions or farmers. Being state righters for the most part, they also condemned suggestions for committing the federal authority to projects of social amelioration. In the main, therefore, they drew their political philosophy from the individualistic Jeffersonian traditions of equality and *laissez faire*.

Standing in contrast and often in opposition was the other wing of the progressive movement, concentrated mainly in the Republican Party in the Middle West and Far West. Nationalistic in outlook, they looked to the federal government as well as to the states for the solution of social and economic problems. Strong believers in the efficacy of collective remedies, they proposed to make the national government incomparably the most powerful force in economic affairs by vesting it with comprehensive regulatory authority. Hence they tended to fear big business less than the Jeffersonian progressives did. Hamiltonian rather than Jeffersonian in their thinking about the exercise of governmental authority, the nationalistic progressives proposed to use political power to benefit so-called submerged or disadvantaged classes.

The conflict between the two wings of progressivism came into the open on an important scale first in 1912. During the Presidential campaign of that year Theodore Roosevelt broke away from the Republican Party when he could not win the Presidential nomination. He then organized the Progressive Party, composed mainly of advanced Republicans and leaders in various movements for social and economic justice. Behind a platform that combined a strong nationalism with an advanced progressivism, Roosevelt made his fight for what he called a New Nationalism— a frank recognition that it was government's duty actively to control, regulate and uplift. Wilson, in contrast, took his stand as the spokesman of the Jeffersonian wing by demanding, not a New Nationalism, which he condemned as paternalism and a dangerous extension of governmental authority, but a New Freedom—a restoration of competition and equality for all comers.

To state the matter briefly, Wilson's leadership and legislation during the first eighteen months of his Presidency was designed to accomplish the destruction of special privileges and to guarantee the restoration of competition, without, however, engaging the federal government in the kind of social and economic experimentation that Roosevelt had proposed. The essential validity of this generalization can be illustrated by referring both to what Wilson achieved and what he refused to undertake during this period.

The Underwood Tariff and the Clayton Acts were both clearly in the liberal New Freedom category, the one attempting to place American manufacturers in a competitive position in the international market, the other attempting to rewrite the rules of the business world to prevent the growth of monopoly and the suppression of competition. The Federal Reserve Act, although it included certain concessions to advanced views, was intended to balance a measure of public supervision over banking and the money supply with a large degree of private initiative and control. The Federal Trade Commission Act was in fact a milder version of the kind of measure that Roosevelt had demanded in 1912; but Wilson approved it largely because it seemed to be the only effective piece of antitrust legislation that he could get through the Senate.

The true character of the New Freedom is better illustrated by an analysis of the measures that Wilson refused to support or actively opposed. He opposed and prevented passage of a measure to establish a federally operated and supported system of long-term rural credits on the ground that it was, as his Secretary of Agriculture said, class legislation "of the most odious type." During the congressional discussions over the Clayton bill, moreover, Wilson refused absolutely to concede organized labor's prime legislative demand, namely, exemption of the activities of labor unions from the prohibitions of the antitrust laws. He vetoed a bill for the limitation of immigration, an objective long demanded by organized labor and strongly supported by many sociologists and social workers. He refused to support a federal child-labor bill on the ground that it invaded the police powers of the states.

Such actions and posturing inevitably brought the President into conflict with advanced political leaders and the spokesmen of groups demanding a bold movement into new social and economic frontiers. These tensions were aggravated when Wilson allowed certain of his Cabinet members to institute segregation in their departments and then defended them publicly in the face of hostile Northern opposition. They were aggravated even further during the spring and summer of 1914, when the President undertook a general campaign to win the confidence of the business community. They were highlighted, finally, when, in a public letter written in November 1914, Wilson declared that the progressive movement on the national level had accomplished its objectives, and that hereafter the main business of statesmanship would be seeking an adjustment between business and the general public.

The truth was, of course, that only the New Freedom and not the national progressive movement had ended in the autumn of

1914. Indeed, the third decisive stage in Wilson's evolution as a domestic leader, when he would abandon his *laissez faire*, state rights inhibitions and stand frankly as the spokesman of advanced progressive nationalism, lay just ahead.

The metamorphosis began in January, 1916, with Wilson's appointment of Louis D. Brandeis, the outstanding legal champion of social and economic reform, to the Supreme Court and occurred with startling rapidity after this date. From the late winter through the early autumn of 1916, the President came out in strong and decisive support of a rural-credits bill, the prohibition of child labor by the federal government, a federal workmen's-compensation bill, a measure establishing a tariff commission, and a bill establishing the eight-hour day as the work standard on interstate railroads. At the same time, he went on to make progressive nationalism one of the chief issues of the Presidential campaign of 1916, and to construct a new progressive coalition that returned him to the White House for a second term.

The reasons for this epochal change are harder to evaluate than they are to find. There was the obvious fact that the Democratic Party was still a minority party, and that its only hope of victory in 1916 lay in drawing into its ranks a large minority of the Progressive Party, which was then in process of disintegration. It is entirely possible, indeed it seems probable, that Wilson shifted from the New Freedom to what was in fact the New Nationalism in order to make a Democratic victory possible in 1916. If this was opportunism, it was opportunism on a high level, for the President sincerely believed that the Democrats alone were capable of leading the nation along the paths of peace and domestic reconstruction. But there was another and perhaps more important reason for Wilson's change, and this was simply the fact that by 1916 he had concluded that limited reform of the New Freedom type was inadequate to solve the enormous domestic problems of twentieth-century society. There are numerous evidences that his thought was running in this direction even during the New Freedom period.

Whatever the causes were, the consequences of Wilson's new leadership remained. He forever ended the division in the progressive ranks over fundamental philosophy and objectives and made it inevitable that the reform movement in its next great surge would be concerned primarily with building secure foundations for economic and social justice in the United States.

After American entrance into the First World War in 1917, Wilson made his most significant contributions in the realm of foreign affairs. In this field, which is beyond the scope of our present discussion, he demonstrated the same capacity for intellectual growth that he had shown in domestic politics. Indeed, Wilson the peacemaker was at the apex of his evolution as a leader and also at the end of his success in leadership. Having built so grandly at Versailles, he returned home to fail in the supreme test of his career, in part because of the bitterness of his opponents, in part also because of his own inflexibility and refusal to compromise the provisions of his treaty. In short, the chief architect of the League of Nations helped prevent the laying of its cornerstone. Thus we conclude this account as we began, on a note of paradox and bafflement. And yet the lasting contributions—Wilson's integrity, idealism and constructive domestic achievements—survived the wreckage of the treaty fight. In this centennial of his birth, Americans of both political parties turn again to this practitioner of responsible leadership and prophet of the future.

The Statesman

CLAUDE G. BOWERS

It is surely the manifest destiny of the United States to lead in the attempt to make this spirit of democracy prevail.

Message to Congress, Dec. 7, 1920 [31]

Right is more precious than peace, and we fight for the things which we have always carried nearest to our hearts, for democracy, for the right of those who submit to authority to have a voice in their own governments, for the rights and liberties of small nations, for a universal dominion of right by such a concert of free peoples as shall bring peace and safety to all nations and make the world at last free.

War Message delivered before Congress, April 2, 1917 [32]

We are at the beginning of an age in which it will be insisted that the same standards of conduct and responsibility for wrong done shall be observed among nations and their governments that are observed among the individual citizens of civilized states.

Message to Congress, April 2, 1917 [33]

—WOODROW WILSON

In 1934, when a guest at "Buena Vista," the country home of Count Romanones, many times Prime Minister and Foreign Minister of the King of Spain, he led me aside from the other visitors and surprised me by saying that he wished to talk with me without interruption about Woodrow Wilson. Romanones had been one of the very few members of the Spanish nobility who favored the Allies in the First World War, and after the war he had made a sentimental pilgrimage to France when Wilson was in Paris to do homage to a statesman he admired. He summed up his impressions in these words: "Woodrow Wilson is one of the truly great men of the centuries. He was a great War President, but posterity will remember him for the fight he made for a lasting peace, resting on the collaboration of all nations in the prevention of senseless wars. Like all prophets he paid the penalty for being wiser than his generation. The criticism of his method is dwindling to a whisper even now. His stature grows every year he recedes from the prejudices and hates that were so powerful in Versailles, and so disastrous in the Senate of your country, and, as time goes on, he will continue to loom larger and larger as the wisest humanitarian and constructive statesman of vision of his age."

This appraisal of a career by Romanones is being constantly justified as history unrolls.

Among the American Presidents, Wilson's career is unique. Most of them trained from early life in partisan conflicts, have been clever politicians in dealing with the surface issues of their day. None of them have been so steeped in the fundamentals of political thinking since Thomas Jefferson, and none, since Jefferson, have thought so profoundly in terms of mankind, or brought to the service of humanity such a rich background of preparation. Until he entered the political arena in New Jersey as the nominee for governor, he was little known to the nation as a whole. He had been secluded many years in the realms of thought, evolving his political philosophy from the accumulated wisdom of the centuries, a companion in the library of the greatest minds.

For a quarter of a century, this man of the cloister had taught politics and government. In teaching, and thinking, he had delved deeply into the fundamentals, and meditated profoundly on the march of history, and the challenging problems of our civilization. During these fruitful years, free from the pushing and shoving of politicians in a hurry who were thinking solely in terms of ephemeral issues in domestic politics, he had actually become a statesman before he became a politician—a reversal of the rule. He knew that to comprehend even these domestic problems, it was useful to know the history from which they evolved, and to understand the significance of their trend. The average politician thinks exclusively in terms of today and of the next election; the statesman in terms of the future. For years, in the serenity of his library, Woodrow Wilson had communed with the political philosophers of the ages. Edmund Burke was a favorite companion of his at the fireside and he based his concept of statesmanship on his example. With him, politics did not mean the mastering of the tricks of low intrigue, or the slippery art of the opportunist in pursuit of personal gain, and least of all did it mean a mere striving after office. He was not a weathercock, changing his principles to make the most of the passing breeze. From the high-toned philosophy he had formulated through years of meditation he never was to deviate to serve a personal end. His thinking had been put in print in books of significance, *Congressional Government*, his *Study in American Politics*, his *Constitutional Government of the United States*, and especially in his *New Freedom*. And his democratic ideology went beyond the spoken word to action. In intellectual circles his stout fight for educational reform and democracy in education at Princeton University had commanded national attention.

It was because of things he found detrimental to the sound functioning of democracy that, at length, in 1910, he turned from the serenity of the closet he had enjoyed, to plunge into the turmoil of practical politics as his party's nominee for governor. This was to advance principles and policies he thought necessary for the general good, not merely to satisfy personal ambition. The cynical politicians who sought to serve their selfish ends behind the prestige of his scholarship were speedily disillusioned. Thrusting them aside, and assuming the responsibility of leadership, he flashed upon the nation almost spectacularly as a new type of leader with ideals and understanding. When he found the public interest thwarted through the underhand maneuvering of men acting for the few against the many, he stripped them to the public view. Corruption to him was tantamount to treason. He did not have to resort to demagogic ranting to conceal ignorance of governmental problems, since he understood them. He went directly to the people in notable speeches, beautifully phrased, temperate as reason, packed with the raw meat of realism, setting forth frankly and courageously what he proposed to do. The public loves novelty, and here was something novel. All over the nation the people read these speeches with admiration, and, within two years after leaving the closet of the scholarly recluse, he was elected President of the United States.

Unfortunately, I think, the brilliant and audacious statesmanship of his first administration has been too much overshadowed by his spectacular leadership in the World War and his dramatic battles for a lasting peace at the close. The policies of his first administration were conceived to place the interests of the whole people above that of a powerful few, without depriving the few of their legitimate rights. He proposed to serve all elements through the creation of a sounder financial and economic system. His program was national, not partisan. He hoped to lift governmental activities to a higher level than they had known in years. His voice was the voice of humanity raised above the clamor of the market place. His work was audacious in that he dared assume that, when the privileges of special interests conflicted with human rights, the latter had the right of way. He felt, and said in memorable speeches that in fighting for the economic rights of the whole people, including the farmers and workers previously neglected, he was serving the interest of the nation as a whole. The reforms he wrought during his first administration have survived the test of time and trial.

From the moment he took the oath of office, his interest was diverted to international affairs by the early vagaries of the great revolution in Mexico. The Mexican people, ground down economically, robbed of their freedoms, and denied the dignity of manhood during the grossly corrupt dictatorship of Diaz, had risen under the leadership of Francisco Madero and overthrown the despotic regime. In their struggle for liberty, democracy and human rights, they had the sympathy of Woodrow Wilson. From his closet he had observed for years our Latin-American policy which violated every principle for which he stood. This policy was predicated on the assumption that citizens of the United States buying concessions from dictators, to the detriment of the Latin-American republics, were above, and beyond, the laws of the nations where the concessions had been bought. Too often these concessions had been bought by foul means and, because bought and paid for, it was taken for granted that our sole obligation was to the concessionaires. Wilson had observed that, by virtue of these concessions, our people thought they had a right to interfere in the domestic politics and affairs of the Latin-American republics. He had been shocked on finding that loans to these nations exacted rates of interest we would not have dared ask of Europe. In his historic speech at Mobile he foreshadowed a new Latin-American policy, attacking our interference in the internal affairs of these nations, and our discrimination against them in the matter of loans. His warning that we would no longer subordinate the rights and liberties of these sister republics to our material advantage thrilled these Americans of the south with hope, and set a pattern for a new relationship with them.

This new Latin-American policy of Wilson's was put to the supreme test in the dawning days of his first administration by the chaotic revolution in Mexico. The cynically reactionary regime of Diaz had been overthrown by the rising of the people under the leadership of Madero, a passionate partisan of the democratic ideology. The reactionaries took up arms against his regime in support of the attempt of General Huerta to re-establish a military dictatorship on the Diaz pattern. President Taft had placed an embargo on arms intended for the enemies of the constitutionally elected government. When Madero was assassinated and Huerta asked recognition for his dictatorship, Wilson extended the embargo completely, and refused to accord recognition to a regime born of military usurpation and assassination. However he set forth conditions for negotiations. These called for the immediate ending of the fighting, for an armistice to be scrupulously observed, for the early holding of free elections, and for Huerta's withdrawal as a candidate. In a report to Congress, Wilson had said that "there can be no certain prospect of peace in America until General Huerta surrenders his usurped power." He would not, however, attempt to impose our will, and having submitted conditions compatible with the democratic process through which the people might regain their freedom, he would "watch and wait."

The lack of a stable organized government, resting on the will of the people, made negotiations extremely difficult. Huerta's hostility to the United States was manifest. He hoped to force us into war. When the paymaster of an American ship landed in Tampico for supplies, he and members of the crew were arrested by Huerta's soldiers. Two of the men had been dragged from the ship which was flying the American flag from stem and stern. Admiral Mayo, commanding the squadron in Tampico waters demanded the release of the sailors and a salute to the flag as an apology from Huerta. The embryo dictator refused just as word reached Wilson that a German ship was arriving in Vera Cruz with fifteen million rounds of ammunition and five hundred rapid-fire guns for the Huerta forces. The word reached Washington between two and three in the morning, and in agreement with the Secretaries of State and of the Navy the word was flashed to our Admiral: "Take Vera Cruz at once."

Here was a situation made to order to serve the purpose of selfish American interests in Mexico. They demanded war to crush the Mexican Revolution and restore the dictatorial regime under which they had flourished at the expense of the mass of the Mexican people, and Wilson replied, "there will be no war with Mexico if I can prevent it." Troops were landed, the Custom House was seized, the arms from Germany were not delivered, and Huerta fled.

When General Carranza took over, Woodrow Wilson again astonished and delighted the Latin-American nations with the acceptance of Brazil, Chile and Argentina as mediators between the United States and Mexico. Thus Wilson aligned ourselves with our

Latin-American neighbors by the confidence we reposed in them. They advised a *de facto* recognition of Carranza and we acquiesced.

But confusion continued south of the Rio Grande, subjecting Wilson to the supreme test of patience. Negotiations were impossible, since the picturesque bandit, Francisco Villa, was leading an armed revolt against the authority of the government in office. When he dashed across the border and murdered some Americans in New Mexico, the clamor for war against Mexico reached its height. Wilson refused to hold Carranza responsible, and least of all the Mexican people, but he ordered troops across the border with instructions to confine their mission to the capture of the bandit.

Denounced as a coward by men with selfish interest intent on the suppression of the revolution, Wilson preferred to play for the verdict of history. While constantly hampered by the actions of factions, he centered his thoughts and hopes on the people's revolution which promised liberty and human dignity to the people for centuries under the iron heel of despotism. He knew that the war hawks at home with axes to grind were asking nothing less than the restoration of the old tyranny by the Army of the United States. "Men forget," he said, "what is back of the struggle. It is the age-long struggle of a people to come into their own, and while we look upon the incidents in the foreground, let us not forget the tragic reality of the background which towers above this whole sad picture. Some of the leaders of the Revolution may often have been mistaken and been violent and selfish, but the Revolution itself was inevitable and right; and so long as they represent, however imperfectly, such a struggle for deliverance I am ready to serve their ends when I can. I am more interested in the fortunes of oppressed men and pitiful women and children than in any property rights whatever."

Thus the Mexican people, who have emerged from their struggle with a democratic regime, owe an immeasurable debt to the wisdom and patience of Woodrow Wilson.

Then, too, while many were thinking in terms of oil wells, Wilson was thinking of the fight in progress in Europe for the preservation of democracy. He knew that we might have to throw our weight into the scale against autocracy and he wanted no diversion to a war with a neighboring nation. Soon his countrymen knew he had been wise when the note of Zimmerman, of the Foreign Office in Berlin, to the German Embassy in Mexico revealed that Germany, too, was eager for our embroilment in a war remote from Europe. "We propose an alliance with Mexico on the following basis," Zimmerman wrote. "That we shall make war together, and together make peace. We shall give general financial support, and it is understood that Mexico is to reconquer the lost territory of New Mexico, Texas and Arizona. You are instructed to inform the President of Mexico in the greatest confidence as soon as it is certain that there will be an outbreak of war with the United States."

Thus, as Wilson's prescience foresaw, the demand for war came from both selfish American interests in Mexico and from Germany which wished us occupied in the Western hemisphere while it conquered the free nations of Europe.

During the turmoil south of the Rio Grande the eyes of Wilson were fixed as well on events in Europe. The assassination in Serbia of a worthless Grand Duke of Austria had involved Europe in a life and death struggle between autocracy and democracy, and Wilson was faced with a problem that was tragedy to him. He hated war. He knew from history that international quarrels are really never settled by guns and bayonets. Being highly civilized, he believed in the arbitrament of reason, but reason had been brushed aside, and insensate hate was riding the whirlwind and directing the storm. Wilson envisioned the slaughter of millions to satisfy the pride of royal houses and to cover the blundering of diplomats without vision.

At this juncture he had two thoughts: one, if compatible with honor, to spare his country the horrors of the slaughter; the other, to use the prestige of the most powerful nation on earth in mediation for an honorable peace. To him this was a conflict that went beyond the surface meaning. He knew it was less a conflict between nations than a struggle between divergent conceptions of civilization, between democracy and autocracy. Hoping he might serve the cause of peace by raising the voice of reason above the clamor of the battlefields, he issued his proclamation of neutrality to leave him free to act.

Thus through many months he tried to lift the voice of the Republic above the shouting of the captains and the cries of the dying on the fields of slaughter. During the intervening months before we declared war, the lonely man in the White House was subjected to the supreme test. His speeches and his notes to the warring nations at this time were noble in substance and crystal clear in phrasing, and the ultimate judgment of history will pronounce them the most prescient of these years—but there was no response from Berlin. The *Lusitania* was sunk without warning, unrestricted submarine warfare was declared by Germany, and the struggle between democracy and autocracy reached its height. Everything that Wilson and the American people cherished had now been challenged, and the preservation of a democratic civilization was demanding action. His appeals to the Germanic powers were masterpieces of enlightened statesmanship that weakened the enemy in the neutral countries, and held forth hope to the allied nations. In both castle and cabin the people knew that a champion of peace, speaking the language of the human heart, had been heard from the loftiest station in the world. Never once did he falter in his hope and purpose. When he asked that the contending nations make their war aims known, he dealt a deadly blow to the Central Powers that did not dare respond. More important—and the importance will increase steadily with the years—was his historic speech three months before we drew the sword, setting forth the conditions on which a real peace could be built. This foreshadowed the Woodrow Wilson of immortality.

His Fourteen Points is one of the most important documents of the century. It was intended to foreshadow a new international order under which the peoples of the earth could live in peace and security, based on justice. Appealing, as it did, to the minds and hearts of the war-weary peoples, they recognized the voice of the supreme leader of the time. Lloyd George had organized and munitioned the magnificent war effort of the British, and Clemenceau had done the same for France, while Wilson, more than either, was peering above the smoke of battle to the time when men could live in security and peace under their vine and fig tree.

As a War President he performed miracles. He chose his collaborators without regard to politics. Expending billions in a hurry, no shadow of corruption stained the record. Pending the preparation of our troops, he gave financial aid to our allies who were bearing the brunt of the battle. War material was poured in for their armies in defiance of the submarines. Within a surprisingly short time a mighty army of fresh American troops reached the battlefields and the tide was turned from almost inevitable defeat to victory. Ancient dynasties crashed, partly due to the philosophy of freedom so brilliantly and movingly expounded by the one war leader who looked beyond the battlefield to a peaceful society resting on the arbitrament of reason in a parliament of man.

At that hour Wilson was the idol of the masses in Europe and millions poured forth in European capitals and cities to pay homage to the man who envisioned a world without war, and who had a plan.

Yes, Wilson had a plan long meditated and prepared in the silence of the closet. He had no illusions about the obstacles he would have to overcome. His plan was revolutionary and without precedent, since this was aimed, not at the protection of dynasties as was that of Vienna, but for the protection of the people against the imperialistic ambitions of dynasties. It was a challenge to tradition, and it ran foul of materialists and cynics. With a keen realization of the opposition he would meet, he determined to cross the sea, sit in the conference of peace, and personally lead the fight for the League of Nations.

This was his greatest hour, but one fraught with danger to his prestige, since his was a challenge to the old blood-caked system of centuries, and his great protagonists, both men of commanding genius, had little faith in the idealism for which he stood. Lloyd George was an opportunist and trader, and the cynicism of Clemenceau was an armor hard to penetrate. If there was to be a League of Nations, Wilson himself would have to bear the brunt of the battle.

Armchair critics have since declared that he should not have gone at all, or, going, should have made his bow at the ceremonial opening and hurried home; or have sent a delegation other than the one he took along. The fact remains that had he not gone there would have been no League of Nations.

He could not have been taken unaware by what he found in Paris. There, as everywhere, were the materialists without vision, thinking in terms of territory to be taken from the fallen foe; and the old-fashioned diplomats thinking of peace in terms of military alliances and a balance of power; and cynics convinced that war is not only inevitable but advantageous; and fanatic nationalists unable to understand that this is now one world, and that in this century no nation can stand aloof and alone. In this atmosphere, a man of Wilson's sensitivity must have passed lonely hours, but he never faltered in his supreme purpose.

We know that it was not without a torture of the spirit that he was forced to accept provisions in the peace treaty that warred with his judgment and sense of exact justice. The birds of prey were hovering over the fallen foe, each bent on getting some part of the carcass. Secret treaties, long concealed, some negotiated during the war behind his back, were dragged into the open to confound him. When unjust items appeared on the agenda he made his protest known, and, if unable to defeat them wholly, he forced compromises; and, if parts of the treaty were bad, they would have been infinitely worse had he not been there. He accepted some things he did not approve to make more certain the adoption of the covenant of the League of Nations. Working incessantly day and night, worn by vigils and worries, he won his battle and the covenant of the League of Nations was included in the peace treaty, which, in part, he had not approved.

With the covenant in his hand Wilson returned home to find that in his absence a crusade to destroy the League had been organized by his enemies. This conspiracy against the League was partly political, but not a little was due to personal jealousies and hates. The mass of the people favored the League in the beginning, but a high-pressure campaign of distortions and misrepresentations had deceived thousands as to the meaning of the covenant. Mothers were made to believe that with its ratification their boys would be hurried back to European battlefields. Racial prejudices were awakened by demagogy. The greatest document for peace in centuries was made to appear an instrument of war.

The debate in the Senate, extending over many months, was prolonged to permit the propagandists to work on the fears of the people. The fight was not wholly partisan, since William Howard Taft moved to Wilson's side with his book on the covenant that should have made its meaning clear to the most confused, and Elihu Root and Charles Evans Hughes gave less militant support. During the long debate, suspicion had been planted in the public mind, but even so, the conspirators, fearful of a downright rejection, moved to the destruction of the League through amendments. These, especially the one on Article X, would have cut the heart from the covenant and left only the carcass. Wilson saw through the purpose and refused to yield.

The opportunist politician concerned solely with his personal prestige predicated on victories, would have jumped at the chance to emerge from the fight with the skeleton in his arms as proof of his triumph. Woodrow Wilson was intellectually and morally incapable of such a pose. No, he would not accept a mutilated covenant but would carry his fight directly to the people from the platform. Worn down by his labors in Paris and the struggle in the Senate, he was warned that a continental tour with speeches every day would cost him his life. He replied that he would gladly give his life to save the League. On this tour he rose to the majestic heights of his cause. The great orations he delivered, presented with clarity, force and eloquence, the passionate appeals of a dedicated man, are among the greatest contributions to American political literature, taking their place in importance with the "Federalist" of Madison and Hamilton. Outpourings of the mind and heart of the man, they mirror his soul.

When in the midst of the grueling crusade, with his flag proudly flying, he fell a victim of his valor, too few realized that humanity had suffered a tragic loss. He fought undaunted to the end until his country, through its Senate, rejected the League of Nations, refused to join, and thereby struck down the fairest hope, until that hour, for the collaboration of all nations to end the curse of war. It was a triumph of the isolationists, a rejection of international collaboration for peace, an acceptance of the old system caked with the blood of centuries.

Wilson had warned that the continuance of war with the constant invention of more deadly weapons of death, extending destruction beyond the battlefields to the homes of civilians, would mean the destruction of civilization, if not the extermination of the greater part of the human race; but the people, lifted to unaccustomed heights of idealism during the war and missing their customary creature comforts were eager to get back to the money making they understood. So for years the ideals of Wilson were brushed aside, and superficially, they seemed dead, but they lived in the hearts of the masses everywhere.

Time passed, and men were slowly learning the hard way when the war he had foreseen, against which he had solemnly warned, came in 1939 to slaughter millions of fine youths, to put civilization in peril, to wipe out monuments of culture. Then the minds of men turned back to Wilson. While the guns were still roaring, Roosevelt and Cordell Hull determined at long last to act on the wisdom and warning of the creator of the League of Nations, and scarcely had the guns been silenced when the nations of the world met in San Francisco and paid belated homage to Woodrow Wilson by the creation of the United Nations.

If the need was great in 1945, it is greater now that science has developed weapons more horrible than anything hitherto imagined by the human mind, capable of destroying civilization and exterminating the race regardless of age or sex, with no differentiation made between the killing of men in battle, and the slaughter of women and children in their homes. Now science and the genius of invention have moved to the side of Wilson to prove his point. Today, with hydrogen and atomic bombs piled high, awaiting another war when millions of men, women and children will be blown to atoms, when densely populated cities will be reduced to rubbage, when our civilization certainly will be destroyed, the world remembers the warning of Woodrow Wilson.

Meditating on the wreckage of his hopes, this statesman and prophet of vision, looking out on the uneasy world from the house on S Street in Washington, repeated his warning as his last word to his country. It is a solemn thought that it has taken the hydrogen and atomic bombs to convince, when the crystal clear reasoning of Wilson failed because we could not lift our minds to the level of his. And so he emerges as not only one of the greatest statesmen in world history, but as the prophet with clear vision, who gave his life to the cause of humanity and blazed a trail through a wilderness of prejudices and hates to the possible peace he sought.

It may be doubted if the people of his generation had a clear insight into the character of Woodrow Wilson. The brilliance of his mind and his intellectual integrity commanded admiration, but the heart of the man was not so well known to the multitude, since he did not carry his heart upon his sleeve. There were recesses in his nature that could not be penetrated at a glance. He had the reticence of true dignity, the keen sensibilities of pride, the humility of one who believed in God. But the appeal he made was to the intellect because he paid humanity the compliment of accepting its intelligence. He did not seek victories through emotions. Thus, in a sense, he appeared to be aloof, on an eminence to which too few could climb. Though he had a delightful sense of humor, this very characteristic which, in Lincoln had drawn the Emancipator close to the people, was not generally known. We are prone to think of Wilson as an Intellect rather than as a Heart, without realizing that it was the Heart behind the Intellect that gave it warmth. His anguish of spirit when the armies were unleashed in Europe and he was passionately seeking a formula to end the slaughter was not on public display. It was not easy for him to draw the sword and send American boys to the battlefields of Europe but we have no idea of his struggle with his conscience, for he hated war and knew that tragedy would darken many a hearth. Only his intimate associates were witnesses of such struggles. That he prayed for guidance as a Christian, we may assume, but he did not commune with God in the market place to be observed by men. He suffered from the slings and arrows of his enemies, but he did not reveal his wounds in public, since he was proud. His secretary has given us one picture that throws a vivid light on his character. The editor of a paper of the opposition had written him a letter that was kindly and sympathetic just before our declaration of war. "That man understood me and sympathized," he said as he drew his handkerchief and wiped tears from his eyes. Then laying his head on the table he sobbed. He faced his enemies with cold pride but a kindly word revealed the heart of the man, a lonely man, facing the necessity of sending American boys to war.

He did not live to see the Second World War he had warned would come because in part his country had rejected the League and foredoomed it to failure. That much he was spared. Chatham, wrapped in his flannels, dragging himself to the parliament in an effort to serve his country in a crisis, is no more dramatic than Woodrow Wilson in the last official act of his regime when, stricken as he was, he went to the Capitol for the closing scene of the last Congress of his administration. He was seated in the chamber of the Vice-President when, in accordance with custom, a Senator appeared at the door to inquire if he had any further word for the Senate. Here was sheer drama. The Senator at the door had organized and unscrupulously directed the fight to mutilate and destroy the League of Nations for which the stricken statesman in the chair had all but given his life. Here was the old system and the new face to face. Coldly, but with dignity, the statesman who had tried to serve mankind dismissed his enemy in a sentence. Pride in what he had tried to do sustained him. Then, too, he was thinking in terms of history.

He then left the Capitol for his retirement to the house on S Street in Washington to linger a little while and die. He could feel the premonitions of another deadly war in the making, but it would not be on his conscience, since he had given warning. It came with all its horrors within twenty years, and the end is not yet, eleven years after the "victory." It was to prevent this threat to civilization that he had given the richness of his mind and the goodness of his heart.

No statesman has ever been more completely vindicated by time. He had played for the verdict of mankind, and it has now been rendered.

The Internationalist

EDGAR EUGENE ROBINSON

Let us pray that vision may come with power.

Article in *Atlantic Monthly*, December 1902 [34]

We are partners of the rest of the world in respecting the territorial integrity and political independence of others.

Address in support of the League of Nations, Sept. 5, 1919 [35]

Only those who are ignorant of the world can believe that any nation, even as great as the United States, can stand alone and play a single part in the history of mankind.

Ibid.[36]

America is made up of the peoples of the world. All the best bloods of the world flow in her veins, all the old affections, all the old and sacred traditions of peoples of every sort throughout the wide world circulate in her veins, and she has said to mankind at her birth "We have come to redeem the world by giving it liberty and justice.

St. Louis, Sept. 5, 1919 [37]

There is often to be found in the life of a great man some point of eminence at which his powers culminate and his character stands best revealed, his characteristic gifts brought to light and illuminated with a sort of dramatic force. Generally it is a moment of success that reveals him, when his will has had its way, and his genius its triumph.

Wilson Woodrow, *Edmund Burke and the French Revolution*, 1901 [38]

—WOODROW WILSON

IF we are to understand the influence of Woodrow Wilson in the history of the United States and of all mankind, we must see his life in twofold perspective. Our view of the years in which he was the leading figure in the world must be balanced by a view of the years of his preparation for his supreme opportunity. Woodrow Wilson was a product of the America of the last half of the nineteenth century. His own life was an adventure in idealism that was in itself the reflection of the idealism of the American people. The prominent leaders of his own generation of college men, whether they entered business or professional life or remained within academic shades, all reflected the driving and enterprising spirit of a nation reaching the zenith of its continental building.

As a college student, as a university professor, and later as president of Princeton, Wilson, the man of thought, was constantly turning to explanations of the purposes and ideals of Americans. His early studies—concentrated though they were upon matters of deep concern to students of government—always placed emphasis upon character, personality, religious conviction and the deep-rooted drives that make nations great.

Fortunately, in the case of this man who was to become the director of his nation's destiny, we have a full record—of his hopes, his aspirations, his disappointments and his dreams. One may search the history of this country in vain to find any American leader rising to eminent place who so completely reflected the inner life of the bustling, eager, energetic people of the United States.

Had Wilson continued to practice law, had he obtained an opening in the Department of State, or had he devoted himself entirely to writing, it would be easier to see just why he contributed so much to the education of his own people in the twentieth century. It is a little difficult for us to comprehend the importance of his thoughtful preparation because our eyes have been, for the most part, upon the great deeds and the great decisions that characterized his Presidency.

When he became President of the United States in March, 1913, he was in frail health, accustomed to the sheltered routine of the university, but driven then, as in his later years, by an indomitable spirit to direct, to control, to rule. His first acts in the Presidency were characterized by a decision that astonished many misled by his apparent lack of preparation for so strenuous a labor. They expected acquiescence and, at best, much slower movement.

It is true that the speeches in Wilson's campaign for the Presidency had been aptly termed fighting speeches. Yet, the issues of that campaign of 1912, compared with the problems about to arise, were very small indeed. The debate that went on between the Progressive candidate, Theodore Roosevelt, and Woodrow Wilson delighted those who enjoyed forensic prowess—for both men had it. It will be remembered that, in the split of the normal Republican vote, there was little likelihood that Wilson would not attain victory, although supported by only a minority of his fellow citizens.

It has been forgotten how small a minority party Wilson led when he came to power in 1913. The new President was given the support of little more than forty per cent of the voters. The majority in Senate and House, organized by Democratic leaders, rested upon minorities. Neither House nor Senate Democratic majorities represented a majority of the population. Indeed, it was widely anticipated that the Democratic Party, which four years earlier was thought of by most commentators as about to disappear, would certainly fail in this, its opportunity, just as soon as the Republicans and Progressives united—as they did.

It was in this situation that President Wilson, in the first year and a half of his administration, performed the act of executive leadership with such alacrity, such skill and such delight, that there was enacted into law in three major fields of dispute the legislation that had been anticipated for nearly a generation.

Now it is an easy explanation that Wilson was enabled to do this by his great art of persuasion. The evidence is all-conclusive that persuasion was Woodrow Wilson's most effective weapon. That he used it with individuals as well as with groups, there is ample evidence.[a] But this would be a superficial explanatoin of what had happened to American liberal tradition by the summer of 1914. What had happened was that Wilson in his speeches, as well as in his action, had been so effective in interpreting what the more thoughtful citizens had been thinking, that his success was that of a popular revolution.

Education is a slow, intricate and baffling process. We do not yet see that Wilson the scholar of deep-rooted convictions, idealistic outlook, and determined resolve, transferred the results of his thoughtful study to the practical affairs of the government of the United States.

The events of the next three years put to a test not only the ideals, but also the methods which Wilson had decided to use in government. Between the outbreak of the European War in August, 1914, and the day on which President Wilson led the United States into that war, he had formulated—out of the perplexities and agonies of his administration—a policy for the United States which was to foreshadow its policy for a generation after his death. This policy was hammered out day by day, week by week, month by month throughout those years, because of the necessity of dealing with the nations at war.

Wilson came to the Presidency no expert in foreign relations. In his voluminous writings down to that date, there is no evidence of deep concern for international affairs. He was not familiar through travel with many parts of the world. He had been in England. His reading had not been that of a man of world outlook. He was an American deeply interested in the history and government of his own country, learned in the principles of the law and politics associated with Anglo-Saxon tradition, imbued with a love of English literature at its best, and particularly enamored of the philosophers and poets who had depicted the hopes and dreams of the liberty-loving peoples of Western civilization.

Yet it could be said that "President Woodrow Wilson's pronouncements on foreign policy were of such a nature as to raise a presumption that a great part of them had been formulated in his long preparation as a scholar." [b]

So it was that this man, faced with a necessity not only of decision but of explanation, formulated his policies on Christian beliefs, Anglo-Saxon principles and American aspirations. He had once said that the Westerner who had been the master of American life was about to disappear. Surely nothing so clearly represented the outcome of the great opportunities that forward-looking minds had found in the new world as this man. He was no explorer, no military leader, no railroad builder, no colonizer, yet an adventurer nevertheless; a man who loved adventure in the world of ideas and knew that—despite temporary defeat—there would be ultimate triumph for those who believed in reason and were given opportunity to lead their fellow men.

In the years of a generation (1924-1956) since Woodrow Wilson's death, many in time of peace—as well as in time of war—have pointed out the significant aspects of his advocacy of the League of Nations and the firm foundation therein laid for the later United Nations. In the launching of the United Nations and in its unhappy history of the past ten years—as in the building of the League and its long and fruitful service to all mankind—too little attention has been given the basic approach which Wilson had taken to what we term "internationalism."

As so often in the appearance of new structures and new instrumentalities in the long history of mankind, the importance of the driving force—without which there is no life—is either unknown or, if discussed, is soon forgotten.

When he came to office as President in 1913, Woodrow Wilson was not an internationalist. Despite the fact that he had spent a professional lifetime in the study of governments and of states which make those governments possible, there was little in the record to indicate that he would break away from the traditional *national* approach to American foreign relations.

As the event proved, issues that were not even mentioned in the Presidential campaign of 1912 came very soon to be the most important problems of his administration. Literally, Woodrow Wilson was educated through emergency into a new world of thought. But here it is that we are mistaken in seeking the orderly development of a foreign policy by Wilson in terms of the doctrine of the more advanced international thinkers of his time. It was long, for example, before he came to accept publicly the League to Enforce Peace. He had never been thought of as a pacifist, as was his Secretary of State, William Jennings Bryan. He had had no wide personal knowledge of the world, as in the case of Herbert Hoover.

Yet, in the creation of the foreign policy which so distinguished his administration, all of this was relatively unimportant. Wilson dealt with the problem placed before him in accordance with certain basic principles of political conduct. It is because he did this, eventually presenting a program based upon such principles, that he came to be for a time the great leader of the thoughtful world seeking an organization for peace.

One is led to conclude that a good way to formulate a policy is to be forced by circumstances to act—and then to explain. This is often what Wilson did in the first three years of his Presidency. Faced with the problem of recognition of a revolutionary government in Mexico; with an ugly situation in race relations in California; with a question of the interpretation of treaty rights in Panama; with the many facets of the problem of neutrality in dealing with Germany and Britain during the war—he stated a policy and then explained it on the basis of principles of American practice.

Looking at this policy now with care, nearly forty years after the event (1917), what is it that we find? The fundamental basis —the unquestionable conviction which was his after years of study —was faith in democracy. He believed as well in democracy among nations; every nation should regard every other nation as its equal. He saw fair dealing as the means of preserving friendship and peace. He assumed that the guidance of established law was essential to fair dealing and international justice. He believed that the proper means of settling disputes was a reasoned consideration before a court. He granted that force should be used to combat criminal aggression.

No one but a convinced democrat could abide by such a program of action. So it came about that when he asked the Congress to declare war, President Wilson asked them to do so because we had to make the world safe for democracy. If democracy should be threatened anywhere, it would be threatened everywhere!

"The idea of America is to serve humanity," Wilson had said to the graduating class of the United States Naval Academy at Annapolis on June 5, 1914, and added, "I hope that wherever you go you will have a generous, comprehending love of the people you come into contact with, and will come back and tell us, if you can, what service the United States can render to the remotest parts of the world."

The deep gulf that lies between the purpose of this President and that of the man who was in due time to succeed him could never be more completely realized than by remembering that Warren G. Harding as Senator held the view with many members of the Senate—and of course with large groups of American people— that we went into the war in 1917 to beat the Germans. In the view of Wilson, then and later, it was a crusade that American men and women essayed in the spring of 1917. And it was a crusade because he had provided the leadership for peace that he now promised to provide in the war.

It should be remembered that it was not—and never has been —clear to many Americans that as a result of Wilson's bold policy, a European quarrel originating obscurely in petty dynastic ambition, in greedy economic rivalry, and in base national hatred, was transformed by the entrance of the United States into a world conflict with the united forces of democracy and international peace ranged squarely against autocracy and aggression. Woodrow Wilson had come to see that a point had been reached in world affairs where war among any nations threatened all other nations. As a result of his leadership, the United States—not England, not France, not new Russia—became the leader, the bearer of the "great light for the guidance of the nations" in the magnificent new venture of democracy to league the peoples of the world together to serve the ends of peace and justice.

As we waged the war on land and sea, and presently in the air, marshaling all the industrial resources of the nation, President Wilson continued to engage in the diplomacy of war. To many, this in itself seemed a strange thing to do, and the critics were numerous. Yet every time the President offered to negotiate or suggested that we might cease before ultimate and final victory was ours, his reason was the same. It was the reason that had actuated Lincoln in the last days of the War Between the States. We had to live in the world with the people with whom we were fighting!

Once it was evident that the war was to be won by the Allies, Wilson's efforts turned quite naturally to bringing into being an organization that would unite all of the liberty-loving peoples of the world and provide a forum for the discussion of disputed questions.

Those who were inclined to object to Wilson's personal participation in the Peace Conference—they had many reasons—overlooked the driving purpose which lay behind the war policy of the President. This purpose was to create an instrumentality for peace as part of the conclusion of the war. If it were to be postponed, there was grave doubt that it would be possible to bring the nations to a point of agreement.

Now that we know all of the disappointment and dissatisfaction and final disaster that came from this Peace Conference, nevertheless we may feel, with Wilson, that the effort was worth the trial. And indeed, the Herculean effort that he made after his return from the Peace Conference up to the time of his tragic breakdown in Colorado, was in itself a manifestation of his conviction that this was his task and that he alone could hope to accomplish the result he sought.

Much attention has been given the defeat in 1920 of the Democratic ticket pledged to the Wilson program and to the triumph of an amalgamation of opposing forces in March, 1921. Yet this did not really weaken the basic pattern of the Wilson leadership. Harsh though it may seem to say it, the Covenant of the League of Nations and the agreements of nations made in the Limitation of Armament Conference of 1922 were only minor aspects of the whole story of the conversion of the thinking of this world from a national basis to an international basis. This conversion was Woodrow Wilson's accomplishment.

Principles based on the convictions of masses of people, seized upon and activated by leaders of great vision, outlast all conferences and covenants and agreements. The principles embodied in the Wilson foreign policy were the principles of a world state, presented as they were by a national statesman dealing with other national statesmen. Yet they were the principles which must and do underlie all permanent agreements for a peaceful world.

This has had dramatic manifestation in the years following Wilson's departure from public life. In the perspective of these years, we have now come to a position where we may realize the significance of Wilson's service to the nation and to the world in the period between his leaving office in March, 1921, and his death in February, 1924. During this period, although apparently disregarded—as his ideals had been rejected by the American people —he was still voicing, with perhaps the most effective voice in all the world, the hopes of those who believed in internationalism.

Notably was this true six months after he turned over the government to his victorious successor, when on Armistice Day, November 11, 1921, Wilson participated in the ceremony commemorating the burial of America's Unknown Soldier at Arlington.

Ex-President Wilson, with Mrs. Wilson, joined the procession that morning at the Capitol, where the coffin containing the body of the Unknown was removed early from the Rotunda and carried to a waiting caisson, to which six jet-black horses with black trappings were attached. The Wilsons were in an old-fashioned horse-drawn victoria with colored driver and footman, symbol of the fact that Wilson was unable to join the procession on foot with the other participants. The Wilson carriage followed the Medal of Honor group, which was preceded by President Harding, General Pershing, Vice-President Coolidge and the Cabinet, and Members of the Senate and House.

As this procession emerged in Lafayette Square, following the military escort of each branch of the service, some of the men in the civilian ranks were obviously in pain from the long march of seventeen blocks. When they reached the White House, most of the civilians dropped out of the procession. President Harding joined Mrs. Harding and her party in a box opposite the west gate of the White House grounds. The President proceeded to greet personally the Medal of Honor men.

This caused the open victoria of the Wilsons to halt directly in front of the main door of the White House, where two Negroes waved to the Wilsons from the inside of the grounds. Other onlookers waved, and presently there was the beginning of applause, then a mild cheer, and finally a succession of cheers given with hearty but subdued enthusiasm. As the cheering continued Wilson, with seeming reluctance, lifted his hat very slowly, grasping a cane to hold himself erect in his seat. He did not smile. Mrs. Wilson looked worried. Several men went out into the street and were greeted by the ex-President. At this point, the footman resumed his seat and the procession moved on as President Harding removed his hat and bowed in the direction of the Wilsons.

In describing the procession, a correspondent of *The New York Times* noted that Wilson had received an ovation all along the route from the Capitol to the White House. "It was apparent," stated the reporter, "that the sight of Wilson, his once strong body broken by ill-health, his limbs too frail to permit his marching with the other great men who followed the Unknown caisson on foot, was a grim reminder that he had been an outstanding figure in the world conflict which today's ceremonial typified."

The prophet . . . no longer without honor in his own country.

On the eve of the Conference for the Limitation of Armament, the *Times* noted further, the multitude persisted and succeeded in making it felt that it was "to Woodrow Wilson as Commander-in-Chief of the great army that went to war to end war for all time, and to Woodrow Wilson, the lover of humanity, who to attain that goal became the exponent of the limitation of armament idea, rather than to Woodrow Wilson, ex-President of the United States, that this informal tribute of admiration, affection and overflowing sympathy was dedicated. . . . He was acclaimed not once but repeatedly as 'the greatest man on earth.' "

Later in the day, a demonstration an hour in length was given by a crowd of several thousand people in front of the Wilson home on S Street. Wilson came out on the porch, walking alone with the aid of a cane. But to descend two steps, as he did to greet three wounded soldiers who were sitting in an automobile, he had to be helped on each side. He shook hands with some vigor, but later when he tried to speak, he uttered only two sentences that could be heard but a short distance away.

It was in the demonstrations of this day—from which Wilson seemed to shrink in embarrassment—that a turning point appeared in the attitude of the public toward the leader they had rejected. The drama and symbolism of his ghostly appearance upon this particular occasion did not escape his admirers in what was possibly the greatest throng of mourners in the history of the nation up to that time.

Wilson's correspondence during the years 1921-23 with his former Assistant Secretary of the Navy, Franklin Delano Roosevelt, shows that the spirit which had animated him as a teacher and again as a public man was still the spirit of Woodrow Wilson, the pioneer. Undoubtedly Roosevelt's vigorous advocacy of the League of Nations in 1920, when he was Vice-Presidential candidate, accounts for the warmth of the correspondence that developed from a discussion of the Woodrow Wilson Foundation, of which Roosevelt became chairman.

On June 5, 1921, Wilson and Roosevelt met in the afternoon, and we may infer from the correspondence ensuing that this was a beginning of a "Woodrow Wilson Fund." On July fourth of that year, Wilson, suggesting certain changes in the plan, wrote Roosevelt objecting to the use of the word "memorial," which, Wilson stated, "suggests a dead one, and . . . I hope in the near future to give frequent evidence that I am not dead." Later in the month the "Woodrow Wilson Foundation" was agreed upon, the word "memorial" being omitted.

Wilson, learning of Roosevelt's illness, wrote to him on September sixteenth, and wrote to Mrs. Roosevelt on November ninth, congratulating her husband on his improvement. On Wilson's birthday, December 28, 1921, Roosevelt telegraphed Wilson the congratulations of the Woodrow Wilson Foundation. On the back of this telegram, on January 5, 1922, Wilson had a reply typed which included the following: "I am exceedingly proud of the proofs of friendship and confidence which the progress of the Foundation affords me, and your own friendship and unselfish devotion to its objects give me, as I hope you know, peculiar gratification. . . ."

Correspondence and occasional visits between the two invalids continued throughout the remainder of Wilson's life. On January 29, 1923, Wilson wrote Roosevelt: "I cannot let tomorrow, your birthday, go by without sending you my heartfelt felicitations and expressing the hope that your health is steadily returning to you, and that with your health will come every desirable blessing. May each return of your birthday be happier than the last."

It was in this year (1923) that Franklin Roosevelt drew up a plan for the creation of a permanent and continuing international conference which he termed the "Society of Nations," designed to replace the League of Nations, which he believed the United States would not join "for many years to come." He later made a memorandum and attached it to a copy of this plan on January 19, 1944. He referred to it again in a memo prepared at Quebec on September 15, 1944.[c]

The contrast between Wilson's conception of a democratic League to provide collective security, and Roosevelt's conception of a world organization in which the leading powers would necessarily reveal their objectives has been shown in the first decade of the United Nations Organization.

During his lifetime, Mr. Wilson remained true to his vision. Yet, that he saw into the future, we have striking proof in two instances. The final year of his life was marked by two utterances which now appear far more prophetic than he himself could have realized.

Writing in the *Atlantic Monthly* (August, 1923), on "The Road Away from Revolution," Woodrow Wilson said what he believed: "The world has been made safe for democracy." He did not foresee, it is true, "any such mad design as that entertained by the insolent and ignorant Hohenzollerns." Wilson was spared the anticipation of Hitler. But he saw further into the future, for he said ". . . democracy has not yet made the world safe against irrational revolution. That supreme task, which is nothing less than the salvation of civilization, now faces democracy, insistent, imperative. There is no escaping it, unless everything we have built up is presently to fall in ruin about us; and the United States, as the greatest of democracies, must undertake it."

He pursued this theme still further. In his last public address, delivered over the radio on November 10, 1923, on "The High Significance of Armistice Day," he said:

The anniversary of Armistice Day should stir us to great exaltation of spirit because of the proud recollection that it was our day . . . which lifted the world to the high levels of vision and achievement upon which the great war for democracy and right was fought and won, although the stimulating memories of that happy triumph are forever marred and embittered for us by the shameful fact that when the victory was won . . . we turned our backs upon our associates and refused to bear any responsible part in the administration of peace . . . and withdrew into a sullen and selfish isolation, which is deeply ignoble because manifestly cowardly and dishonorable. . . .

The affairs of the world can be set straight only by the firmest and most determined exhibition of the will to lead and make right prevail.

Happily, the present situation in the world of affairs affords us the opportunity to retrieve the past and to render to mankind the inestimable service of proving that there is at least one great and powerful nation which can turn away from programs of self-interest and devote itself to practicing and establishing the highest ideals of disinterested service and the consistent standards of conscience and of right.

The only way in which we can worthily give proof of our appreciation of the high significance of Armistice Day is by resolving to put self-interest away and once more formulate and act upon the highest ideals and purposes of international policy.

Thus, and only thus, can we return to the true traditions of America.

The death of Woodrow Wilson on February 3, 1924, was the occasion for an outpouring of eulogy. Yet there appears to have been little realization at the time of the nature of the contribution which this American had made to the world. Wilson throughout his life had so preached a doctrine of Americanism that it has become the doctrine of internationalism. Only one deeply imbued with the Christian faith and fully cognizant of the dominant forces that had made America what it is could have projected into the world this view with such conviction that it became a part of the thinking of all mankind.

We can see how utterly inconceivable would have been the United States in the role of crusader in World War I, had Wilson not been President. For he had led the United States in a great revolution in thought between 1914 and 1917. All men, when called to public office, find that they must act. Few indeed find that, in acting, conscience forces them to think and preach and prophesy. It is these few who win lasting place as leaders of the people.

Wilson's contribution to humanity is derived from two dominant aspects of his own personal experience. The first of these was his idealistic outlook based on his ancestral background. The second was his historical outlook based on a professional life of thirty years. The new internationalism had to be rooted in fundamental ideas presented to the American people as the bases of their own existence.

For example, "Wilson believed that in upholding freedom of the seas, long identified with American foreign policy, the United States was maintaining the vitality of international law. The idea that security is a function of law and morality is deeply ingrained in our internal affairs. . . . This conviction Wilson projected from the domestic to the international area of politics." [a]

When President Wilson revealed himself fully as a statesman of international vision, as he did in the formulation of the principles embodied in the League of Nations, he lost not only his hold upon the leaders of national states in Europe and Asia, but also—and more important—his leadership of the American people. They were not internationalists.

But what Wilson never fully admitted, and what the American people never saw, was the flaw in American thinking revealed by the struggle over American adherence to the League of Nations. It was not partisan consideration that called for Wilson's defeat; it was not historical precedent for the view of the isolationists. It was the failure of the majority of Americans to face the compelling issues of the future raised by an international community. This international community already existed in 1919, but they did not see it.

Wilson formulated his creed of leadership in a democracy. He asked much of his fellow citizens, and he believed profoundly in the considered judgment of the common man. He had a mystic faith closely akin to that of Lincoln, remarking, "You cannot resist Providence."

Wilson remained an internationalist until his dying day. He prophesied with amazing clarity the events of the ensuing thirty years. His successors, as they have caught his vision, have succeeded not only in creating a United Nations Organization, but also in leading the peoples of the world to a new hope of democracy, both as an ideal and as a practice. We must look forward to the day when we have not only a forum in the United Nations, with its appendage UNESCO engaged in work for the health—mental, moral, and physical—of mankind, but an international government devoted to resolving the differences which arise among all mankind. We must anticipate international political parties. In the papers taken to the Paris Conference by Woodrow Wilson in December, 1918, was a manuscript prepared by Frederick Jackson Turner entitled "International Political Parties in a Durable League of Nations." [e] And we must anticipate such a curtailment of national sovereignty that the national jealousies and prejudices that occupy so much of our time will seem relatively unimportant.

For more than a generation a question that pressed upon many a participant in public debate was this: "Was Wilson Wrong?" The answer is that in his vision of war internationalized to control aggressors, and in his vision of the foundations of international peace, he was, as the events of the past thirty years have proved, right.

The Man in History

KATHARINE E. BRAND

". . . shall we not constantly recall our reassuring past, reminding one another again and again, as our memories fail us, of the significant incidents of the long journey we have already come, in order that we may be cheered and guided upon the road we have yet to choose and follow?"

Article in *Atlantic Monthly*, 1897 [39]

After all, a University has as its only legitimate object intellectual attainment. I do not mean that there should not go along with that a great deal that is delightful in the way of comradeship; but I am sure that men never thoroughly enjoy each other if they merely touch superficially. I do not believe that men ever thoroughly know or enjoy each other until they lay their minds along side each other and make real test of their quality.

Chicago, Illinois March 12, 1908 [40]

—WOODROW WILSON

I N December of this year, a century will have passed since the birth of Woodrow Wilson. And what a century! A Civil War, World Wars, uneasy intervals of peace, scientific advance beyond what would have seemed the limits of possibility in 1856—and certainly beyond the limits to which the spirit of man can even now easily adjust.

Much of this upheaval Wilson missed, in point of time. He began his life in the leisurely South, among gentlefolk, deeply religious people. He remembered the effects of the Civil War, yes, but for the most part these were not searing memories. And he came to maturity—he "came to himself"—in quiet academic communities which, with all the bitter controversy, were still somewhat removed from the noise of business, of politics. Wilson himself felt this keenly. "Experience in affairs, I feel, is what I most imperatively need . . ." he wrote, from his first teaching post. "I love the stir of the world."

The advent of World War I was a shocking thing to most men. What must it have been to a President newly come into the place of highest responsibility, to a "literary politician" who instinctively resisted, but had finally to accept, the task of leading his country into and through and out of the maelstrom! It is interesting enough to speculate upon what Wilson would have been—what, indeed, Washington, or Lincoln, or Franklin D. Roosevelt would have been —without the circumstances of their respective times. It is interesting, but futile. The times forged the men; each man in his own way put his indelible stamp upon his time.

Of first importance, then, is the study of the leader, not only within his own personal framework but within his own time. This has been possible for many years in the case of Washington, of Lincoln, and the others; it is now becoming increasingly possible with the more recent figures.

This chapter is reprinted, in part, from The Library of Congress Quarterly Journal of Current Acquisitions. Vol. 13, Feb. 1956, No. 2.

When the first reader opened his first box of Woodrow Wilson papers * in the Library of Congress some fifteen years ago, he was venturing into more or less new territory. Until the previous year, most of them had been in the custody of the authorized biographer, in Amherst, Mass.

Five tons of papers!" said Ray Stannard Baker, when he peered into the truck which had brought them to the New England town where he lived. And, even allowing for the overemphasis of the moment, they must have presented an awesome sight, in their cartons, drawers, bundles and trunks. Filing cases had come from the White House, boxes from a Washington warehouse, more boxes and cases and packages from the Wilson home on S Street in Washington. Here, then, was a miscellaneous assortment containing pure gold for the historian and the biographer, as well as a considerable amount of what would look, to many investigators, like dead wood. It was, in short, a typical collection of personal papers, but with this difference: the man who had worked with these had been President of the United States, and had led the people of his country not only through a domestic program of great importance, but through the First World War and the peace conference which followed. Here, it seemed, was Woodrow Wilson's record, a part of the evidence by which he was to be judged, and with him, the country he served.

During their sojourn in Amherst, from 1925 to 1939, the papers were kept, some of them in the substantial fireproof building of the Converse Memorial Library at Amherst College, or of the Jones Library, in the town; and some in appropriate quarters at the Baker residence, which Mr. Baker had especially constructed to house them. Toward the end of their stay in Amherst, a fire in the Baker house served to test the effectiveness of the latter arrangements. As a roaring in the chimney gave the first indication of danger, fireproof cabinets, standing on their concrete floors, were shut and locked, a fireproof door swung closed, and, within two minutes, the papers were safe, leaving the excited and helpful townspeople who gathered at once in a great crowd on the lawn, free to form a human chain which swiftly disposed in a heap upon the driveway outside not only

---

* An asterisk (*) following the name of a collection will hereafter indicate that those papers may be used only by special permission, which should be sought through the Chief of the Library's Manuscripts Division.

household articles of all kinds, but also the printed books relating to Wilson which the biographer had been collecting for many years. The present writer, who took part in all this activity, well remembers the weary hours required to trundle this confused miscellany back into the house, and replace the volumes on their shelves!

The story of the Wilson papers during their Amherst years, interesting though it was, need not be told here. In the spring of 1939, when Mr. Baker's work had been completed, the collection passed temporarily into the custody of one of his assistants and, by Mrs. Wilson's direction, was prepared during that summer for presentation to the Library of Congress. In the fall of the year, the physical transfer took place, a bonded truck being dispatched by the Library for the purpose.

Upon reaching their destination the papers were shifted, with as much speed as possible, to the red box portfolios so familiar to those who knew the Library's Manuscripts Division at that time; but they were not made immediately available to readers. Some ten months passed—from October, 1939 to July of the following year —before they were declared open for research, under special conditions. In the interval before that announcement was made, the arrangement which had been maintained for the biographer's use was somewhat altered. Original groupings were kept so far as possible, in accordance with the policy of the Library, but certain changes were effected in the interest of what would be, it was hoped, a permanent archival structure.

As of 1956, the main body of the Wilson Papers appears in nine series, an arrangement which will probably stand. The series are:

I—*Miscellaneous Papers*, including among other things, such diaries as have survived; II—a *Chronological File*, including both letters received and carbon copies of many letters sent, the latter controlled by a card index; III—*Notes, Manuscripts of Books and Articles, Proofs*, and so on; IV—*Correspondence* between Woodrow Wilson and Ellen Axson Wilson (entirely restricted for the present); V—a *New Jersey File*, covering a few months in the winter of 1912-1913; VI—an *Official File*, kept at the Executive Office during Wilson's administration (a numbered file, controlled by indexes); VII— a series of *Letterpress Volumes*, containing copies of perhaps 28,000 of Wilson's letters-sent, with a self-index at the front of each volume; VIII—the *Peace Conference Papers*; and IX—the "*S Street File*," kept after Mr. Wilson's retirement.

From the papers before they reached Washington in 1939, there had come Ray Stannard Baker's three volumes of just-off-the-fire Versailles Peace Conference history, which he called *Woodrow Wilson and World Settlement* [f] eight volumes of his biography, *Woodrow Wilson, Life and Letters* [g] which carries the story through World War I only; and, jointly edited by Baker and William E. Dodd, six volumes of *The Public Papers of Woodrow Wilson*.[h] But this mass of published material, valuable though it was, represented in the main one man's selection and interpretation. For many others there now remained the exciting business of looking into the papers for the first time. For the eager biographer—and there have been many—it meant realignment of the story, readjustment of emphasis after the passage of time, and, in a sense, the straining of known facts through a new personality. For the specialist in economic history it meant the discovery or rediscovery of materials which had been little used or used not at all. For the student of political philosophy it meant tracing again, perhaps, the dramatic 1912 convention at Baltimore, which few writers can resist; or the curious campaign of 1916; or the election of 1920, in some ways tragic, with the President still in the White House but broken by illness; or the final days of retirement, which saw Wilson's last straining effort, in which a few of his friends participated with kindness and a kind of desperate hope, to exercise some final political guidance in the years before his death.

But the Wilson collection did not remain static upon coming to the Library of Congress, as many do. The working papers which Baker had assembled during his fifteen years of work on the biography came also, and were organized; and almost at once, Wilson's friends and associates began sending to the Library letters or copies of letters received from him, retained copies of which, if they were of the early years, had not been preserved in the Wilson papers.

But quite aside from these valuable accretions to the Library's manuscript holdings, the Wilson papers themselves have been gradually increased. Long unused trunks, boxes and bundles in the Wilson residence have been uncovered from time to time and examined. Those containing manuscripts were sent to the Library at once by Mrs. Wilson, whose constant effort for more than thirty years has been to effect a public-spirited disposition of her husband's papers. These completely new materials (some eighteen thousand pieces), constituting a true part of the papers of Woodrow Wilson, have not yet, in most cases, been integrated in the original materials, which became available for use in the summer of 1940. They have been thrown, rather, as a matter of deliberate policy, into a rough chronological arrangement to facilitate their use, and have been kept entirely separate, so that those who came earlier to the Manuscripts Division, and sat day after day in the Reading Room scanning each paper, need not, upon a return visit, be confronted with the necessity of going again through the entire collection to discover the fresh materials. But now, since the latest, and almost certainly the final, large addition was made in the fall of 1954, a definitive reorganization and integration of all the papers within a year or two is contemplated.

The new material covers a wide date-span (roughly 1875-1924, with a few earlier and later papers) and constitutes a varied and fascinating assortment, from early notebooks kept while Wilson was still in college to hundreds of letters and messages which poured in after his death in 1924. The latter are carefully mounted in several volumes of an extensive scrapbook series * kept by John Randolph Bolling, Mrs. Wilson's brother and assistant through many years.

Practically all the letters found in this new group were addressed to Wilson. There are family letters, from his father, his brother and sisters, his uncles and his cousins. There are letters from many friends: R. Heath Dabney and Charles W. Kent, of the University of Virginia days; Herbert B. Adams and Albert Shaw, whom he knew at Johns Hopkins; James W. Hazen, a Middletown friend of the Wesleyan period; Princeton classmates such as Robert Bridges, Hiram Woods and Charles Talcott, as well as the friends and associates of his later Princeton years—Winthrop M. Daniels, Henry B. Fine, Andrew F. West, Henry van Dyke, Cyrus H. McCormick, Edward R. Sheldon, Lawrence Woods, and others. There are letters from John Grier Hibben, who followed Wilson in the presidency of Princeton, and from Francis L. Patton, who preceded him; and a handwritten note from old Dr. James McCosh, stalwart friend of the Wilson family and, at the time of Wilson's appointment to the Princeton faculty, President Emeritus:

I am glad they are bringing you back to your old college. You will receive a welcome here and will have a wide field of usefulness. You will enter it and possess it.

There are letters also from Edward Ireland Renick, Wilson's first law partner, who remained his warm friend to the time of his death in 1902; and, from the early months in Atlanta, a power of attorney given to Wilson by his mother and father, and written out in careful longhand by the young lawyer himself.

Then, too, there is correspondence from associates in the publishing world, such as Walter Hines Page and Horace E. Scudder; letters relating to efforts made by universities—William and Mary, Virginia, and Texas, among them—to draw Wilson away from Princeton; letters from colleagues in his own and related fields, including Frederick J. Turner, A. Lawrence Lowell, John Bates Clark of Smith College, John H. Latane, and even one—strictly businesslike and to the point—from President M. Carey Thomas of Bryn Mawr! And here and there one finds a surprising note, such, for example, as this letter of September 14, 1891:

Dear Sir

Allow me to express the pleasure with which I have read your paper in the *Atlantic*. Your literary touch is so light and sure that you ought by no means to confine yourself to public questions which so many others are treating. We have few who possess the literary touch.

I should not venture to write this, but that the best reward of literature lies in the acknowledgments it brings from strangers.

> Cordially yours,
> Thomas Wentworth Higginson

We must regret that Wilson, at this point in his career, was so little inclined to view himself as a man confined "to public questions" that he failed, as far as can be discovered, to make and retain a copy of his own reply.

Included also are drafts of early essays, some of which never got beyond their youthful author's desk; and, laid between the pages of an 1876 notebook, careful pencil drawings of sailing ships, Wilson's interest in which was stimulated when, at the age of eighteen, he moved with his family to the coastal town of Wilmington, N. C. There are many pages of practice notes, painstakingly written out and preserved in the course of the study of Graham shorthand, which Wilson undertook when he was still in school, and used consistently to the end of his life in the preparation of lectures, articles, books and public addresses. And there are essays toward diary-keeping which broke off, as did all his later efforts of the same kind, after the first few entries. One of the latter was written at Bryn Mawr College, where he began his long academic career by lecturing to women—an exercise which appears to have confirmed this young Southern intellectual in what was already a deep-seated point of view. His comment was set down on October 20, 1887, evidently in some exasperation of spirit:

Lecturing to young women of the present generation on the history and principles of politics is about as appropriate and profitable as would be lecturing to stone-masons on the evolution of fashion in dress. There is a painful *absenteeism* of mind on the part of the audience. Passing through a vacuum, your speech generates no heat. Perhaps it is some of it due to undergraduateism, not all to femininity.

I have devoted myself to a literary life; but I do not see how a literary life can be built up on foundations of undergraduate instruction. That instruction compels one to live with the commonplaces, the A. B. C., of every subject, to dwell upon these with an emphasis and an invention altogether disproportionate to their intrinsic weight and importance; it keeps one on the dusty, century-travelled high-roads of every subject, from which one gets no outlooks except those that are catalogued and vulgarized in every guide-book. One gets weary plodding and yet grows habituated to it and finds all excursions aside more and more difficult. What is a fellow to do? How is he to earn bread and at the same time find leisure and (in the toils of such a routine) disposition of mind for thoughts entirely detached from and elevated high above the topics of his trade?

Also from the academic years, but representative of a more mature Wilson, are notes, examination questions, various exchanges in regard to college administrative matters, and other letters from friends and colleagues. As controversies at Princeton waxed hotter, they drew increasing notice from other academic centers about the country, and mail poured in. One point of view, at least, is represented by a letter from David Starr Jordan of Leland Stanford University—"I believe most sincerely in the things that you are trying to do at Princeton." The manuscripts relating to the Princeton years must be used, of course, in conjunction with the collection of such materials in the Princeton University Library.

The fresh material of the governorship period is perhaps of especial value, since the documentation for those years has been, in the past, much too sparse. In the concentration of new materials for 1910-12, for example—some twenty-five hundred pieces—there are many communications from H. E. Alexander of the Trenton *True American* and several from George Harvey, as well as scattered letters from Richard S. Childs of the Short Ballot Association, James Kerney of the Trenton *Evening Times*, Dan Fellows Platt, Martin P. Devlin, Thomas B. Love, and others who were in one way or another concerned with Wilson's candidacy.

We find him, in the spring of 1910, being asked by the Democratic State Central Committee of Pennsylvania to draft a Democratic platform. "Of course, this is entirely confidential," wrote A. G. Dewalt, Chairman of the Committee, "and I will never mention your name, unless you give me permission to do so."

The deed was done, and on April twelfth Dewalt returned enthusiastic thanks: "The planks that you have constructed are so tersely and succinctly drawn that they met with unanimous approbation."

Unfortunately, Wilson's drafts for his own part of this exchange have not yet been identified, though they may well be found among the shorthand notes in the papers, not yet transcribed.

On July fifteenth, it will be remembered, Wilson finally "took the plunge," as one of his biographers relates, and sent a statement regarding his candidacy for the governorship of New Jersey to the Trenton *True American*. His draft for this statement is among the new papers, as is a letter from his friend, Alexander, who wrote: "Your 'statement' was exactly the thing. In my opinion it prepares the way for your unanimous nomination and election and then!

It means a political revolution in New Jersey and every man who has any political sense so understands it."

And the next day, the practical-minded Alexander wrote: "As a matter of policy, so far as possible we speak of you as plain Woodrow Wilson, eliminating 'the President' and 'Dr.'"

The passage from academic halls to politics was fairly swift, once the "plunge" had been taken! From then on, events moved fast. We find among the additional materials Wilson's much-revised draft of his letter of October 24, 1910, to George Record, which proved so effective in the governorship campaign. It is interesting to note that in this draft, following the well-known statement, "If I am elected, I shall understand that I am chosen leader of my party and the direct representative of the whole people in the conduct of the government," the words "No person or organization will twice try to dictate to me" are crossed out—one wonders at what point in the revision, or by whose advice.

There are, too, early letters from many who became influential in the years of the Presidency: from Josephus Daniels, who wrote of the 1910 election, "My wife joins me in hearty and sincere congratulations on your victory. Will hearten all men everywhere who are tired of government by favoritism"; from Charles A. Talcott, Princeton classmate, whose letter began, "My dear old boy—I am glad New Jersey is to be all right"; from Lindley M. Garrison, later Wilson's Secretary of War, who considered the election to be "a demonstration of the inherent sanity and wisdom of the people." Senator John Sharp Williams, that remarkable old character who became one of Wilson's warm friends, wrote with some prescience: "You will succeed in public life because you have the knack of striking off 'key-note' sentences. . . ."

As the governorship wore along into the Presidential campaign, new names appeared: William G. McAdoo, who was to become Secretary of the Treasury; Frank I. Cobb of the New York *World* ("Whether we win or lose at Baltimore we can at least make a real fight for a real principle"); Carter Glass, asking, two days after the election, for a brief interview on the revision of the currency system.

From Louis D. Brandeis there came a characteristic note on November 6:

Your great victory, so nobly won, fills me with a deep sense of gratitude; and I feel that every American should be congratulated, except possibly yourself.

May strength be given you to bear the heavy burden.

And James Bryce, an old friend now become British Ambassador to the United States, wrote a letter which must have warmed the heart of the newly elected President:

Though I am debarred from congratulating a victor in a political campaign, there is nothing to prevent me from sending sincere good wishes and earnest hopes to an old friend who, being a scholar and a man of learning has obtained a rare and splendid opportunity of shewing in the amplest sphere of action what the possession of thought and learning may accomplish for the good of a nation in the field of practical statesmanship. This opportunity is yours, and I may wish you joy the more heartily because I feel confident that your attainments and character promise success. Few have ever reached your high office equally qualified, in both respects, to discharge its duties worthily.

The new materials for the Presidential years are not extensive, which is understandable in view of the heavy documentation of that period in the main body of the Wilson papers. They do, however, contain additional letters from Edward M. House, a good many of William J. Bryan's sprawling, handwritten communications (which were, in the beginning, transcribed on the typewriter for the President by one of the White House clerks), and material relating to Mexican problems, including a number of reports from John Lind. There are also a number of Wilson's drafts—for letters, public statements and addresses—suggesting, in some cases, the development of his thought. A hand-corrected early draft of his letter of February 5, 1913, to A. Mitchell Palmer, for example, on the matter of a second term for Presidents, was found to contain the following words, crossed out in pen by Wilson:

At the outset, and in order to clear the ground, let me say that I do not understand this discussion to have anything whatever to do with the question of a third term. That I take it may now be regarded as beyond debate. Nothing that I shall have to say will touch that.

There are a few documents which may throw some additional light upon this country's foreign policy in the last years of the administration. And there is a remarkable collection of memorabilia, mainly of the Peace Conference period. Petitions are there, and diplomas from the Universities of Brussels, Padua, Cracow, Pisa, Ghent and others; illuminated manuscripts are there, and unique documents in hand-tooled leather cases, and honorary citizenships. These, with the hundreds of letters and messages in the main body of the Wilson papers, which came to the President in 1919 from the little people of many countries, written in many languages—all these, one must suppose, represent part of the outpouring of relief and hope and, for a time, faith, with which Woodrow Wilson was greeted in Europe at the close of World War I.

But, fortunately for scholarship, the Woodrow Wilson papers by no means stand alone. The Library of Congress, which has for many years been assembling personal papers of public figures in order to round out and supplement its Presidential collections, now has, for the Wilson period, much closely related Cabinet material, personal papers of Senators and Representatives whose service in Congress included the Wilson administration, Versailles Peace Conference papers, and, in addition, the significant but often more peripheral papers of military and naval figures, bankers, labor leaders, social workers and others.

This aggregation of historical source material has become, in consequence, a Mecca for scholars concerned with the history of the first quarter of the twentieth century.

The papers of Cabinet members should perhaps be given first attention. Of the nineteen men whom Wilson brought into his Cabinet between 1913 and 1921, the papers, or all that remain, of ten are in the Library of Congress, and the papers, or all that remain, of five are in other repositories.

The Bryan, Lansing, and Colby * collections are in the Library, thus completely covering the Secretaryship of State for the two administrations which included World War I and the Versailles Peace Conference. Each, of course, has special contributions to make: the Bryan papers, with regard to foreign service appointments, the administration's early policies in Latin America, arbitration treaties, and the increasingly difficult neutrality problems; [i]

the Lansing papers in the continuing area of neutrality, followed by the war and the Peace Conference; the Colby papers in the final days of the administration, when this country's relations with Russia were of vital concern and when the President's hope for a League of Nations in which the United States would play a strong part were being gradually beaten down. The Colby papers also contain some material relating to his law partnership with Woodrow Wilson, after the latter's retirement from office.

While the papers of Lindley M. Garrison, Wilson's first Secretary of War, are not in the Library, they have been preserved and made available in the Firestone Library at Princeton University. The main body of the papers of Newton D. Baker,* who followed Garrison as Secretary of War and saw the country through its first major world struggle, have been in the Library of Congress for some years, and a considerable addition to the collection is expected in the near future. These have, perhaps, an especial interest for the biographer and the student of military history, since the minds of the Commander-in-Chief and his Secretary of War ran parallel on many matters of principle and the application of principle. The papers of William G. McAdoo,* first of Wilson's three Secretaries of the Treasury and longest in that office, are also in the Library, but by the donor's wish, are closed to research until July 1, 1959. In the Alderman Library at the nearby University of Virginia are the papers of Senator Carter Glass, second of Wilson's Secretaries of the Treasury and, before that, his close associate in the battle for the Federal Reserve Act; and also the papers of Justice James C. McReynolds, first Attorney General and, later, by Wilson's appointment, Associate Justice of the Supreme Court of the United States. The papers of David F. Houston, who served as Secretary of Agriculture, leaving that post in 1920 to succeed Glass in the Treasury, have not, unfortunately for scholars, been preserved in a unified group. The official records of his Cabinet department during his incumbency may of course be found, with similar official records of all such departments, in the National Archives; a group of his correspondence is in the custody of the Widener Library at Harvard; and some materials presumably are still in family hands. The Thomas W. Gregory papers, not a large collection but all have been preserved, are also in the Library, as are a series of letters—

mainly from Woodrow Wilson—to A. Mitchell Palmer, who, as Wilson's Third Attorney General, succeeded Gregory in 1919. The main body of the Palmer papers has not so far been found.

The papers of Josephus Daniels and of Albert S. Burleson, Secretary of the Navy and Postmaster General, respectively, during both Wilson administrations, are in the Library. Of these, the Daniels papers are by far the most extensive, pertaining as they do not only to his service under Wilson but also to his years as Ambassador to Mexico in the administration of Franklin D. Roosevelt, and to his own work, in the years between these posts, as owner and editor of the Raleigh *News and Observer*. His papers include a substantial amount of diary material, which adds much to an already valuable collection. The Burleson papers, bound in chronological order, relate not only to the affairs of the Post Office Department but also, as would be expected, to the matter of lesser appointments and to relations between the President and his colleagues on Capitol Hill. The collection also includes some eighty letters addressed to the President, but sent by him to his Postmaster General, under "buck-slips," for information or comment or action, and never returned to the White House.

Of the remaining six Cabinet members, the papers of William B. Wilson, Secretary of Labor through both administrations, are in the Historical Society of Pennsylvania, in Philadelphia; such of the papers of Franklin K. Lane, Secretary of the Interior, as have been preserved are in the custody of the University of California at Berkeley; and a small group of John Barton Payne papers remain with the American Red Cross, in which organization he held the post of chairman of the Central Committee from 1921 until his death in 1935. His papers pertain for the most part to that portion of his career. The family of Edwin T. Meredith, who succeeded Houston in the Department of Agriculture, is searching for his papers, but none have been found as yet. Such papers of William C. Redfield (Secretary of Commerce, 1913-17) as have been preserved are in the custody of the Library of Congress, but they are sadly few in number; and the papers of J. S. Alexander, Redfield's successor in office, were, it is believed, destroyed many years ago in an office fire.

So stands the Cabinet record as of 1956. It is probably safe to say that more than two-thirds of the personal papers accumulated by Cabinet members during the Wilson administration have been preserved in the Library of Congress or in non-governmental repositories. There is still hope that papers now missing altogether will eventually be found, since the Wilson administration, in historical terms at least, is recent, and experience has shown that both care and patience are needed in order to discover and draw together the documentation of an era.

The Library's manuscripts relating to the Peace Conference of 1919 are likewise voluminous. Of the five American Commissioners to Negotiate Peace, the Library owns the papers of four—Wilson, Lansing, Henry White and Tasker H. Bliss. The papers of the fifth, Col. Edward M. House, are at Yale University, as are those of Frank L. Polk, Acting Secretary of State during Lansing's absence from the country at the Peace Conference. Among other Conference papers in the Library are: an indexed collection of House "Inquiry" materials, consisting mainly of studies prepared by various of its members; the papers of David Hunter Miller,* international lawyer and member of the "Inquiry," whose twenty-one-volume diary, privately printed, has long been an extremely useful part of the Conference documentation; the papers of Leland Harrison, Diplomatic Secretary to the American Commission to Negotiate Peace and subsequently a distinguished career diplomat; the papers of Ray Stannard Baker,* who was head of the American Press Bureau in Paris during the Conference and later became Wilson's biographer; and the papers of Norman H. Davis,* financial adviser to President Wilson at Paris and, like Harrison, an outstanding member of this country's diplomatic corps. The papers of Miss Edith Benham * [now Mrs. James M. Helm], Mrs. Wilson's secretary, who accompanied the President's party to Europe, and of Irwin H. Hoover, Head Usher at the White House, who functioned under many Presidents and who was also a member of the Presidential party in 1919, will furnish many details which would be difficult to come at elsewhere.

Among the collections of Members of Congress who were active during the Wilson administration, there should be mentioned those of Senator Gilbert F. Hitchcock, leader of the pro-League of Nations forces in the treaty fight of 1919-20—a small group, but valuable for that period; of Philander C. Knox, then Senator and a member of the opposition; of John Sharp Williams, Senator from Mississippi; of Henry D. Flood, Chairman of the House Foreign Affairs Committee during World War I, whose papers are voluminous but unfortunately lack, for the most part, materials relating to the powerful committee which he headed; of James Hay, Chairman of the House Committee on Military Affairs until 1917, whose papers, though very few in number, do relate to the preparedness program; of Robert M. LaFollette, Sr.,* whose voluminous and detailed collection is invaluable on many counts, not the least of which is its usefulness as a kind of corrective in the study of various moot points; of Cordell Hull,* later Secretary of State under Franklin D. Roosevelt, but during the Wilson administration a member of the Democratic National Committee, and of William E. Borah, George W. Norris, Thomas J. Walsh, Charles L. McNary, Key Pittman, Tom Connally, and others, each of whom played a part in the country's legislative history during all or part of the Wilson administration.

Then, too, there are in the Library the papers of many other figures whose careers impinged upon that of Wilson. These collections, like most of those already mentioned, furnish widely varying materials for research, some having only restricted bearing upon the Wilson story; but, for the student of Wilson's broad career, each does have certain contributions to make.

Among these are the papers of John J. Pershing,* General of the Armies, and of the other high-ranking military and naval figures —Hugh L. Scott, James G. Harbord, Leonard Wood,* Robert Lee Bullard, Mark L. Bristol, Albert Gleaves, and Washington I. Chambers, and a first installment of the Peyton C. March collection, relating to World War I and the 1919 Conference, to Mexican border difficulties, and many other matters. There are the papers of Charles Evans Hughes,* distinguished jurist, Secretary of State under Harding and Coolidge, and Chief Justice of the United States, who ran against Wilson in the campaign of 1916, and two years later headed, by Presidential appointment, the Aircraft Investigation which was sparked by that fiery sculptor, Gutzon Borglum. And there are the papers of Borglum,* himself. There are also the papers of Breckinridge Long,* Third Assistant Secretary of State and specialist in Far Eastern questions in Wilson's time, and subsequently a member of the country's diplomatic corps, and those of Harry A. Garfield,* whom Wilson called to Washington during the war to be Fuel Administrator. There are the papers of Elihu Root, Secretary of War under McKinley, Secretary of State under Theodore Roosevelt, and for six years United States Senator from New York, whose career crossed Wilson's at more than one point but nowhere more surprisingly than when he was made, by Presidential appointment, the head of the United States Commission to Russia in 1917; and the papers of Charles Edward Russell, member of the same Commission. The papers of William E. Dodd, one of Wilson's early biographers long before his appointment by Franklin D. Roosevelt to the Ambassadorship of Germany, are in the Library, as are the papers of such newspapermen as "Marse Henry" Watterson, Frederick William Wile, Stanley Washburn and William Allen White. There also are journals, like that kept by Chandler P. Anderson from 1914 to 1927, which remains in his papers, and there are the long and chatty diaries and the exhaustive scrapbook series of Charles Sumner Hamlin, which concern not only the early days of the Federal Reserve System but also various political and social facets of the Wilson and other administrations.

The papers of George Creel, writer and head of the Committee on Public Information during World War I, are also in the Library. Creel was not one to save correspondence, but he did preserve and have bound, in three handsome leather-backed volumes, his Wilson letters, as well as such drafts and memoranda as concerned their association and his own work on the C.P.I. This material continues to be the heart of the Creel correspondence, though his remaining papers, which came to the Library after his death, include much that pertains to his long career as a writer.

There are, too, the papers of Brand Whitlock, Minister to Belgium, and of Henry Morgenthau, Sr., Ambassador to Turkey, both appointed by Wilson, and of Oscar S. Straus, Ambassador to Turkey, Cabinet member under earlier administrations, and a member of Wilson's Second Industrial Conference. And there are the papers of Andrew Carnegie, whose relations with the war President, beginning in the Princeton days, included a visit to Carnegie's Scottish "castle," and lasted to the end of Carnegie's life.

"I know how your heart must rejoice at the dawn of peace after these terrible years of struggle," Wilson wrote Carnegie in the winter of 1918, "for I know how long and how earnestly you have worked for and desired such conditions as I pray God it may now be possible for us to establish. The meeting place of the Peace Conference has not yet been selected, but even if it is not held at The Hague, I am sure that you will be present in spirit."

Last but not least are the papers of other Presidents of the United States, without which a study of Woodrow Wilson would be the poorer: Grover Cleveland, for some years Wilson's friend and neighbor in Princeton; Theodore Roosevelt, whom he knew in friendly fashion long before the exigencies of the Presidency drove the two men poles apart; William Howard Taft, whom he followed in the White House and from whose views in the matter of a League of Nations he diverged less widely, at one period, than might have been expected; and Calvin Coolidge,* with whom he had little or nothing in common, but whose administration must often serve (the Harding papers being to all intents and purposes nonexistent) to point up the changes wrought in the country and in its viewpoint under changed political leadership. Then, too, there are in the Library the papers of earlier Presidents, about whom Wilson himself wrote much and eloquently during his academic years, when he could afford the luxury of leisurely historical writing —Washington, Jefferson, Lincoln and the others. Of the twenty-eight Presidents from Washington through Coolidge, the Library has the papers, or the best collection of papers that has been preserved, of twenty-three, and it also has the papers of many Cabinet members. These collections, easily available as they are, have been found invaluable by scholars concerned with the development of the thinking, and the principles, and the practices of our Chief Executives.

All these papers, and others too, offer rich source material for a study of late nineteenth- and early twentieth-century history and biography. Such a network of interlocking (and constantly increasing) manuscripts for research tends at times to drive the conscientious scholar into a fine frenzy as he approaches the end of the time he has allotted for himself, but it tends also to bring him back again and again to the reading tables of the Manuscripts Division.

From these materials and others in the Library—Wilson's books in the Woodrow Wilson Room, photographs in the Prints and Photographs Division, maps, music, periodicals, Government publications, and other materials in the collections—much history, much biography in the Wilson period, has already been written. More than three hundred fifty persons have been given permission to consult the papers of Woodrow Wilson since their opening in the summer of 1940, and there have been few days, except when the Manuscripts Division was closed to research for a time during World War II, which have not seen at least one student at work there upon the Wilson and related collections. A good many studies of special phases of Wilson's career have been published, or, in the case of doctoral dissertations, made available otherwise, as have also a large number of widely varied historical studies, and biographies or autobiographies of Wilson's contemporaries. And twenty or more writers have consulted the papers with the intention of preparing biographies of Wilson or editions of his works. Ten such volumes have already been published, and it is expected that at least three or four more will appear during this centennial year.

In reviewing the notable printed record and manuscript resources of an era, one cannot fail to be impressed over and over again with the continuing pertinence of many of Woodrow Wilson's words—not for his time only, but for the years between and for our own generation. There are set down below certain of his sentences, which illustrate this curious ability to speak of the present and at the same time for the future:

The great malady of public life is cowardice. Most men are not untrue, but they are afraid. Most of the errors of public life, if my observation is to be trusted, come, not because men are morally bad, but because they are afraid of somebody. (Address of June 13, 1914, to the Princeton Class of 1879.)

. . . every man can see that the opportunity of America is going to be unparalleled and that the resources of America must be put at the service of the world as they never were put at its service before. Therefore, it is imperative that no impediments should be put in the way of commerce with the rest of the world. You cannot sell unless you buy.

Commerce is only an exalted kind of barter. (Speech of December 10, 1915, to the Columbus, Ohio, Chamber of Commerce.)

I can imagine no greater disservice to the country than to establish a system of censorship that would deny to the people of a free republic like our own their indisputable right to criticise their own public officials. (Letter of April 25, 1917, to Arthur Brisbane.)

. . . I want to utter my earnest protest against any manifestation of the spirit of lawlessness anywhere or in any cause. . . . We claim to be the greatest democratic people in the world, and democracy means first of all that we can govern ourselves. If our men have not self-control, then they are not capable of that great thing which we call democratic government. (Address of November 12, 1917, to the American Federation of Labor.)

I have not lost faith in the Russian outcome by any means. Russia, like France in a past century, will no doubt have to go through deep waters but she will come out upon firm land on the other side and her great people, for they are a great people, will in my opinion take their proper place in the world. (Letter of November 13, 1917, to Frank Clark.)

. . . when I pronounced for open diplomacy I meant not that there should be no private discussions of delicate matters, but that no secret agreement of any sort should be entered into and that all international relations, when fixed, should be open, aboveboard, and explicit. (Letter of March 12, 1918, to Robert Lansing.)

I feel that it is very dangerous to raise questions of loyalty unnecessarily, though I believe in raising them very emphatically when it is necessary. I am afraid that we are getting in a suspicious attitude towards people who are not really disloyal but merely unreasonable. We never know until a crisis like this how many of them there are in the country, and yet upon reflection it is evident that most of them do very little harm. (Letter of May 1, 1918, to Anita McCormick Blaine.)

We proudly claim to be the champions of democracy. If we really are, in deed and in truth, let us see to it that we do not discredit our own. I say plainly that every American who takes part in the action of a mob or gives it any sort of countenance is no true son of this great democracy, but its betrayer. . . . How shall we commend democracy to the acceptance of other peoples, if we disgrace our own by proving that it is, after all, no protection to the weak? (Statement of July 26, 1918.)

It will now be our fortunate duty to assist by example, by sober, friendly counsel and by material aid in the establishment of just democracy throughout the world. (Announcement of the signing of an armistice, November 11, 1918.)

It is moral force that is irresistible. It is moral force as much as physical that has defeated the effort to subdue the world. (Address of December 29, 1918, at the Lowther Street Congregational Church, Carlisle, England.)

I am not hopeful that the individual items of the settlements which we are about to attempt will be altogether satisfactory. One has but to apply his mind to any one of the questions of boundary and of altered sovereignty and of racial aspiration to do something more than conjecture that there is no man and no body of men who know just how it ought to be settled. . . .

So that we must provide a machinery of readjustment. . . . (Address of December 30, 1918, at Manchester, England.)

Force can always be conquered, but the spirit of liberty never can be . . . (Speech of January 5, 1919, at La Scala, in Milan, Italy.)

If America were at this juncture to fail the world, what would come of it? . . . I do not mean any disrespect to any other great people when I say that America is the hope of the world. And if she does not justify that hope results are unthinkable. (Address of February 24, 1919, in Boston, Mass.)

An admirable spirit of self-sacrifice, of patriotic devotion, and of community action guided and inspired us while the fighting was on. We shall need all these now, and need them in a heightened degree, if we are to accomplish the first tasks of peace. They are more difficult than the tasks of war,—more complex, less easily understood;—and require more intelligence, patience, and sobriety. (Reply of August 25, 1919, to representatives of the Railway Employees' Department of the American Federation of Labor.)

America is necessary to the peace of the world. And reverse the proposition: The peace and good will of the world are necessary to America. (Address of September 8, 1919, at Sioux Falls, S. D.)

Our choice in this great enterprise of mankind . . . is only this: Shall we go in and assist as trusted partners or shall we stay out and act as suspected rivals? We have got to do one or the other. We have got to be either provincials or statesmen. (Address of September 9, 1919, at Minneapolis, Minn.)

The immediate need of this country and of the world is peace not only, but settled peace, peace upon a definite and well-understood foundation, supported by such covenants as men can depend upon, supported by such purposes as will permit of a concert of action throughout all the free peoples of the world. (Address of September 18, 1919, at San Francisco, Calif.)

Stop for a moment to think about the next war, if there should be one. I do not hesitate to say that the war we have just been through, though it was shot through with terror of every kind, is not to be compared with the war we would have to face next time. (Address of September 25, 1919, at Denver, Colo.)

. . . there is only one way to assure the world of peace; that is by making it so dangerous to break the peace that no other nation will have the audacity to attempt it. (Address of October 27, 1920, to Pro-League Republicans.)

The sum of the whole matter is this, that our civilization cannot survive materially unless it be redeemed spiritually. (Wilson's last published article, "The Road Away from Revolution," August 1923.)

The Prophet

WILSON TO ASIA
WILSON TO SOUTH AMERICA
WILSON TO EUROPE
WILSON TO THE UNITED NATIONS

Just as in the Biblical parallel of Elijah, the prophet of inspiration, and Elisha, the prophet of action, on whose shoulders the mantle of Elijah's vision fell—so it seems that in this 20th Century, Wilson is the prophet of inspiration whose mantle of vision is falling on the shoulders of people of action throughout the world, people in far and near places who are striving each in his or her own way to perpetuate Wilson's call to faith, honor and peace among all men. Thus as "The Prophet" is Wilson honored by the catholic authors of the following chapter.

—EDITOR'S NOTE

Wilson to Asia

MADAME CHIANG KAI-SHEK

To recall the wisdom, the philosophy, and the high idealism of Woodrow Wilson is to note in contrast the international amorality of his day. In retrospect Wilson's ethics stand out strikingly against a background of cynicism, a mad scramble on the part of other national leaders for spheres of influence in China or for colonies in Southeast Asia.

Some of these statesmen resorted to tricks in international affairs which in private dealings they would probably have been the first to condemn. Exploitation, chicanery and secret deals were the order of the day, for the criterion of diplomacy was not honor but political advantage. To be sure, this attitude was nothing new, since for centuries the survival-of-the-fittest theory implied that all was fair in political and economic domination of weaker peoples.

Although the Monroe Doctrine and John Hay's Open Door Policy bespoke a different American concept in international affairs, it was not until Wilson advocated building on right and justice to all nations, weak or strong, that the world at large began to realize that a new order might replace the old. Like shafts of lightning his oft-enunciated principles that peoples are not pawns, that governments must rest on the consent of the governed, that small nations as well as great powers have the right of self-determination, illuminated the murkiness of the international horizon. He had a conviction that America was founded to show mankind the way to liberty. "To conquer with arms," he said to Congress on Armistice Day, 1918, "is to make only a temporary conquest; to conquer the world by earning its esteem is to make permanent conquest." (j)

Wilson was explicit that on temporal things (what might be called nonessentials) it was permissible to yield ground, shift one's viewpoint, or even give up the struggle, but in matters of eternal principle, where one is dealing with ultimate truths, no compromise is possible. In anticipation of the end of the war, he said: "There can be but one issue. The settlement must be final. There can be no compromise. No halfway decision is conceivable. These are the ends for which the associated peoples of the world are fighting, and which must be conceded before there can be peace." (k) Adamant as Wilson was against Clemenceau's proposal of crushing Germany, and aware that Lloyd George was re-elected premier on the slogan "Be tough on Germany," he could doggedly resist the kind of settlement which would "leave a sting, a resentment, a bitter memory" (l) and yet at the same time avoid the compromises and concessions which would rob the peoples of both sides of the rights and liberties which he regarded as their birthright.

Although faced with the stubborn opposition of "a small willful group of men" (m) within his own government as well as the obstruction of some of the allied statesmen (who paid lip-service to his proposed League of Nations while jockeying for territorial advantage behind the scenes), he persevered in bringing the international organization into being. He sought to appeal directly to the peoples of the world over the heads of their rulers for a secure and permanent peace based on right and justice, and a League of Nations with the power of collective security to keep the peace. "Justice," he avowed, "has nothing to do with expediency, justice has nothing to do with any temporary standard whatsoever. It is rooted and grounded in the fundamental instincts of humanity." (n)

Everything President Wilson had to say about making the world safe for democracy, and about a new covenant in a League of Nations to ensure peace, was wholeheartedly approved and accepted by China. China had suffered so much from unjust treaties imposed from without, and from the carving of the Chinese melon (the spheres of influence) among the great powers, that a peace based on equality between nations, of mutual guarantees of political independence and territorial integrity, to great and small, strong and weak alike, was warmly received in China. All that Wilson said about "tranquility of the spirit and a sense of justice, of freedom and of right" [o] was harmonious with the Confucian ethics of China.

A nation which had not been warlike welcomed the proposal that nations should avoid armament races. A nation, where spheres of special rights had been established by rival powers, welcomed Wilson's idea that the Monroe Doctrine should become a world doctrine, with each nation left free to determine its own policy, unhindered, unthreatened and unafraid.

But perhaps China's hopes for a new era did not soar as high as those of other Asian nations because of the immediate disillusionment felt among the entire Chinese people when Shantung was allowed by the Versailles Treaty to become Japan's sphere of influence. President Wilson, vexed with problems at home, thwarted at the Peace Conference, thought it the best settlement that could be achieved at the time. He hoped that his dreamed-of League of Nations could later adjust the inequities of the Treaty.

But to the Chinese people this was the most sacred province of all China, the national shrine of our great sage Confucius. It was a rich agricultural province with fine seaports and harbors. If all that had been said about one nation supporting another's just rights, even when its own interests were involved, meant anything, then the West would see to it that Japan gave back to China at once what was indisputably China's territory, now wrested from Germany. This was China's first and great disillusionment with the New Order. An unharried Wilson might have been able to secure justice for China in Shantung, but Wilson was beset before and behind. Backstage Japan was bent on hegemony at the expense of China and allied statesmen were determined to crush Germany. Back home a handful of powerful men determined to keep America out of the League of Nations.

His influence on Asia, however, was like the planting of seeds. Taking a long-range view, it is perhaps unimportant that the harvest did not ripen during his lifetime. At least his moral standards were impeccable, and from that time all Asian peoples have yearned for the fulfillment of his ideals.

In application Wilson's ideas were sometimes impractical for the times. Or, as in the case of Asia, his ideas were misapplied for lack of knowledge and understanding of the situation. His intentions toward China were of the best, but—like others who have followed him—he was not a close student of the Far East. Hence there were at least two unfortunate paradoxes.

In his desire not to infringe on China's political integrity, he reversed the policy of his predecessor Taft and caused the withdrawal of America from the six-nation consortium. It left five powers with less noble designs on China to vie with each other for an economic stranglehold on our country. The paradox was that later Wilson found it necessary to reverse his own position and initiate a new consortium.

A second paradox was his tacit approval of Yuan Shih-kai's abortive monarchical movement. Yuan was a selfish and wily politician of the feudal type. Sun Yat-sen was struggling to establish government on the very principles of right and justice which the American President so ardently espoused. But because Sun Yat-sen's colleagues, the very men who caused the downfall of the Manchus and established the fledgling Chinese Republic, were young and inexperienced, Wilson dismissed them as hotheads disturbing internal unity and peace which he considered of paramount importance, and hence failed to aid the democratic process in China. Again his motives were of the best; his knowledge of Chinese affairs limited. This has happened so many times in the course of Chinese-American relations that it cannot be overlooked.

No doubt the ideals of self-determination, self-government, independence, territorial integrity and political freedom proclaimed by Woodrow Wilson affected the peoples of all Asia, including the underdeveloped areas and the colonies. To varying degrees they caught his vision, they glimpsed the goal. Perhaps someday an exhaustive study may be made picking up the threads in such countries as India, Indonesia, Burma, Thailand and Korea, to weave a pattern of the whole. In the meantime, the free nations of both East and West might do well to review the high ideals of international morality and integrity inherent in Woodrow Wilson's ideology, and thus restore hope and faith in peoples who have again and again been "thrown back upon the bitterness of disappointment not only, but also the bitterness of despair." (p) Only in this way can the people of Asia aspire to reach the goal envisioned in the lightninglike flashes of Wilson's clear pronouncements; only in this way can the hopes of the peoples of the world be fulfilled.

Wilson to South America

LUIS QUINTANILLA

IN order to consider exclusively the historical contribution of Woodrow Wilson to the idea of a League of Nations and his concept of a world order, I will leave out altogether any reference to controversial aspects of Wilson's foreign policy which affected seriously various countries of Latin America.

International order, as embodied in the United Nations and long before that in the Pan-American movement, is a Western Hemisphere contribution to world politics. It was in America where, for the first time, governments decided to set up an international organization: the "Union of the American Republics." At present, in view of the spectacular position occupied by the United Nations, few people seem aware of the American antecedents of the world organization; but we Americans, North and South, can never forget them.

Over a century ago the South American Liberator, Simon Bolivar advocated an inter-American association—he liked to refer to it as "The Nation"—in which all the new Republics of America would find themselves so united as to ensure each other's sovereignty. At his invitation, the first International Conference of the American Republics met in Panama in 1826. Anticipating the event, Bolivar said, in 1815: "May God grant that some day we may have the happiness of installing there an august Congress to discuss and study the high interests of peace and war with the nations of the world." And, in a document dated February, 1826, Bolivar predicted: "The New World will be composed of independent nations, all bound together by a common law that will determine their external relations.

. . . Perhaps in the march of centuries *one* nation alone—the Federal Nation—will embrace the universe." That is to say, Bolivar envisioned both a regional organization and an eventual world organization. The inter-American system would, for him, serve as an inspiration for the future world organization; in fact, Bolivar had expressed such ideas since 1812 and 1815. A century later, Wilson knowingly or unknowingly followed Bolivar's plan. True, other people in America, as well as in Europe, had thought of maintaining international peace through some kind of world organization, but Bolivar and Wilson, as Chief Executives, not only advocated the idea, they implemented it.

In Bolivar's proposal for the coming Congress in Panama, he predicted that "The day our Plenipotentiaries make the exchanges of their powers, will stamp in the diplomatic history of the world an immortal epoch." And he added: "When after centuries posterity shall search for the origin of our public law and shall remember the compacts that solidify its destiny, they will finger with respect the Protocols of Panama. In them they will find the plan of the first alliance that shall sketch the mark of our relations with the universe." In later instructions issued by him on May 18, 1825, Bolivar stated: "You shall make every effort to secure the great compact of Union, League and Perpetual Confederation. . . . You shall see that the proclamation . . . contains an energetic and efficient declaration . . . in regard to the necessity . . . of abandoning all ideas of further colonization on this continent, and in opposition to the principle of intervention in our domestic affairs. . . . You shall endeavor to negotiate a Treaty by which all the new American states be united in a close alliance. . . . You shall see that the Treaties agreed upon at the Great Federal Congress of the American States . . . be promulgated as the public law of America."

In the document of February, 1826, mentioned earlier, Bolivar further summarized his view on the coming inter-American Assembly: "This Congress seems destined to form the largest, most extraordinary, and strongest *League* [ital. by ed.] that has yet appeared on the face of the earth. . . . Mankind will give a thousand blessings to this League. . . . Political society will be given a Code of Public Law to be used as a rule of universal conduct in their relations. . . . The very life of these new states will receive new guarantees. . . . None will be inferior to others and none stronger. A perfect equilibrium will be established in this truly new order of things. The power of all would come to the rescue of any that might suffer from external aggression. . . . Differences of origin and race will lose influence and strength. . . . Social reform will be reached under the holy auspices of liberty and social peace. . . ." Here we have, in the year 1826, about a century before the League of Nations, the substance of international order and world organization. Even the name *League* of nations was there! And those were not just words; Bolivar did not rest until the Panama Congress took place.

Four treaties were approved at Panama, the most important one being that of Perpetual Union, League and Confederation (July 15, 1826). The three others were: an agreement providing that the permanent inter-American Congress should meet periodically in Mexico; a Convention fixing the contingent of troops of each Republic for a permanent inter-American army of eighty thousand men; and an agreement additional to the conventional contingents, regarding the organization of the army. Only Colombia approved them partially; the Congresses of Peru, Mexico and Guatemala failed to ratify them. The United States, whose Congress had bitterly opposed Bolivar's initiative on the grounds that the North American Republic was against commitments which could limit its freedom of action, was not represented at Panama, although it did send finally and most reluctantly two plenipotentiaries; one died during the trip and when the other finally reached Panama, the meeting had ended.

The main Treaty approved in Panama contained twenty-one Articles. It embodied and implemented the principle of what is now known as "collective security." Its objective, reads the Pact, "will be to maintain in common, defensively and offensively, should occasion arise, the sovereignty and independence of all and each of the confederated powers. . . . To secure to them from this time forward the enjoyment of unalterable peace and to promote in this behalf better harmony and good understanding. . . . The contracting Parties obligate and bind themselves mutually to defend themselves against against every attack which shall endanger their political existence, and employ against the enemies of the independence of all or any of them, their influence, resources, and naval and land forces which . . . each is bound to contribute for maintaining the common cause." What could the League of Nations, the United Nations, or the Organization of American States add to Bolivar's Pact? Very little, indeed! Rather, those three international organizations are still trailing behind Bolivar's initial plan; for the Bolivarian Pact, aside from introducing collective security, included the creaton of an international army, the adoption of conciliation and arbitration for the settlement of *all* disputes between governments, the protection of human rights, the condemnation of all forms of colonialism, the adoption of continental citizenship, and various other significant measures. A hundred years later another great American, this time a President of the United States, renewed Bolivar's fight.

Wilson met the same tenacious opposition that Bolivar had encountered a century before; the selfish power of national interests, the shortsightedness of local politicians, the lure of isolation. But, like Bolivar, Wilson was in reality never defeated. It merely took time for America to understand both.

Wilson's original contribution to the League of Nations was basically the controversial Article XI of the League Covenant, concerning collective security; a principle previously and clearly proclaimed by Bolivar in Article III of the Panama Treaty. Yet, there existed fundamental differences between Bolivar and Wilson. Bolivar was a Liberator, a warrior. His sword emancipated from the Spanish Crown the territory of what are today six Latin-American countries, including his own Venezuela. Wilson shared Bolivar's broad international vision but he was a moralist, a missionary of democracy. One should never separate his devotion for international order from his passion for democracy. Thus his firm determination to place internationalism at the service of democracy was certainly Woodrow Wilson's distinction.

He was unquestionably a dedicated and militant democrat. He yearned for democracy, not only in his own United States but in the world at large; democracy, of course, as Wilson understood it, democracy as reflected in the American way of life. No one can doubt the nobility of his purpose. It resulted, however, in many a predicament for the Washington government. Interventionism is interventionism, whether it be "good" or "bad." Latin Americans rightfully considered Wilson's inter-American policy as just another form of interventionism. Yet, in all fairness, one must keep in mind that Wilson was personally a sincere believer in the principle of self-determination; in fact, he urged all nations to associate themselves in the League of Nations, so as to ensure permanently their respective independence and sovereignty.

Wilson's self-contradictions are the product of his two currents of thought. On the one hand, he wanted an international organization in order to maintain a permanent international peace which would guarantee the freedom of all countries and their absolute sovereignty. On the other hand he endeavored, with equal zeal, to extend democratic rule to peoples of the entire world. Both these motives are praiseworthy, but their combination proved difficult because unless all countries spontaneously adopted a similar type of democracy, how could a world organization impose a universal type of democracy without infringing upon national sovereignty?

On March 11, 1913, Wilson made a Declaration of Policy in regard to Latin America, in which he explained: "Co-operation among the American Republics, is possible only when supported at every turn by the orderly process of just government based upon law, not upon arbitrary or irregular force. We hold . . . that just government rests always upon the consent of the governed . . . we can have no sympathy with those who seek to seize the power of government to advance their own personal interests or ambition. . . . As friends, therefore, we shall prefer those who . . . respect the restraints of constitutional provision." The outspoken Declaration was transmitted to all the United States diplomatic officials abroad.

Latin America served as Woodrow Wilson's proving ground not only for his policy of internationalism but for his policy of *democratic* internationalism. This explains Wilson's use of non-recognition as a sanction against militaristic *coups d'état*, a practice which, again, was criticized as intervention for different reasons. The messianic United States President once exclaimed: "We intend to teach the Latin-American countries to have good rulers." His thirst for moral leadership, his apostolic spirit, made him embark the Washington administration upon a crusade for good government;

it being understood that "good" was the North American model, and "bad" was whatever departed from it.

In his address before the Southern Commercial Congress at Mobile, Alabama, on October 27, 1913, President Wilson, referring to Pan Americanism—to which, in spite of his mistakes in hemisphere policy, he was sincerely devoted—said that the future was "going to be very different for this Hemisphere than the past"; that the states lying to the south would be "drawn closer to us by innumerable ties" into a spiritual union, so that the opening of the Panama Canal would also open the world to "a commerce . . . of intelligence, thought, and sympathy between North and South."

The countries of Latin America, he then said, were also going to see an emancipation from subordination to foreign enterprise, such as had resulted from the granting of "concessions" to foreign capitalists. The United States ought to be the first to take part in assisting Latin America in that emancipation. "Human rights, national integrity and opportunity as against material interests"; this, in Wilson's memorable words, was the issue to be faced.

One of the charges formerly leveled at Latin-American governments was that they seem slow or unwilling to pay their loans. It should be said in all fairness, commented Wilson, that quite often those abusive loans could never be repaid. Speaking of Mexico, he pointed out: "What Mexico needs more than anything else is financial support which will not involve the sale of her liberties and the enslavement of her people. I am speaking of a system and not uttering an indictment. The system by which Mexico has been financially assisted has in the past generally bound her hand and foot. . . . It has almost in every instance deprived her people of the part they were entitled to play in the determination of their own destiny and development." Coming from a United States President, that is indeed a courageous criticism.

In a message to the Congress, on December 7, 1915, Wilson concluded: "The moral is, that the states of America are not hostile rivals but co-operating friends, and that their growing sense of community of interest, alike in matters political and in matters economic, is likely to give them a new significance as factors of international affairs and in the political history of the world. It presents them as in a very deep and true sense a unit in world affairs, spiritual partners, standing together because thinking together, quick with common sympathies and common ideals. Separated, they are subject to all the crosscurrents of the confused politics of a world of hostile rivalries; united in spirit and purpose, they cannot be disappointed of their peaceful destiny. This is Pan-Americanism. It has none of the spirit of Empire in it. It is the embodiment, the effectual embodiment, of the spirit of law and independence and liberty and mutual service." And Woodrow Wilson went further. In the winter of 1914-15 the President sounded out the representatives of some Latin-American countries at Washington as to the possibility of signing with the United States a Treaty for "the mutual guarantee of territorial integrity and political independence, under republican forms of government." Later on, the sensational proposal was officially transmitted to all the governments of the Western Hemisphere. The proposed draft of Wilson's Pan-American Treaty should be well known to all those interested in the growth of international organization. It reads as follows:

"Article I. That the high contracting Parties of this solemn covenant and agreement, hereby join one another in a common and mutual *guarantee of territorial integrity and of political independence* under republican forms of government.

"Article II. To give definite application to the guarantee set forth in Article I, the high contracting Parties severally covenant to endeavor forthwith to reach a *settlement of all disputes* as to boundary of territory now pending between them by amicable agreement or by means of international arbitration.

"Article III. That the high contracting Parties further agree: first, that all questions, of whatever character, arising between two or more of them which cannot be settled by the ordinary means of diplomatic correspondence shall, before any declaration of war or beginning of hostilities, be first submitted to a *permanent international commission for investigation,* one year being allowed for such investigation; and second, that, if the dispute is not settled by investigation, to submit the same to arbitration, provided the question in dispute does not affect the honor, independence or vital interests of the nations concerned or the interests of third Parties.

"Article IV. To the end that domestic tranquility may prevail within their territories the high contracting Parties further severally covenant and agree that they will not permit the departure from their respective jurisdictions of any *military or naval expedition* hostile to the established government of any of the high contracting parties, and that they will prevent the exportation from their respective jurisdictions of arms, ammunition or other munitions of war destined to or for the use of any person or persons notified to be in insurrection or revolt against the established government of any of the high contracting Parties."

Together with the all-embracing Treaty of Confederation drafted by Bolivar and signed at the historic Assembly of Panama in 1826, this project submitted by Wilson is one of the most important documents in the growth of Pan-Americanism. It contains an implicit abandonment of the narrow, unilateral spirit of the Monroe Doctrine. Pan-Americanism, as outlined by Wilson, was a policy of "partners," with no self-appointed "guardian" as beneficiary. That Wilson had his Pan-American Pact very much at heart, is evident. A scholarly interpreter of the great President's policy, Ray Stannard Baker, wrote: "His heart was indeed set upon the achievement of the new pact, for its implications were far flung. If he were to ask the war-torn world to accept the basic elements of such an agreement in forming a League of Nations, he must omit no effort to apply it practically in the Western Hemisphere. It would make us 'partners' with South and Central America, 'rather than guardians.' He thought it a 'great step in advance.' " And indeed it was.

No other Chief of State, not even Bolivar, had been more emphatically world-minded. And it adds to Wilson's credit that he was a citizen of a most powerful country. Had he simply followed the easy trend of nationalism, Wilson could have committed the United States to a continuation of the ruthless "Big Stick" policy. Instead, he chose to stand as a defender of international justice. The physical might of his great country never intoxicated his spirit. More than anything else, mankind was his concern. Listen to his voice: "We are participants, whether we would or not, in the life of the world. The interests of all nations are our own also. . . . What affects mankind is inevitably our affair. . . . The principle of public right must henceforth take precedence over the individual interests of particular nations. . . . Alliance must not be set up against alliance. . . . The nations of the world have become each other's neighbors. . . . This is undoubtedly the thought of America. . . . We believe these fundamental things: *first*, that every people has a right to choose the sovereignty under which they shall live. Like other nations, we have ourselves no doubt once and again offended against that principle. . . . *Second*, that the small States of the world have a right to enjoy the same respect for their sovereignty and for their territorial integrity that great and powerful nations expect and insist upon. *Third*, that the world has a right to be free from every disturbance of its peace that has its origin in aggression. . . ."

Two years after, Wilson delivered his famous Fourteen Points message in which he defined the philosophy and structure of the League of Nations. "We entered this war," he emphasized, "because violations of right have occurred. . . . What we demand . . . is nothing peculiar to ourselves. It is that the world be made fit and safe to live in. . . . All the peoples of the world are . . . partners in this interest, and for our own part we see very clearly that unless justice be done to others it will not be done to us. . . . A general association of nations must be formed under specific covenants for the purpose of affording mutual guarantees of political independence and territorial integrity to great and small states alike." In this last, fourteenth point of that immortal message, one finds the gist of Article X of the League's final Covenant, the drafting of which is believed by many to constitute the outstanding original contribution made by Woodrow Wilson to the text of the Covenant.

Article X is fundamental because it expresses the essence of the world League. It stipulates that "the members of the League undertake to respect and preserve as against external aggression the territorial integrity and existing political independence of all members of the League"; and that "in case of any such aggression, the council shall advise upon the means by which this obligation shall be fulfilled." In 1826, in his Pact of Panama, Bolívar had proclaimed an identical principle. Article II of said Pact stated: "The object of this perpetual contract will be to maintain in common . . . the sovereignty and independence of all and each . . . and to secure to themselves . . . the enjoyment of unalterable peace." And Article III read: "The contracting Parties obligate and bind themselves mutually to defend themselves against every attack which shall endanger their political existence. . . ." The similitude between the Bolivarian and the Wilsonian Articles is striking, but, as we must always keep in mind, Wilson was not alone a soldier of universal Peace, he was basically an evangelist of Democracy. On January 25, 1919, in an address before the second plenary session of the Peace Conference, Wilson stressed the democratic philosophy of his proposed League: "I may say . . . that we are not Representatives of governments but representatives of peoples. It will not suffice to satisfy governmental circles anywhere. It is necessary that we should satisfy the opinion of mankind. . . ." And to underline the popular character of true democracy and democratic diplomacy, Wilson went on to say: "Gentlemen, the select classes of mankind are no longer the governors of mankind. The fortunes of mankind are now in the hands of the plain people of the whole world, and you have justified their confidence not only, but established peace. Fail to satisfy them, and no arrangement that you can make will either set up or steady the peace of the world." We could never overestimate the timeliness and the soundness of Wilson's warning. He is the ideological bridge between Abraham Lincoln and Franklin D. Roosevelt: three genuine North American leaders of the people. The people, democracy and international peace were, in Wilson's mind, inseparable. This philosophy led him to come out against militarism, not only as a danger to international peace but as a definite danger to national democratic institutions at home. In a memorable passage of a lengthy address to the United States Senate on July 10, 1919, when the President was submitting the peace treaty for ratification, he emphasized: "Restive peoples had been told (before World War I) that fleets and armies, which they toiled to sustain, meant peace; and they now know that they had been lied to; that fleets and armies had been maintained to promote national ambitions and meant war. They knew that no old policy meant anything else but force, force—always force. And they knew that it was intolerable. Every true heart in the world, and every enlighted judgment demanded that . . . every government . . . should lend itself to a new purpose and utterly destroy the old order of international politics." Wilson believed in reason. He was an intellectual. He spoke with deep concern of the "terror that lay concealed in every Balance of Power." He was for a "Concert of power," and not for a "Balance" which could only lead (and history is there to back

Wilson's contention) to bigger and more dreadful wars. The League was to end for all time "power politics" and precarious "balances," or antagonistic alliances. The strengthening of national armies would, in his opinion, undermine the nature and the mechanism of the world organization.

In a statement to the members of the Senate Committee on Foreign Relations (August 19, 1919), the wartime President linked national with international security, and made it very clear that we cannot, as nations, know how big an army we need "until we know how peace is to be sustained, whether by the arms of single nations or by the concert of all the great peoples."

Revolutions did not scare him too much. At Columbus, Ohio, on September 4, 1919, he asked: "Have you ever reflected, my fellow countrymen, on the real source of revolution?" And here are the answers he gave us: "Men do not start revolution in a sudden fashion. . . . Revolutions do not spring up over night. Revolutions come from the long suppression of the human spirit. Revolutions come because men know that they have rights and that they are disregarded. . . . We are going to leave it to the people themselves, as we should have done, what government they shall live under." Two days later, at Kansas City, Missouri, Wilson dealt again with the danger of militarism. In a long address, which will remain as a masterpiece of democratic theory, he patiently explained why sincere democrats ought to fear military power. "You know, my fellow citizens," said he, "what armaments mean? Great standing armies and great stores of war material. They do not mean burdensome taxation merely, they do not mean merely compulsory military service which saps the economic strength of the nation, but they mean also the building up of a military class. . . . So soon as you have a military class, it does not make any difference what your form of government is. If you are determined to be armed to the teeth, you must obey the orders and directions of the only men who can control the great machinery of war. Elections are of minor importance. . . . That is the meaning of armaments. It is not merely the cost of it, though that is overwhelming, but it is the spirit of it, and America has never and I hope, in the providence of God, never will have that spirit. . . ." It was natural for a universal intellect, like Wilson possessed, to oppose "classes" of all kind, whether military or economic. Referring to the latter, he spoke in this same speech with equal courage: "My fellow citizens," said Wilson, "it does not make any difference what kind of a minority governs you if it is a minority, and the thing we must see to is that no minority anywhere masters the majority. If it is proved that any class, any group, anywhere, is, without the suffrage of their fellow citizens, in control of our affairs, then I am with you to destroy the power of that group." Since Abraham Lincoln, no Chief Executive had spoken with deeper revolutionary conviction.

The democratic fire burning in Wilson's heart made him place the interests of mankind always above any other. Could it be argued that, because of such position, he underrated the national interest? It would be most unfair to answer that question affirmatively. The patriotism of the eminent President cannot be questioned by any sane person. Wilson was at all times a great patriot. But he never saw a reason why the interest of his own United States could not adjust itself to the interest of mankind. On the contrary, he felt that international security, based on a world order and a League of Nations, was not only the best but the only guaranty of permanent security for the United States or any other country. In other words, only justice could bring security, never sheer force. In Mobile, on October 27, 1913, the moralist President denounced expediency: "It is a very perilous thing to determine the foreign policy of a nation in the terms of material interests. . . . We dare not turn from the principle that morality and not expediency is the thing that must guide us, and that we will never condone inequity because it is most convenient to do so." As indicated in Professor Morgenthau's recent survey of "American Foreign Policy," Wilson's wartime speeches are but an elaboration of this philosophy. On September 27, 1918, Wilson once more criticized military alliances and power politics: "There can be no leagues or alliances or special convenants and understandings within the general and common family of the League of Nations. . . . Special alliances and economic rivalries and hostilities have been the prolific source in the modern world of the plans and passions that produce war. It would be an insincere as well as insecure peace that did not exclude them in definite and binding terms. . . . This is a people's war, not a statesmen's." And then followed this other typically Wilsonian warning: "Statesmen must follow the clarified common thought, or be broken."

Wilson knew that, whether popular or not during his life time, the peace policy proclaimed by him from Washington was going to start a new chapter of history, and shape more constructively the world of tomorrow. Never, thought he, could we go back. He had infinite faith in human progress. Mankind would never remain still, and it could only go forward. "The day we have left behind us," he proclaimed at Los Angeles on September 20, 1919, "was a day of balances of power. It was a day of every nation take care of itself or make a partnership with some other nation or group of nations to hold the peace of the world steady or to dominate the weaker portions of the world." The American voice that spoke to future generations with such insight, clarity and bravery, will continue to be heard for centuries to come. And the world of tomorrow, living at last without fear, will forever remember Woodrow Wilson's fight to establish on this earth of ours a universal order which will ensure mankind the happiness of peace, and the blessings of democracy.

Wilson to Europe

BOGUMIL VOSNJAK

I HAD during my life the chance to meet three really great men: Leo Tolstoi in Jasnaja poljana, Thomas G. Masaryk and Woodrow Wilson. These three men shaped in a certain way the destiny of Europe. Being a great artist, Christian and writer Tolstoi was a foe of the state. He was partially responsible that the Russian elite began to hate the state, paving unconsciously the way for the Bolshevik revolution. Masaryk on the contrary, imbued by the traditions of Hussitism, received from these traditions the baptism of Czech nationalism, but he possessed also a sound conception of what modern state life has to be. Born in a Presbyterian manse Wilson was, like Tolstoi, a follower of Christ, a really great Christian, but he, the Professor of Political Science, had naturally a positive attitude to the state. It cannot be otherwise because he is reared in the traditions of democracy, so familiar to the great Virginians of the pattern of a Thomas Jefferson.

All three are prophets. As we have radio speakers, columnists, men who are making public opinion, so had Israel its prophets. Naturally the mechanized trend of modern life creates the slant toward platitude. Therefore there will never be shaped out of modern makers of public opinion such formidable leaders of their people as were the Jewish prophets. These real first democrats were the representatives of their peoples who accused the unlawful rulers, who defended the downtrodden, the poor and oppressed. But their fate was often tragic. Betrayed by those for whose sake they sacrificed themselves their lives were martyrdom and often they paid with their lives for the high ideals they proclaimed for the sake of their peoples.

The destiny of these three leaders of mankind is different. Tolstoi is by birth an aristocrat who shares all the privileges of his caste but ravaged by some internal unrest he leaves his Jasnaja poljana and dies in the shabby room of a stationmaster far away from the comfort he was accustomed to enjoy during his life, far away from his family.

Masaryk was a happy man. Of humble origin, a controversial figure in the life of his nation before the outbreak of the First World War, he hoarded in his life such a wealth of ideals that the prophet emerged when the hour struck. Destiny determined that he became in the spirit of Plato, a ruler-philosopher. He created a happy democratic commonwealth for a people which adored him. But his life on the zenith of his achievement is in the shadow of a tragedy. As triumphant he entered Prag, he found his wife mentally alienated as the consequence of police persecution. But nevertheless he was able in a high age to rule his people efficiently in a thoroughly democratic way. Again fate was in his favor. He died just in time not to be a witness of the downfall of the republic.

The case of Woodrow Wilson is another one. Late he is entering public life. He is admirably trained by his father to give to his thoughts a brilliant shape. He reaches without great effort the highest honor an American can reach, the Presidency. Seldom a man was so prepared to take over such responsibilities. Ideal is his conscientiousness to perform his duties towards America and mankind. He gives in his speeches the greatest eulogy of America an American ever uttered. He declared in Washington April 19, 1915: "We are interested in the United States, politically speaking, in nothing but human liberty." "We are custodians of the spirit of righteousness, of the spirit of equal handed justice, of the spirit of the law with the perfectibility of human life itself," (Washington, D.C., October 20, 1914.) "We are the predestined mediators of mankind," (St. Paul, Minn. September 9, 1919.) "America is not ahead of other nations because she is rich. Nothing makes America great except her thoughts, except her ideals . . ." (Denver, May 7, 1911.) Seldom in an American statesman the conception prevailed so strongly as in Wilson that America is the leader of mankind, because she is the representative of the highest democratic traditions.

Among these three men Wilson is not favored by the goddess who distributes good and evil men have to endure. The acknowledged leader of this people is not able to realize his own vision of a happy commonwealth of men. In the deciding moment the leading power left the arena and the consequences were disastrous for mankind. The ailing President in his residence in S Street, in the capital of the United States, must be a witness of the temporary breakdown of his ideals. But too strong were the foundations of the edifice he built. The ideas of Wilson are today stronger than they were in the days of his greatest triumph. They are living. He is revenged.

The clear conception what to do with the Empire of the Habsburgs did not ripen suddenly in the mind of Wilson. There are years of hesitation. Germany is for him the great aggressor, not Austria-Hungary.

The thesis of the Czechoslovaks and Yugoslavs was that only the dissolution of the Monarchy was the unique political solution of the Habsburg problem. In May arrived Masaryk in Washington. It is a pity that among the Wilson papers in the Library of Congress no report about the talks between Wilson and Masaryk exists. The witness who brought Masaryk to the first visit in the White House told me that the audience had to be very short, but it lasted hours and hours. During this audience in the White House the destiny of the Dual Monarchy was decided.

On June 29, 1918, the Department of State issued notice that it was the wish of the President and of the secretary that all branches of the Slav race be made completely free of German and Austrian rule.

The great slogan, the "self-determination of nations," reached the Adriatic Sea and the Balkan peninsula. Wilson was pleading for the agreement of the people in all questions of reciprocal relations, eventually by means of a plebiscite. War against secret diplomacy was another Wilsonian endeavor.

Woodrow Wilson declared already in Washington, D.C. on May 27, 1916: "We believe these fundamental things: First, that every people has a right to choose the sovereignty under which they shall live. . . . Second, that the small states have a right to enjoy the same respect for their sovereignty and their territorial integrity that great and powerful nations expect and insist upon."

Again, Woodrow Wilson declared in April, 1917: "We are glad . . . to fight for the liberation of all peoples—the German people included—for the rights of nations great and small and the privilege of men everywhere to choose their way of life and of obedience."

Such words of the acknowledged leader of American democracy was dynamite for the public life of Austria-Hungary. The miraculous oratory of Wilson in fact dismembered the monarchy.

To illustrate the spirit which pervaded the Yugoslavs in Europe and America in those days, I will give the text of two documents I found among the Wilson Papers in the Library of Congress. The first is the Declaration submitted by the Yugoslav National Council in Washington, D.C., speaking in the name of the Yugoslavs in the United States and also those of the Austro-Hungarian monarchy, to Woodrow Wilson on July 4, 1919: "The principle of self-determination of nations which you, Mr. President, in the name of American democracy so solemnly proclaimed to the whole world, is on its victorious march, and there is no force that could prevent its complete triumph. In the victory of this principle our nation sees its salvation. Encouraged by the strong and indomitable will of the United States to fight under your leadership for this lofty principle to the bitter end, our people, within and without Austria-Hungary are ready to sacrifice all for their liberty and for the victory of democracy over autocracy.

"Our nation, exhausted after centuries of bloody struggle against German imperialism and after countless sacrifices for liberty but still unbroken spirit, is looking to you, Mr. President, to lead it into the final battle. For this struggle our nation is offering without reserve all its energies, its life and wealth."

And second—the solemn Declaration of the Czechoslovak people to the Republic of the U.S.A. and its great President, on July 4, 1918: "We loyal Czechoslovaks of America . . . stand with all the might we possess behind you and your President. . . . We came here from the land of suffering and oppression. It is on this account that we hailed America like a rising sun after the dark night of humiliation. And she received us from the first moment we set foot on her soil—the big sun of a freer, happier life than that we had lived in our oppressed native land. There was the voice of a man speaking the message of God's brightest angel: 'The world must be made safe for Democracy.' . . . Millions of eyes of the suffering nations look to you over the oceans—ten millions of our people in Europe, one million of sons and daughters of this land . . . greet their new Country."

The feeling of the common man of Slav origin of those days is expressed wonderfully in the letter of an anonymous, unkown young Slovene soldier which has been submitted by the Secretary of Defense, Newton D. Baker, from Cleveland to the President May 3, 1918. This unknown soldier writes to his parents: "Indeed, how I love my young healthy life, how I long to be free again, going on my own way, but alas, am I justified to think of my own liberty and happy life when the moment is here that calls on every young man to bring liberty to others? Away, you selfish thoughts! On, in the battle! I am a Slovene myself and my father and my grandfathers never had an opportunity to fight for liberty; indeed they fought for hundreds of years under the command of the Habsburgs to continue slavery and tyranny. Good by, my beloved young life. I shall not return to my happy home until the day has come when I can proudly see liberated Yugoslavia in a liberated world. Then I shall return, conscious that I have done my duty. If I shall perish—I am afraid I will—let it be so. The only thing I am sorry about is that I do not possess hundreds of lives to give them all for liberty."

Can there be stronger proof of the formidable democratic forces created by the great prophet of democracy and a new world order, Woodrow Wilson, than this letter of a plain Slovene boy who fought for the United States and its ideals?

In his fight for a new world order, in those days in which his physical collapse was near, not only a prophet, but also a martyr as were so many of his predecessors on the soil of Israel, Woodrow Wilson said in St. Louis, September 9, 1919: "America is made up of the peoples of the world. All the best bloods of the world flow in her veins, all the old affections, all the old and sacred traditions of peoples of every sort throughout the wide world circulate in her veins and she has said to mankind at her birth: 'We have come to redeem the world by giving it liberty and justice.' "

Wilson to the United Nations

THOMAS CONNALLY

I FIRST saw Woodrow Wilson in the fall of 1911 at Dallas, Texas, where he delivered an address. This was before his nomination for the Presidency while he was on a tour through the country. I came from Texas to attend his first inauguration and heard his magnificent address at his installation. I saw him again on March 4, 1917, at his second inauguration. I also, of course, saw him in 1917 when he addressed Congress advocating United States entrance into the World War. In Paris in 1919 during the Peace Conference I, along with a number of other Congressmen, saw him where he received us at his residence and freely and widely conversed with us regarding the progress of the Conference. I saw him again when he returned to Washington from Paris for a short time, and conferred with members of the Senate Foreign Relations Committee and of the House Foreign Affairs Committee. Of course, I saw him on a number of occasions at state dinners and other functions.

The European War burst upon the world in 1914 with tremendous shock and carnage. The reckless and barbarous submarine warfare of Germany upon the shipping of neutral nations as well as its enemy resulted in the murder of American citizens and was a supreme challenge to the doctrine of the freedom of the seas as championed by the United States over the years. It was a war upon peaceful nations and their citizens while engaged in lawful pursuits on the high seas. More than that, it was a supreme challenge to free peoples and free nations by autocracy and tyranny.

President Wilson, fortressed by his sublime convictions and sustained by the united sentiments of the people of the United States, on April 2, 1917, stood in the House of Representatives and addressed a joint session of the Congress. He spoke inspired words. He marshalled the opinion not only of his countrymen but of free men everywhere. He led our Republic into war and laid before the public opinion of Europe and America the tremendous issues which our nation championed. He thrilled the hearts of our allies. He was heard round the world. As a new member of Congress I sat in the House Chamber and witnessed his calm courage and firmness and heard his challenging words. Wilson, a liberal statesman and guardian of his country's honor was urging the American people to take up the sword against arrogant tyranny and the violation of American rights on the seas and on the land. He was speaking for the righting of wrongs, he was pleading for the reconsecration and the rededication of the liberties of the American people. He was declaring for the rights of nations and free people. He was conscious of the responsibility resting upon the United States. He had always been an advocate of peace with justice and honor but when the infamous violations of the liberties and safety of the people of the United States were thrust upon us, he spoke in clarion tones.

When the outrageous and malignant submarine warfare convinced him that it must be resisted by military might, that resistance alone could preserve the peace and safety of the free world, he declared that America must retaliate with all of its strength and power. He asked the Congress to adopt a declaration of war against Germany.

I was a new member of the House Committee on Foreign Affairs to which was referred the resolution to declare war. My membership imposed upon me a terrible responsibility. To me it was a solemn and overwhelming decision. On my knees I sought guidance and direction. A few days later the Committee voted for reporting a declaration of war and I was among the Members who supported the resolution. It was adopted. It later was adopted by the House of Representatives and the Senate. The United States was at war.

In early 1918, President Wilson appeared again before Congress and submitted his famous "fourteen points of peace." This great State paper deserved a place among the historic charters that have advanced the liberties of mankind through the ages. His speeches and State papers inspired our soldiers at the front and advanced our battle lines. His voice became the voice of free peoples. His words impressed the world with the grandeur of his aims and high purposes.

The progress of the war and Wilson's superb leadership guaranteed that kings and emperors would abdicate and under allied triumph the war would come to an end. An armistice was declared followed by a peace conference. Under the President's leadership, and the unity of our people, and the courage and bravery of its armies, victory had come to the cause of the United States and its allies.

In late 1918, President Wilson landed on French shores and took part in a conference assembled to chart and guarantee the peace following the war. It seemed to Wilson that it was his duty to go to Europe, heedless of the dangers which might face him. High was his hope for the establishment of a council among free and democratic nations which might result in a parliament of nations.

At Paris he fought for his ideals and hopes. He wanted to see brute force disenthroned as the rule among nations and peoples. He labored bravely for these noble sentiments and principles. He wanted the League of Nations to administer the principles of international justice. Wilson was faced by the leaders, not only of our allies, but of the enemy. Tremendous problems stared him in the face. Not alone a Peace Treaty to end the war, but future problems in international affairs challenged him at every step that he took. He secured all that was possible. The liberal features of the Versailles Treaty had his support and championship. His great spirit was revealed in those aspects of the Treaty. The American people wanted the Treaty to embrace some kind of project to

The Prophet 235

guarantee the peace in future years. There was latent a small group
who opposed any sort of international treaty with regard thereto.
Wilson returned to the United States with wide acclaim. He returned to America offering his country's leadership in the noble
cause of peace.

During the pendency of the Peace Conference, President Wilson returned to the United States for a short time to attend to Presidential duties. He had a conference at the White House. He invited the members of the Committees on Foreign Relations of the
Senate and Foreign Affairs of the House. As a member of the House
Committee on Foreign Affairs, I attended that conference. The
President related to those assembled the matters with which the
Conference was struggling. He outlined his own views and purposes. He was clear and firm. He was highly hopeful. He was frank
and gave a detailed report of the progress of the Conference. He
then returned to Paris to engage again in the labors of the Conference.

While he was in Europe, he visited several countries. He was
enthusiastically and widely acclaimed in Italy, France and in other
areas wherever he went. The people of Europe in tremendous numbers welcomed him as their deliverer from tyranny and aggressive
war. They looked upon him as the champion of a new order that
would guarantee their safety and the peace of the world.

Upon the adjournment of the Conference and the signing of
the Peace Treaty Wilson returned to Washington. He was faced
with enemies bent upon his defeat. The Treaty of Peace as
finally signed was appropriately submitted to the Senate of the
United States. Here a battle was to be fought in Committee and
later on the Floor. Here the opponents of the Treaty, organized
and militant, were to begin an attack particularly upon the clauses
regarding the League of Nations. Opponents submitted involved
and confusing reservations to the League's provisions to weaken and
destroy it. They were designed to alarm the people and to arouse
their prejudices and to inflame their fears and passions. Political
agitation and bewildering debate were broadcast throughout the
land.

The League was never proposed as a partisan or Democratic

political maneuver. It was an appeal to all of the American people. But all the wiles and devices of partisanship were brought forward to condemn it and to denounce Wilson. The miners and sappers were at work overtime. Some of his most bitter opponents were prominent public figures who theretofore had advocated a "league to enforce peace." Some of them had toured the country in support of such an international agency. The public records will today reveal their support and promotion of such a project. But their overpowering political and personal hatred of Wilson drove them into the camp of his enemies and the league which he had helped to write.

The President soon was aware of the tremendous and bitter forces that were marshalled against the Treaty and against him. He believed that the people of the United States wanted a League of Nations. He believed they hungered for world peace. He believed that they wanted international treaties binding the nations to resort to the League to settle quarrels and to prevent war. He felt it his duty to lay before the American people the issues involved and to secure their approval of his conduct at the Peace Conference. There followed a long and bitter debate in the United States Senate over the Treaty and particularly those clauses relating to the League.

In September, 1919, he undertook a Western tour, seeking approval of his work in Europe. Woodrow Wilson was stricken as though in battle at Pueblo, Colorado, on September 25, 1919. The United States Senate on March 20, 1920, rejected the Treaty. Without the United States as a member the League was foredoomed to failure. After a few years of ineffective and spasmodic effort it ceased to exist. It was superseded not directly but in fact by the United Nations.

Though it was widely asserted that Wilson failed in his efforts for an international organization to preserve peace, it must be remembered that finally in 1945 the United Nations Charter, which embraced the ideal that was in his heart, was adopted at San Francisco and later formally ratified by the United States Senate. In 1945, I was the ranking delegate next to the Secretary of State to the International Conference at San Francisco for the consideration of the charter of the United Nations. *It was gen-*

erally and definitely recognized that the organization created there was a reflection of the high purposes of Woodrow Wilson. Though in detail it differed from his conception, it may be stated that his inspiration prompted its adoption by the United States Senate and the American people. Though his cold and pulseless form rested in the Washington Cathedral, his spirit, his noble purpose, his high concept of an agency for world peace marched on and revived in anxious hearts the desire for a world organization. Today, notwithstanding its weakness in some respects and its shortcomings in others, the United Nations is the best hope of the world to prevent wars and to safeguard and guarantee peace. It may be amended and strengthened. It embodies in essence the concept of Woodrow Wilson for the establishment and preservation of international peace.

The Immortal

E. WALTON OPIE

. . . The cheers of the moment are not what a man ought to think about, but the verdict of his conscience and of the consciences of mankind.

Speech delivered in Brooklyn Navy Yard, 1914 [41]

The following eulogy was delivered in memorial ceremony held at Wilson's tomb in the National Cathedral, Washington, D.C., February 3, 1956, upon anniversary of Wilson's death, under auspices Woodrow Wilson Centennial Celebration Commission. THE EDITOR

IT is with humbleness that we enter today the radiant light of the tomb where rests one of the noblest leaders of mankind. The spirit which once dwelt in the mortal shell enshrined in this sacred edifice lives on to inspire new generations.

A new birth has been given to Woodrow Wilson's aspirations for peace, world order and brotherhood. The time will come when his full vision, the march toward which was slowed only by the blindness and fears of others, becomes a reality. Right and justice will yet rule the world, and wars will be no more.

Such were the goals of Wilson. He climbed toward them with steps which never faltered, though at last the body proved unequal to the demands of the spirit.

We know that this man drew his inspiration from God, of whom he learned at his mother's knee and whose will and ways his reverend father taught him. He lived close to God throughout his days, and found in Him the faith, the courage, and the wisdom which won him place among the world's immortals.

As we observe the centennial of Woodrow Wilson's birth, and today the anniversary of his passing, it is well to think of how thoroughly he prepared himself for the tasks destiny set him. It is well to recall his unfailing adherence to principles, though compromising when need be as to methods. We should ponder, too, his love for mankind, his selflessness, and the achievements which flowed from these attributes—laws which blessed this country with new freedom and better government; the successful prosecution of what was then the most all-embracing war in history; the crystallization of all people's longing for freedom, self-government and peace; the launching of the "parliament of man," which, until Wilson, was but the figment of imagination.

Yes, we stand in a brilliant light today in what some would call the shadows of a tomb. Millions of Americans will become better acquainted this centennial year with the greatness and nobility that were Wilson's. Thus they will be better Christian citizens—some of them leaders strong in the spirit of this son of Virginia.

St. Paul said: "Death is swallowed up in victory." Those words were never truer than they are of Woodrow Wilson, whose victory is of both the world and the spirit.

A Salute

DAG HAMMARSKJOLD

The world must be made safe for democracy. Its peace must be planted upon the tested foundations of political liberty.

War Message to Congress, April 2, 1917 [42]

—WOODROW WILSON

The following tribute was delivered as an address for ceremonies in the Hall of Fame, New York University, upon unveiling of the Woodrow Wilson bust and tablet in commemoration of the Wilson Centennial, May 20, 1956.

THE EDITOR

M AY I first of all thank you for inviting me to join in this ceremony. An occasion such as this in the Hall of Fame for Great Americans belongs in a very special way to the American people. This is a national shrine. The men who are honored here have helped to make the history which is your national heritage. They are bone of your bones and flesh of your flesh.

In asking an international official—the Secretary-General of the United Nations—to speak on this occasion, you have, I am told, broken a precedent of long standing. I am deeply grateful for the generous thought which prompted your invitation. You have done so because of Woodrow Wilson's pioneering leadership in the struggle to achieve a just and peaceful international order.

Woodrow Wilson came to that leadership as an authentic and eloquent spokesman to the world of the spirit of American idealism. That spirit, expressed anew from generation to generation, is deeply rooted in your own national culture. But because it also reflects and shares ideals that are universal, it has often been an inspiring and enriching influence for all mankind.

This is the case with the great idealists of any age and culture. This was the case with Woodrow Wilson's advocacy of world organization. From the very first, he spoke in terms of universal ideals and of the common interest. His first public commitment to the idea of a League of Nations was made just forty years ago this month. It was made when he spoke on May 27, 1916, to a meeting of a group of world-minded Americans who had banded together as the League to Enforce Peace.

Why was an association of nations needed? Because, he said, "the peace of the world must henceforth depend upon a new and more wholesome diplomacy;" because "the principle of public right must henceforth take precedence over the individual interests of particular nations;" because "the nations of the world must in some way band themselves together to see that that right prevails as against any sort of selfish aggression;" because "there must be a common agreement for a common object" and "at the heart of that common object must lie the inviolable rights of peoples and of mankind."

In this same speech he defined some of these rights: the right of every people "to choose the sovereignty under which they shall live;" the right of small States "to enjoy the same respect for their sovereignty and territorial integrity as the great nations" and the right to be free from every disturbance of the peace "that has its origin in aggression and disregard of the rights of peoples and nations."

These statements of the reasons for, and purposes of, world organization are as much to the point today as when they were made forty years ago. In his stress upon the precedence of "public right" over "the individual interests of particular nations" and upon "common agreement for a common object"—that is for the rights of peoples—Woodrow Wilson went to the heart of the matter.

As he so clearly understood, the international interest had to be institutionalized if it were to have a reasonable hope of prevailing in the course of time. No matter how solemn the engagement to common purposes and universal aims, whether expressed in a Covenant for a League of Nations or in a Charter for the United Nations, institutions functioning continuously in the service of these purposes would be needed to give them effect. When he opened discussion of plans for a League of Nations at the Paris Peace Conference in January, 1919, Wilson called for the creation of an organization that should, he stressed, be "not merely a formal thing, not an occasional thing, not a thing sometimes called into life to meet an exigency" but that should have a "vital continuity" of function. He summed it up in these expressive words: "It should be the eye of the nations to keep watch upon the common interest, an eye that does not slumber, an eye that is everywhere watchful and attentive."

Forty years after Woodrow Wilson first uttered these words, the idea of world organization is far more firmly established than it ever was in the years of the League of Nations. The mere fact that the United Nations, unlike the League, has never lost a

Member State, and now, with seventy-six Members, seems to be moving inexorably toward true universality, speaks for this. But we are still seeking ways to make our international institutions fulfill more effectively the fundamental purpose expressed in Woodrow Wilson's words—"to be the eye of the nations to keep watch upon the common interest."

I have no doubt that forty years from now we shall also be engaged in the same pursuit. How could we expect otherwise? World organization is still a new adventure in human history. It needs much perfecting in the crucible of experience and there is no substitute for time in that respect.

Two of our most common human failings, indeed, seem to be our disrespect for the slow processes of time and our tendency to shift responsibility from ourselves to our institutions. It is too often our habit to see the goal, to declare it and, in declaring it, to assume that we shall automatically achieve it. This leads us to confuse ends with means, to label as failure what is in fact an historic step forward, and in general to mistake the lesser for the greater thing.

Thus Woodrow Wilson, in the years between the wars, was commonly considered to have failed because the United States refused to join the League of Nations. Yet, in fact, he had made history, great history, by being the principal founder of the first world orgainization.

The League itself was labeled a failure because its existence did not prevent a second World War. Yet the failure lay not in the League, but in the nations which failed to live up to their pledged word and also failed to infuse into the League as an institution the vitality and strength that Wilson had pleaded for in 1919.

In our day too, we often hear it said that the United Nations has succeeded here, or has failed there. What do we mean? Do we refer to the purposes of the Charter? They are expressions of universally shared ideals which cannot fail us, though we, alas, often fail them. Or do we think of the institutions of the United Nations? They are our tools. We fashioned them. We use them. It is our responsibility to remedy any flaws there may be in them. It is our responsibility to correct any failures in our use of them. And we must expect the responsibility for remedying the flaws and correcting the failures to go on and on, as long as human beings are imperfect and human institutions likewise.

This is a difficult lesson for both idealists and realists, though for different reasons. I suppose that, just as the first temptation of the realist is the illusion of cynicism, so the first temptation of the idealist is the illusion of Utopia. As an idealist, it was natural that Woodrow Wilson also did not entirely escape his temptation, any more than have most of the idealists of history. In his valiant fight for the cause of the League of Nations, he went beyond the concept of an institution acting for the common interest of the peoples of the world. He visualized the establishment of the League as ending the old system of the balance of power and substituting what he called a "community of power."

The creation of a true community of power to serve the common interest is, indeed, the goal—now as it was in Woodrow Wilson's day. But the establishment of the League of Nations did not, and could not, of itself bring such a community of power into being. It did not, nor could it, end at one stroke the system of the balance of power in international affairs.

The League was an association of sovereign nation-states, just as the United Nations is today. In such an association, the play of the balance of power is inevitable. And it should be said that one of the most serious remaining obstacles in the way of public understanding of the true role of the United Nations today results from a similar tendency to picture the United Nations of 1945 as establishing collective security for the world.

Now, as then, it is important for all of us to understand that true collective security, in the sense of an international police power engaged to defend the peace of the world, is to be found at the end, not at the beginning, of the effort to create and use world institutions that are effective in the service of the common interest.

The spirit and practice of world community must first gain in strength and custom by processes of organic growth. It is to the helping along of these processes of growth that we should devote all our ingenuity and our effort. To the extent that we are able to increase the weight of the common interest as against the weight of special interests, and therefore of the power of the whole community to guide the course of events, we shall be approaching that much nearer to the goal.

This is, in fact, the most essential message of the career of Woodrow Wilson for the present day, whether we think of him as educator, as President of the United States, or as the pioneer of world organization.

Throughout his life he was the eloquent spokesman and dedicated champion of the general welfare both within his nation and among the nations of the world. Though his hopes for the enforcement of peace through collective security were ahead of the times, he also saw that international organization should rely primarily upon moral force, because—in his words—it was "intended as a constitution of peace, not as a league of war."

He understood very well what was at the root of the difficulty with making world organization work more effectively in the common interest, and he expressed it in words that we would do well to turn into the first person plural and repeat to ourselves in our own times: "They have thought too much of the interests that were near them and they have not listened to the voices of their neighbors."

Woodrow Wilson could denounce such selfishness, as powerfully as he could evoke a vision of "pastures of quietness and peace such as the world never dreamed of before." He could also give movingly human expressions to his deep-seated faith in the processes of democracy. Just before he died in 1924, he told a friend: "I am not sorry I broke down. As it is coming now, the American people are thinking their way through and reaching their own decision, and that is the better way for it to come."

It is not only the American people, of course, but the peoples of many nations, who have been thinking their way through and reaching their own decision since Woodrow Wilson first showed the way. The United Nations stands as evidence of the direction of their thinking and of their decision.

How would Woodrow Wilson have reacted to the recent developments in the life of the United Nations?

Would he not have hailed the atomic conference at Geneva last summer as evidence of the possibilities of co-operation even in a divided world, when a major interest common to all is at stake? Would he not have been happy that this co-operation developed within the framework of an organization owing so much to his original conception?

Would he not have hailed the development of the membership, which shows the vitality of the concept of universality at the present juncture in the growth of internationalism?

And, although he certainly would have been deeply worried by the underlying problems, would he not have been happy to see how in the Middle East the United Nations machinery could help Member Governments in crystallizing their wish to re-establish order?

I think he would, but I think he also would have found reason for criticism. He would have been surprised to see how far we have yet failed to bring international conflicts effectively under the rule of law.

Although the spokesman for "open covenants openly arrived at" —for democracy in international negotiation—he would also, I think, not have approved all of the applications given to that sound principle. Knowing too well the ways of man to believe in his ability to resist selfish or shortsighted public pressures, he would certainly have found it appropriate to plead for a combination of the new methods of diplomacy, of which he was in favor, with such of those time-honored political techniques as would give us the result best serving the interests of peace.

It is a true measure of the leadership and idealism of Woodrow Wilson that it is not a vain pastime in this way to give some thought to the question of how he would have looked at our endeavors, our failures and our successes, in the fields to which he devoted the best of his life. He is not only the first and foremost spokesman for true international organization. He is one of those who helped to create an international conscience which is, and will remain, a living force in all attempts to build a world of order.

My dream is that as the years go on and the world knows more and more of America it will also drink at these fountains of youth and renewal; that it also will turn to America for those moral inspirations which lie at the basis of all freedom; that the world will never fear America unless it feels that it is engaged in some enterprise which is inconsistent with the rights of humanity; and that America will come into the full light of the day when all shall know that she puts human rights above all other rights and that her flag is the flag not only of America but of humanity.

What other great people has devoted itself to this exalted ideal? To what other nation in the world can all eyes look for an instant sympathy that thrills the whole body politic when men anywhere are fighting for their rights? I do not know that there will ever be a "declaration of independence and of grievances for mankind," but I believe that if any such document is ever drawn it will be drawn in the spirit of the American Declaration of Independence, and that America has lifted high the light which will shine unto all generations and guide the feet of mankind to the goal of justice and liberty and peace.

Woodrow Wilson

Address delivered at Independence Hall, Philadelphia, July 4, 1914

Biographical Outline

1856, Dec. 28	Born in Staunton, Virginia
1858	Family moved to Augusta, Georgia
1870	Family moved to Columbia, South Carolina
1873, Sept.	Entered Davidson College, North Carolina
1874, June	Left Davidson; returned home to build up his health and prepare for Princeton.
1874	Moved with family to Wilmington, North Carolina
1875, Sept.	Entered Princeton
1879	Graduated from Princeton, A.B.
1879, Sept.	Entered law school at University of Virginia
1881	Graduated in law at University of Virginia
1882-83	Practiced law at Atlanta, Georgia
1883, Sept.	Entered Johns Hopkins University
1885, June 24	Married Ellen Axson of Rome, Georgia
1885-1888	Associate professor of History and Political Economy at Bryn Mawr College
1886	Ph.D., Johns Hopkins University
1888-1890	Professor at Wesleyan University
1890	Professor of Jurisprudence at Princeton
1902, Aug. 1	Appointed President of Princeton University
1910, Sept. 15	Nominated for Governor of New Jersey
1910, Nov.	Elected Governor of New Jersey
1912, July 2	Nominated Democratic candidate for the Presidency
1912, Nov. 5	Elected President of the United States
1913, March 4	Inaugurated President of the United States
1914, Aug. 6	Death of Mrs. Wilson
1915, Oct. 7	Engaged to Mrs. Norman Galt (née Edith Bolling)
1915, Dec. 18	Married Mrs. Galt
1916, Nov. 7	Elected for second term
1917, Mar. 5	Inaugural address

1917, Apr. 2	Delivered message to special session of Congress advising declaration of war
1917, Apr. 6	Signed joint resolution and proclaimed state of war with Germany
1918, Jan. 8	Proclaimed Fourteen Points as a basis of world peace
1918, Nov. 11	Armistice proclaimed in address to Congress
1918, Dec. 4	Sailed for Europe to attend Peace Conference
1919, Jan. 16	Opened Peace Conference
1919, Feb. 14	Addressed Peace Conference on draft of League Covenant
1919, Feb. 24	Landed at Boston on return from Peace Conference
1919, March 3	Thirty-seven Senators with Senator Lodge against Covenant of League of Nations as drafted
1919, Mar. 5	Sailed for Europe to resume participation Peace Conference
1919, June 28	Peace Treaty signed
1919, July 8	Arrived in New York from Peace Conference
1919, Sept. 3	Started on Western trip to appeal to people for ratification of Versailles Treaty
1919, Sept. 25	Collapse at Pueblo, Colorado; trip ordered stopped by Admiral Grayson, Wilson's physician
1920, Mar. 20	Treaty returned to President with resolution that it could not get necessary two-thirds vote
1921, March 4	Left White House to enter private life; inauguration of Harding
1923, Nov. 10	Delivered last public address by radio from his home, reaffirming faith in League of Nations
1924, Feb. 3	Died at 11:15 a.m. at his home, 2340 S. Street in Washington, D.C.
1924, Feb. 6	Buried in crypt of National Cathedral, Washington, D.C.

Bibliographical Sketch

HARRY CLEMONS

Librarian Retired, University of Virginia

THE collection, preservation, and accessibility of material connected with the thirty-three distinguished individuals who have attained to the presidency of the United States have in recent years become matters of increasing concern. Indeed for several of these collections special libraries have been established or are being planned, and publication on a large scale has been undertaken. For the most part such collections consist of public papers and correspondence. But other subjects are to be found—such as Thomas Jefferson's *Notes on the State of Virginia* and Herbert Hoover's translation of Georg Agricola's *De Re Metallica*. In the cases of two of the Presidents, Theodore Roosevelt and Woodrow Wilson, there is in addition an impressive array of books and articles in biography, history, political science, and the personalized essay.

Woodrow Wilson had gained eminent distinction as an author prior to his political career. Besides numerous articles there had been these works in book form:

Congressional Government: a Study in American Politics. Houghton, Mifflin, 1885.
The State: Elements of Historical and Practical Politics. Heath, 1889.
Division and Reunion, 1829-1889: Epochs of American History. Longmans, 1893.
An Old Master, and Other Political Essays. Scribner, 1893.
Mere Literature and Other Essays. Houghton, Mifflin, 1896.
George Washington. Harper, 1897.
A History of the American People. Five volumes. Harper, 1902.
Constitutional Government in the United States. Columbia University Press, 1908.

With the publication in 1913 by Doubleday of *The New Freedom*, edited by William Bayard Hale, there began the issue in book form of various collections of Woodrow Wilson's addresses and public papers. The most comprehensive of these, covering both the educational and the political periods, was the six volume *Public Papers of Woodrow Wilson*, edited by Ray Stannard Baker and William Edward Dodd and issued by Harper in 1925-1927.

Such books and collections, however, amount to only a part of the total. The most recent record, Laura Shearer Turnbull's *Woodrow Wilson: a Selected Bibliography of His Published Writings, Addresses, and Public Papers*, issued by the Princeton University Press in 1948, lists no fewer than 1,061 items. In addition there are in this useful little volume seventy-six entries of "Newspaper Reports of Woodrow Wilson's Speeches, Statements, and Papers, 1910-1912" compiled by Arthur Stanley Link, and 106 "Books in the Woodrow Wilson Field" selected by Katharine Edith Brand.

Other bibliographies are available for consultation. One is included in volumes two, four, and six of *The Public Papers* compiled by Baker and Dodd, and another is attached to the sketch of Woodrow Wilson by Charles Seymour in volume twenty of the *Dictionary of American Biography*.

For books about Woodrow Wilson, a controversial figure both as an educator and as a statesman, one hesitates to make selection. The reader will be well advised to experiment with choices of his own from the titles in the bibliographies. It would seem clear, however, that the biographical studies by four of the writers already mentioned, Baker, Dodd, Link, and Seymour, merit recommendation. The Charles Seymour article in the *Dictionary of American Biography* is excellent for a brief initial study of the whole life. At the opposite pole in extent is the eight volume *Woodrow Wilson, Life and Letters*, written by Ray Stannard Baker from his access to a mass of source material and published by Doubleday, Doran 1927-1939. Charles Scribner's Sons issued a seven volume edition of this in 1946. The William Edward Dodd contribution, *Woodrow Wilson and His Work*, appeared with a Doubleday, Page imprint in 1920. A revised edition was published by Peter Smith in 1932. By Arthur Stanley Link there have more recently appeared two studies: *Wilson, Road to the White House*, published by the Princeton University Press in 1947, and *Woodrow Wilson and the Progressive Era*, published by Harper in 1954.

The criticisms, favorable and unfavorable, of the Wilsonian policies and pronouncements greatly augmented the list of works about this international figure. Events that have crowded the three decades since his death, particularly the second world war and the framing and testing of the United Nations organization, have afforded a clearer perspective for appraisal of his aims and achievements; and there has been a considerable accumulation of studies reflecting the later and more seasoned approach. Among the writers of these recent works are Thomas Andrew Bailey, Herbert Clifford Francis Bell, Harold Garnett Black, Edward Henry Buehrig, Ruth Cranston, Josephus Daniels, Edward Maurice Hugh-Jones, and Gerald White Johnson.

For a masterpiece of appreciation there is the memorial address delivered before a joint session of the two houses of Congress on 15 December 1924 by Edwin Anderson Alderman. This was printed as a government document and also, in 1925, as a separate book by Doubleday, Page. There are several other excellent appraisals among the pamphlets printed and distributed by the Woodrow Wilson Foundation, an example being *The Story of Woodrow Wilson* by David Loth, issued in revised form in 1954.

It is fortunate that for a rounded picture of Woodrow Wilson's personality there is access also to several enjoyable book portraits by members of his family. Among these are Margaret Randolph Elliott's *My Aunt Louisa and Woodrow Wilson* (University of North Carolina Press, 1944), Eleanor Randolph McAdoo's *The Woodrow Wilsons* (written in collaboration with Margaret Gaffey and published by Macmillan in 1937), and Edith Bolling Wilson's *My Memoir* (Bobbs-Merrill, 1939).

The career of this President would not seem, at least at first glance, to offer material for an exciting story for young readers. Yet commendable attempts within the "juvenile" classification have been made in book form by Alden Hatch (Holt, 1947) and by Helen Albee Monsell (Bobbs-Merrill, 1950).

These bibliographical reminders bring us to this centennial year, 1956, of Wilson's birth. It is known that a number of new works—collections, biographies, and critical studies—are in the making. One that has already appeared—*The Politics of Woodrow Wilson*, edited by August Heckscher and published by Harper—affords promise that among such contributions there will be valuable additions to the long Wilsonian list. The continued growth of that list seems inevitable. This commemorative volume will itself be an invaluable addition. Woodrow Wilson's devotion was to the underlying and permanent truths; and we have painfully learned that making the world safe for democracy must needs be an unending task.

Biographical Notes on Contributors

EISENHOWER, DWIGHT DAVID, President of the United States. B.S. U.S. Military Academy, 1915; Allied Commander-in-Chief, North Africa, 1942; Commanding General Allied Powers E.T.O., 1943; General of the Army, December, 1944; Commander, U.S. Occupational Forces in Germany, 1945; Chief of Staff, U.S. Army, 1945-1948; President Columbia University, 1948-1952; Supreme Commander Allied Powers, Europe, 1951; inaugurated President of the United States Jan. 20, 1953. Recipient honorary degrees from institutions in United States and abroad; foreign and United States orders, decorations and medals.

DOWDEY, CLIFFORD, JR. Author. Student Columbia University, 1923-25; reporter, book reviewer Richmond News Leader, 1925-26; editorial staff Munseys and Argosy; book reviewer N.Y. Sun, 1926-28; editor pulp magazines Dell Publishing Co., 1928-29, 1933-35; free lance writer 1929-33 and since 1935. Awarded Guggenheim fellowship 1938. Author "Bugles Blow No More," 1937; "Experiment in Rebellion," 1936; "Weep for my Brother," 1950; "Jasmine Street," 1952; "The Proud Retreat," 1953; "The Land They Fought For," 1955. Contributor to McCall's, Ladies Home Journal, Holiday, Colliers, American Mercury, Saturday Evening Post, Atlantic Monthly, Saturday Review.

DABNEY, VIRGINIUS, Newspaper Editor. A.B. University of Virginia, 1920; A.M. 1921; D.Litt. (honorary) University of Richmond, 1940; LL.D. Lynchburg College, College William and Mary, 1944. Editor Times-Dispatch since 1936. Spent six months in Central Europe in 1934 under grant from Oberlaender Trust. Winner Lee Editorial

Award of Virginia Press Association and Lee School of Journalism, Washington and Lee for "distinguished editorial writing during the year 1937." Pulitzer Prize for editorial writing, 1947. Author "Liberalism in the South," 1932; "Below the Potomac," 1942; "Dry Messiah: the Life of Bishop Cannon," 1949. Contributor to National Magazines.

LEWIS, FRANK BELL, Professor, Union Theological Seminary, Richmond, Virginia. A.B., M.A. Washington & Lee University, University of Virginia, 1932 and 1933; B.D., Th.M., Union Theological Seminary, Richmond, Virginia, 1936 and 1937; Ph.D. Duke University, 1946; attended University of Edinburgh. Pastor, Presbyterian Church, 1937-42; Professor Religion and Philosophy Davis and Elkins College, Elkins, West Virginia, 1942-47; President, Mary Baldwin College, 1947-54.

DODDS, HAROLD WILLIS, President Princeton University. A.B. Grove City (Pennsylvania) College, 1909; A.M. Princeton University, 1914; Ph.D. University of Pennsylvania, 1917; LL.D., Grove City College, 1931; Yale, Dickinson, American University, Rutgers, New York University, Harvard and Williams, 1934; Cincinnati, 1935, University of Pennsylvania, 1936; Dartmouth College, 1937; Purdue, 1938; Tulane, 1941; Tusculum, 1945; North Carolina, 1946; Oberlin College, 1947; Toronto University, 1947; Washington and Lee University, 1949; University of Glasgow, 1951; University of California, 1955. Litt.D., Columbia, 1934; Hahnemann Medical College, 1937; University of Hawaii, 1949; Dr. Humane Letters, Hobart College, 1936; Dr. Humanities, Wooster, 1938. President Princeton University since 1933. Executive Secretary U.S. Food Administration, Pennsylvania, 1917-19; Consultant to Cuban Government in election law and procedure, 1935; Chairman President's Commission on Integration of Medical Services of the Government, 1946; Chairman Task Force on Personnel, 2nd Hoover Commission, 1954-55; Trustee, Carnegie Foundation for Advancement of Teaching, 1935; Chairman, American delegation, Anglo-American Conference on the Refugee problem, Bermuda, 1943. Author "Out of This Nettle . . . Danger," 1943; member of the President's Advisory Commission on universal training, 1945 . . . numerous articles, surveys and reports in political science.

LIPPMANN, WALTER Editor, Author. A.B. Harvard, 1909; graduate student in philosophy, 1910. Formerly Associate Editor, The New Republic; writer, New York World until 1931; now special writer for

New York Herald-Tribune and other newspapers. Assistant to Secretary of War, 1917; Secretary of organization directed by E. M. House to prepare data for Peace Conference; Captain, U.S. Army Military Intelligence, attached to 2nd Sect. General Staff, Gen. Hdqrs. A.E.F., and American Commission to Negotiate Peace. Author "A Preface to Politics," 1913; "Drift and Mastery," 1914; "The Stakes of Diplomacy," 1915; "The Political Scene," 1919; "Liberty and the News," 1920; "Public Opinion," 1922; "Men of Destiny," 1927; "American Inquisitors," 1928; "A Preface to Morals," 1929; "The U.S. in World Affairs" (with William O. Scroggs), 1931, 1932, 1933; "The Method of Freedom," 1934; "The New Imperative," 1935; "The Good Society," 1937; "Some Notes on War and Peace," 1940; "U.S. Foreign Policy: Shield of the Republic," 1943; "U.S. War Aims," 1944; "The Cold War," 1947; "Isolation and Alliances," 1952; "The Public Philosophy," 1955. Contributor to magazines including Atlantic, Yale Review, Harpers, Life. Editor, The Poems of Paul Mariett, 1913.

McGILL, RALPH EMERSON, Editor Atlanta Constitution. Student Vanderbilt University, 1917-19-22. LL.D. University of Miami 1919. Served with U.S. Marine Corps, 1918-19. Awarded Rosenwald fellowship for travel in Europe, 1937-38; Editor, Atlanta Constitution since 1942. Author "Israel Revisited" 1951. Contributor: *Saturday Evening Post, Atlantic Monthly, Harper's, Reader's Digest.*

WHITE, WILLIAM ALLEN, editor, author (1868-1944). Born in Emporia, Kansas. Educated at the University of Kansas. Ph.D. Washburn, Oberlin and Beloit Colleges, and Baker, Brown, Columbia and Harvard Universities. Proprietor and Editor, Emporia Gazette from 1895. President American Society of Newspaper Editors, 1938; member of board of Book-of-the-Month Club from its inception. Sent to France as observer by American Red Cross, 1917; delegate to Russian Conference at Prinkipo, 1919; member President's Commission to Haiti; Member President's Commission on Organization for Unemployment Relief, 1931. Trustee, College of Emporia, Will Rogers Memorial Association, Rockefeller Foundation and Roosevelt Memorial Association. Author of four books of short stories, three novels, three biographies and five books of political essays, among them "The Real Issue," 1896; "The Court of Boyville," 1899, "In Our Town," 1906; "Woodrow Wilson, the Man, the Times and His Task," 1924; "Calvin Coolidge: the Man Who Is President," 1925; "Forty Years on Main Street," 1937; "A Puritan in Babylon," 1938; "The Changing West," 1939.

LINK, ARTHUR S., Professor of History at Northwestern University. A.B. 1941, Ph.D. 1945, University of North Carolina; graduate studies at Columbia University; Guggenheim Fellow 1950-1951; Member of the Institute for Advanced Study, Princeton, New Jersey, 1954-55; member of faculty of Northwestern University since 1949. Author, "American Epoch," 1955; "Woodrow Wilson and the Progressive Era," 1954; "Wilson—the Road to the White House," 1947; "Wilson—the New Freedom," 1956; co-author and co-editor "Problems in American History, 1952; articles in American Historical Review, Mississippi Valley Historical Review; Journal of Southern History, Journal of Negro History, Yale Review, American Scholar and numerous state journals.

BOWERS, CLAUDE GERNADE, Historian, diplomat. Educated public schools and private tutors; honorary M.A. Tufts, 1926; LL.D. Notre Dame, 1930; University of South Carolina, 1930; University of North Carolina, 1941; Litt.D., Holy Cross College, 1930; Doctor Honoris Causa Philosophy and letters, Catholic University, Chile, 1951; University of Indiana. Editorial writer, New York World, 1923–31; political columnist, New York Journal, 1931-33; ambassador extraordinary and plenipotentiary to Spain, 1933-39; ambassador to Chile, 1939-53. Chairman American Delegation to Conference of Inter-American Institute of Cartography, Geography and History, Santiago, 1950. Recipient Jefferson medal at formal dedication of Monticello, July 4, 1926; honorary president, Andrew Jackson Society; Chairman Society for Relief of Spanish children in Spanish War; acted as intermediary for exchange of prisoners. Author: "The Party Battles of the Jackson Period," 1922; "Jefferson and Hamilton—the Struggle for Democracy in America," 1925; "The Tragic Era—the Revolution after Lincoln," 1929; "Jefferson in Power—the Death Struggle of the Federalists," 1936; "The Young Jefferson," 1945. Editor, Diary of Elbridge Gerry, Jr., 1927; "Making Democracy a Reality," 1954; "My Mission to Spain," 1954; "Spanish Adventures of Washington Irving," 1940.

ROBINSON, EDGAR EUGENE, Historian. A.B. University of Wisconsin, 1908; fellow in American History, A.M., 1910; LL.D., 1942. Assistant Professor American History, 1911-18; Associate Professor, 1918-23; Professor since 1923, also Executive Head of Department, 1929; Margaret Byrne Professor of American History, 1931, Stanford University. Director, Institute American History, Stanford University, 1943-52; Director, Franklin D. Roosevelt study under J. Brooks B. Parker Award, 1952-54; Recipient, Freedoms Foundation Award, 1950.

Author "The Foreign Policy of Woodrow Wilson" (with V. J. West), 1917; "Evolution of American Political Parties," 1924; "The Presidential Vote (1896-1932)," 1934; "American Democracy in Time of Crisis," 1934; "Independent Study at Stanford University," 1937; "The Presidential Vote (1936)," 1940; "The New United States," 1946; "They Voted for Roosevelt," 1947; "Scholarship and Cataclysm," 1947; "The Roosevelt Leadership (1935-45)," 1955. Contributor of articles to History of the United States, Encyclopedia Britannica, Book of the Year, 1950-53.

BRAND, KATHARINE E., A.B. Smith College, 1921. Assistant to Ray Stannard Baker, 1925-39; Curator Woodrow Wilson papers, Library of Congress on behalf Mrs. Wilson, 1939-44. Head, Recent Manuscripts Section, Manuscripts Division, Library of Congress. (Retired as of February 28, 1956.) "Books in the Woodrow Wilson Field," in *Woodrow Wilson Bibliography* . . . by Laura S. Turnbull; " 'The Inside Friend': Woodrow Wilson to Robert Bridges," The Library of Congress *Quarterly Journal of Current Acquisitions*, May, 1953; other articles in field.

CHIANG, KAI-SHEK, MADAME (Mayling Soong Chiang); Chinese sociologist, youngest daughter C. J. Soong; married Chiang Kai-Shek, 1927. Honor graduate, Wellesley College; Phi Beta Kappa. Engaged in social service work in China; first woman member Child Labor Commission; inaugurated Moral Endeavor Association, Chinese Women's Clubs; established schools for orphans, Nanking. Director General Women's Department, New Life Movement. Former Member Legislative Yuan; Secretary-General Chinese Commission Aeronautical Affairs; Founder: National Chinese Women's Association for War Relief, Refugee Children; Chinese Women's Anti-Aggression League; Director General Women's Department Kuomintang; first Chinese woman decorated by national government in China. Recipient American Alumni Council first annual award of merit to outstanding graduate of American College or University, 1944. Recipient highest military and civil decorations. Author, "China in Peace and War," 1939; "China Shall Rise Again," 1939; "This Is Our China," 1940; "The Sure Victory," 1956.

QUINTANILLA, LUIS, Mexican diplomat. Ambassador Extraordinary and Plenipotentiary to USSR, 1942; Colombia, 1945; Delegate San Francisco Conference, 1945; U.N. Second Assembly, 1947; Chairman, Inter-American Peace Commission, 1948; Fact Finding Committees in Central America, 1948-55; Council of Organization of American States, 1949; Professor of Political Science, George Washington University; Ambassador Extraordinary and Minister Plenipotentiary to the Organization of American States, Washington, since 1945. Author "Latin America Speaks."

VOSNJAK, BOGUMIL, former Professor Government, University of California. Member Yugoslav Commission, London (1915-19). Represented the Slovenes at the Corfu Conference, 1917. Helped draft the Corfu Declaration. Secretary General of the Yugoslav Peace Delegation, Paris, 1919. Member of the Yugoslav Constitutional Assembly, 1920. Member of Parliament, 1931-35. Member of the Slovene National Committee, since 1945 in exile. Author 30 books on the history of Yugoslavia.

CONNALLY, THOMAS TERRY, former U.S. Senator. A.B. Baylor University, Waco, Texas, 1896; LL.B., University of Texas, 1898; LL.D., Baylor University, 1936, Howard Payne University, 1936. U.S. Senator, 1929-53. Chairman Senate Foreign Relations Committee, 1941-46, and 1949-53; Delegate Inter-Parliamentary Union, Geneva, 1924, London, 1930, Constantinople, 1934, Rome, 1948, Bern, 1952. Chairman, U.S. Delegation to U.N. Conference on International Organization, San Francisco Conference, 1945; served as member U.S. Delegation to First General Assembly of U.N., London General Assembly, 1946. Served as Advisor to Secretary of State at sessions of Council of Foreign Ministers, Paris, France, 1946. Served as representative of the U.S. to General Assembly of the U.N. 1946. Author, "My Name is Tom Connally," 1954.

OPIE, EVARTS WALTON, Major-General retired, Newspaper publisher. Graduate Staunton Military Academy, 1908-11; graduate Command and General Staff College, 1936. General Manager and Publisher, The Evening Leader and the News Leader, daily newspapers of Staunton, Virginia. Trustee, Woodrow Wilson Birthplace Foundation. Chairman, U.S. Woodrow Wilson Centennial Celebration Commission, 1956.

HAMMARSKJÖLD, DAG HJALMAR AGNE CARL, Secretary General, United Nations. Born Jönköping, Sweden, July 29, 1905. B.A. Uppsala University, 1925; LL.B., 1930; Ph.D., Stockholm University, 1934; LL.D. University of Pennsylvania, Amherst College, Columbia University, Johns Hopkins University, University of California; Carleton College, McGill, Canada. Assistant Professor Political Economy, Stockholm University, 1933; Secretary Bank of Sweden, 1935-36, Chairman Board, 1941-48. Under-Secretary of State, Ministry of Finance, 1936-45; Appointed Envoy Extraordinary, Financial Advisor, Ministry Foreign Affairs, 1946; Delegate, Paris Conference, 1947-48; Delegate Organization for European Economic Co-operation (OEEC) 1948-53, Vice-Chairman, Executive Committee, 1948-49; Under-Secretary of State, 1949; Deputy Foreign Minister, 1951-53; General Assembly United Nations, 1949, 51-53; Member, Swedish Academy 1954.

CLEMONS, HARRY, Librarian, Retired, University of Virginia; writer. Born Corry, Pennsylvania, September 9, 1879. A.B. Wesleyan University, 1902, A.M., 1905, Litt. D., 1942. Scribner fellow, Princeton University, 1903-4; A.M., 1905. Jacobus fellow of Princeton at Oxford University, England, 1906-7. Instructor in English, Princeton, 1904-8, reference librarian, 1908-13. Professor of English, University of Nanking, China, 1913-20, librarian, 1914-27. Librarian, University of Virginia, 1927-50, Consultant in Library resources since 1950. Official representative, A.L.A. in charge of Library war service, A.E.F., Siberia, 1918-19; Special cataloger Chinese section Library of Congress, 1922. Member Virginia Library Association (President, 1931-32), Raven Society, Phi Beta Kappa, Omicron Delta Kappa, Pi Delta Epsilon. Author "An Essay Towards a Bibliography of the Public Writings and Addresses of Woodrow Wilson (1875-1910)," 1913; "The A.L.A. in Siberia," 1917; "A Survey of Research Materials in Virginia's Libraries," 1936-37, 1938; "Story of Jeffersonian Foundation," 1954.

Notes

‡ My earliest recollection of conversations below, while I perched on the bannisters above, is of impassioned, resounding discussion of the efficacy of the League of Nations. Politics have always been meat and drink to old families in the Old Dominion; it is a compulsive inheritance from their Whig ancestors in England, augmented by their American ancestors' continuing participation. In our home, there was no question but that the world "*had* to be made safe for democracy!" and we had to convert any guest who failed to see the vision. I can hear my mother's mellifluously intense and challenging voice now; while my father's soothing bass would insist, "It is all self-evident," using Lincoln's phrase deliberately. It was even clear to me. Had not my uncle by God's grace alone just returned safely from "the front"? And what would happen in twenty years, he himself demanded, if I "ever had a brother." What pain was the memory of that prophecy when that very brother, who had never been out of the United States before, was killed by a German in sub-zero cold on an Italian mountaintop in the middle of the night, December 7, 1943.

My grandfather who had served in the Virginia legislature went to the state democratic convention in Norfolk in 1912 to fight for the Virginia delegation's support of Wilson. A Presbyterian and an intellectual himself, he felt always a close affinity with the candidate. When the delegation went to Baltimore in June, instructed to vote for Champ Clark instead of Wilson, he was devastated by their "myopia" and spent the rest of his life fighting for Wilsonian principles.

‡‡ Five years later, May 1, 1862, on a modest farm twelve miles up the "Valley Pike" north of Staunton, Ida Elizabeth Stover Eisenhower, mother of President Dwight D. Eisenhower, was born. Her birthplace and the schoolhouse she attended are also still standing. (Editor)

Appendix A

The quotations from Wilson's writings and addresses on pages xvi, 2, 16, 36, 50, 66, 80, 138, 152, 168, 184, 240, 244, 251, are from the following sources:

1. Jackson Day Address, Indianapolis, January 8, 1915. Quoted by Ray Stannard Baker and William E. Dodd, eds., *The Public Papers of Woodrow Wilson: The New Democracy*. Vol. I (1926), p. 247. Hereafter cited as: *Public Papers*.

2. Address to the Grand Army of the Republic, Washington, D.C., September 28, 1915. Quoted in the *Public Papers: The New Democracy*. Vol. I, p. 371.

3. Address at the Tercentenary Celebration of the Translation of the Bible into the English Language, Denver, Colorado, May 7, 1911. Quoted in the *Public Papers: College and State*. Vol. II, p. 298.

4. Letter to Frank E. Doremus, September 4, 1914. Woodrow Wilson Papers, Series III-A, Box 11. Library of Congress.

5. On April 29, 1912 in a speech at the Lyric Theater in Baltimore, Wilson said, "All that fair flower, that luscious fruitage that comes out like quaint ornaments upon the bough has found its source in the operations of the soil, in the roots that you do not see. . . ."

6. Address before Pennsylvania State Sabbath School Association, Oct. 13, 1904.

7. Address at the First Annual Banquet of the Motion Picture Board of Trade, Hotel Biltmore, New York, January 27, 1916. Quoted in the *Public Papers: The New Democracy*. Vol. I, p. 448.

8. Address to the National Press Club, May 15, 1916. Woodrow Wilson Papers, Series III-A, Box 12. Library of Congress.

9. Woodrow Wilson, *The New Freedom* (1913), p. 220.

10. Woodrow Wilson, "When a Man Comes To Himself," *The Century Magazine* LXII (June 1901), p. 273.

11. "Robert E. Lee: An Interpretation." Delivered on the occasion

of the Hundredth Anniversary of the birth of Robert E. Lee, at the University of North Carolina, January 19, 1909. Quoted in the *Public Papers: College and State*. Vol. II, p. 69.

12. Woodrow Wilson, "The Road Away From Revolution," *Atlantic Monthly* CXXXII (August 1923), p. 146.

13. Address before the New Jersey State Teachers Association, December 28, 1909. Typed copy in Woodrow Wilson Papers, Series III, Box 6. Library of Congress.

14. Address delivered to the High School Teachers Association of New York, January 9, 1909. Copy in the Woodrow Wilson Papers, Series III, Box 5. Library of Congress.

15. Address at Princeton Sesquicentennial Celebration, October 21, 1896. Published in *The Forum* XXII (December 1896), p. 461.

16. "The Spirit of Learning." Address delivered before the Phi Beta Kappa Chapter at Cambridge, July 1, 1909. From *Harvard Graduates' Magazine* XVIII (September 1909), p. 7.

17. *Ibid.* p. 14.

18. Woodrow Wilson, "University Training and Citizenship," *The Forum* XVIII (September 1894), p. 109.

19. Address delivered in New Jersey when candidate for governor.

20. Annapolis, June 5, 1914.

21. Address delivered before the General Assembly of Virginia in Richmond, February 1, 1912. As quoted in *Public Papers: College and State*, Vol. II, p. 379.

22. Address from the platform of train, Richmond, Ind., Sept. 4, 1919.

23. Woodrow Wilson, "Democracy and Efficiency," *Atlantic Monthly* LXXXVII (March 1901), p. 296.

24. Inaugural Address, March 4, 1913. *Public Papers: The New Democracy*, Vol. III, pp. 5–6.

25. Address when Governor of New Jersey, 1911.

26. Ray Stannard Baker, *Woodrow Wilson; Life and Letters: President*, 1913–1914. Vol. IV, p. 66.

27. Address at the Woodrow Wilson Birthplace, Staunton, Virginia, Dec. 28, 1912. On anniversary of his birth fifty-six years before.

28. Woodrow Wilson, *The Fortnightly Review* XCIII (February 1913), pp. 216–217.

29. Address at Biltmore Hotel, New York, May 17, 1915. *Public Papers: The New Democracy*, Vol. I, p. 330.

30. Address from platform of train at Richmond, Indiana, September 4, 1919. *Public Papers: War and Peace*, Vol. I, p. 106.

31. Annual Message to Congress, December 7, 1920. *Public Papers: War and Peace*, Vol. II, p. 514.

32. War Message delivered to Joint Sessions of Congress, April 2, 1917. *Public Papers: War and Peace*, Vol. I, p. 16.

33. War Message delivered to Joint Sessions of Congress, April 2, 1917. *Public Papers: War and Peace*, Vol. I, p. 11.

34. Woodrow Wilson, "The Ideals of America," *Atlantic Monthly* XC (December 1902), p. 734.

35. Address in support of the League of Nations, St. Louis, Missouri, September 5, 1919. *Public Papers: War and Peace*, Vol. I, p. 631.

36. Address at Coliseum, St. Louis, Missouri, September 5, 1919. *Public Papers: War and Peace*, Vol. I, p. 635.

37. Address at Coliseum, St. Louis, Missouri, September 5, 1919. *Public Papers: War and Peace*, Vol. I, p. 645.

38. Woodrow Wilson, "Edmund Burke and the French Revolution," *The Century Magazine* LXII (September 1901), p. 784.

39. Woodrow Wilson, "The Making of the Nation," *Atlantic Monthly*, July 1897.

40. Address before University Club, Chicago, March 12, 1908. Ray Stannard Baker, *Woodrow Wilson; Life and Letters: Princeton, 1890–1910*, Vol. II, p. 213.

41. Address delivered at the Brooklyn Navy Yard, May 11, 1914. Quoted in *Public Papers: The New Democracy*. Vol. I, p. 105.

42. Address delivered at a Joint Session of the Two Houses of Congress, April 2, 1917. Quoted in *Public Papers: War and Peace*. Vol. I, p. 14.

43. Address at Independence Hall, Philadelphia, Pennsylvania. July 4, 1914. *Public Papers: The New Democracy*, Vol. I, pp. 147–48.

Appendix B

(a) Charles Seymour, Woodrow Wilson in Perspective, in *Foreign Affairs*, January, 1956, pp. 175-186.

(b) Harley Notter, *The Origins of the Foreign Policy of Woodrow Wilson*, p. v.

(c) Edgar Eugene Robinson, *The Roosevelt Leadership 1933-1945*, Ftn. 9, p. 44.

(d) Edward H. Buehrig, *Woodrow Wilson and the Balance of Power*, p. 106.

(e) Published for the first time by William Diamond in *The American Historical Review*, April 1942, XLVII, pp. 545-551.

(f) Ray Stannard Baker, *Woodrow Wilson and World Settlement*, Doubleday, Page & Company, Garden City, N.Y., 1922.

(g) ————, *Woodrow Wilson, Life and Letters*, Doubleday, Doran & Company, Inc., Garden City, N.Y., 1927-39. 8 vols.

(h) Ray Stannard Baker and William E. Dodd, editors: *The Public Papers of Woodrow Wilson*, Harper & Brothers, New York and London, 1925-27. 6 vols.

(i) The library has also a small group of papers relating to the fabulous expedition of the Ford Peace Ship.

(j) Woodrow Wilson, Address to Congress, November 11, 1918.

(k) ————, Wilson's "Fourteen Points."

(l) ————, Address to the Senate, January 22, 1917: "Peace Without Victory."

(m) ————, Statement of March 4, 1917.

(n) ————, Address to Gridiron Club, February 26, 1916.

(o) ————, Address to the Senate, January 22, 1917: "Peace Without Victory."

(p) ————, Response to Welcome on Return from Europe, February 24, 1919.

Acknowledgments

ALTHOUGH the conception and execution of this volume has been my own—a fact in which I take pride both as my contribution to President Wilson's Centennial and as a memorial to my brother who gave his life in the last world war—primary credit of course goes to those who so generously responded to my requests for chapter contributions and focused their in-some-cases-illimitable authority on the specific Wilson period indicated. But the volume has also been assisted by others whose interest and co-operation have given it immeasurable encouragement—and to them I wish to express a continuing gratitude: Kevin McCann, Special Assistant to the President; James M. Cox, former Governor of Ohio; David K. E. Bruce, former Ambassador to France; Congressman Burr Powell Harrison of Virginia; Katharine Brand, of the Library of Congress; Louis Bromfield (in appreciative memory); Darryl F. Zanuck, producer of 20th Century Fox Films motion picture, *Wilson*; the Messrs. Clemons, Connally, Quintanilla, and Vosnjak; Conrad Wirth, Director of the National Park Service; Lewis F. Powell, Jr., of Richmond; Edwin Congor of Staunton; the *Virginia Quarterly Review*; the staff of Rinehart & Company, Inc.; Miss Kathleen Hornsberger of The Birthplace and Miss Florence Bodurtha of the Richmond Public Library; Mrs. Molly Brooks, uniquely resourceful as a secretary, and the staff of the Episcopal church office surrounding her. I wish to add my hope that this tribute meets with the kind approval of Mrs. William Gibbs McAdoo, the former Eleanor Wilson.

No one, no firm whose name appears between these covers has been reimbursed in any way (with a single exception for secretarial aid). All proceeds go directly to the Woodrow Wilson Birthplace Memorial Fund, Staunton, Virginia. It is evidence of the admiration of all for Wilsonian ideals that this is a true memorial to our great twenty-eighth President.

THE EDITOR